The Irresistible Fairy Tale

The Irresistible Fairy Tale

The Cultural and Social History of a Genre

Jack Zipes

PRINCETON UNIVERSITY PRESS

Princeton and Oxford

Copyright © 2012 by Princeton University Press
Published by Princeton University Press, 41 William Street,
Princeton, New Jersey 08540
In the United Kingdom: Princeton University Press, 6 Oxford Street,
Woodstock, Oxfordshire OX20 1TW

press.princeton.edu

Cover art: Kiki Smith, *Born*, 2002. Lithograph in 12 colors on Saunders Watercolor HP from St.
Cuthberts Mill. 68 x 56 in (172.7 x 142.2 cm). Photo courtesy Universal Limited Art Editions, Inc.
© Kiki Smith and Universal Limited Art Editions, Inc.

Fourth printing, and first paperback printing, 2013
Paperback ISBN 978-0-691-15955-3

The Library of Congress has cataloged the cloth edition of this book as follows

Zipes, Jack, 1937-
The irresistible fairy tale : the cultural and social history of a genre / Jack Zipes.
   p.   cm.
Includes bibliographical references and index.
ISBN 978-0-691-15338-4 (hardcover : alk. paper) 1. Fairy tales—History and criticism.
2. Fairy tales—Social aspects. I. Title.
GR550.Z59 2012
398.209--dc23   2011040188

British Library Cataloging-in-Publication Data is available

This book has been composed in Minion Pro

Printed on acid-free paper. ∞

Printed in the United States of America

10 9 8 7 6 5 4

To Klaus Doderer, friend and mentor

Contents

Illustrations

Preface

During the past fifty years, the scholarly study of oral folk and literary fairy tales throughout the world has flourished and appears to have expanded commensurately with the irresistible rise of fairy tales in almost all cultural and commercial fields. Though many different approaches to folk and fairy tales have stood in conflict with one another, and though universities have eliminated many folklore programs, there has generally been a peaceful, if not tolerant, attitude among the disputing sides in the academic world. Nobody has ever claimed to know everything about the oral wonder tale or literary fairy tale. Most folklorists and literary critics have, in fact, largely agreed that the fairy tale emanated from oral traditions, and that the history of tale types related to the fairy tale is complex and cannot be reduced to simple or positivist explanations. The diversity of analytic approaches to folk and fairy tales has generally enriched the fields of anthropology, comparative literature, cultural studies, children's literature, psychology, philosophy and others. If there is any single genre that has captured the imagination of people in all walks of life throughout the world, it is the fairy tale, and yet we still have great difficulty in explaining its historical origins, how it evolved and spread, and why we cannot resist its appeal, no matter what form it takes.

In my own case, during the past forty years I have tried to forge a greater link with the social and natural sciences to explain the fairy tale's irresistible and inexplicable appeal. I have sought, in particular, to widen my own sociopolitical approach to folk and fairy tales, and have explored new developments in evolutionary psychology, cultural anthropology, biology, memetics, cognitive philosophy, and linguistics. For the most part, I have endeavored to demonstrate that the historical evolution of storytelling reflects struggles of human beings worldwide to adapt to their changing natural and social environments. The cultural evolution of the fairy tale is closely bound historically to all kinds of storytelling and different civilizing processes that have undergirded the formation of nation-states.

I do not believe in the notion of progress, or that we come to a greater understanding of the arts through improved technological advances and greater rationalized civilizing processes. But I certainly believe in evolution, adaptation, innovation, and transformation that can be traced in diverse cultural patterns and hark back to ancient societies long before the rise of nation-states. I am fascinated by the mediation of writing, print, the visual arts (painting and illustration), electronics, photography, film, and the Internet that has enabled the fairy tale to change as well as expand in unusual, innovative ways. In this regard, I have explored how Richard Dawkins's notion of memes might be useful for explaining the replication, evolution, and dissemination of folk and fairy tales, and I have also been influenced by other theorists of cultural evolution.

In 2006, I published *Why Fairy Tales Stick: The Evolution and Relevance of a Genre*, in which I tried to ground the fairy tale's development in oral traditions based on the biological and cultural dispositions of human beings. Since its publication numerous significant studies have appeared in a short time, dealing with cultural evolution, memes, socionarratology, the origins of storytelling, and the history of fairy tales. These studies have a bearing on how we understand the nature and history of the fairy tale. They have by and large reinforced my belief that we can never explain the inexplicable fairy tales, but we can learn to fathom how and why they evolved in oral and literary traditions, and why we are impelled and compelled to use them to make meaning out of our lives.

In some ways we live and breathe fairy tales, or, as Arthur Frank insists in his highly stimulating book *Letting Stories Breathe: A Socio-Narratology*, stories have lives of their own, which we then embody. Though there was no such thing as a fairy tale as we understand it today when humans developed the capacity to speak, communicate, and tell tales thousands of years ago, there were certainly metaphoric linguistic seeds in their communications that contributed to the gradual formation of oral wonder tales. This book explores the history of the mediations that have enabled fairy-tale seeds to blossom, flourish, and become one of the most irresistible as well as inexplicable cultural genres in the world. My book also responds to some deplorable scholarly endeavors that have sought to dismiss the fairy tale's oral roots and reduce it to a genre that privileges print over orality. I have reviewed these works in the two appendixes to make my position firm and clear, for it is important, I believe, not to be silent when misleading ideas are circulated as fact.

The first chapter, "The Cultural Evolution of Storytelling and Tales: Human Communication and Memetics," expands on my most recent books, *Why Fairy Tales Stick* and *Relentless Progress*, and includes new research by Michael Tomasello, Michael Trout, Kate Distin, Frank, and other scholars interested in interdisciplinary approaches to cultural evolution. It clarifies why and how tales were created and told, and formed the basis of culture. In my opinion oral tales were imitated and replicated as memes in antiquity to form the fiber of culture and tradition. Taxonomies in the nineteenth century were established in response to recognizable features of tales as well as to organize and order types of stories. "Modern" genres originated during the Enlightenment and are basically social institutions that have defined cultural artifacts and patterns, divided them rationally into disciplines, and established rules and regulations for their study. In many ways, the fairy tale defies such definition and categorization.

Chapter 2, "The Meaning of Fairy Tale within the Evolution of Culture," focuses on the significance of Madame Catherine-Anne d'Aulnoy and the French writers of fairy tales in the 1690s. It demonstrates how orality combined with literature to form the basis for most, if not all, short narrative forms that were appropriated and adapted for print. I maintain that orality is still highly relevant for the creation and dissemination of fairy tales.

The third chapter, "Remaking 'Bluebeard,' or Good-bye to Perrault," argues that Catherine Breillat's filmic appropriation of Charles Perrault's "Bluebeard" is part of a memetic process that entails imitation, innovation, and transformation. Her interpretation of Perrault's tale is a contestation, and while she seeks to replace Perrault's version with a double rendition of his tale, she also emphasizes the significance of Perrault's tale and demonstrates how all Bluebeard tales are part of a singular discursive process within the larger genre of the fairy tale. Interestingly, both Perrault and Breillat become merely markers in the evolutionary history of a tale type about mass murders that continues to breathe and demand our attention through supernormal stimuli.[1]

Chapter 4, "Witch as Fairy/Fairy as Witch: Unfathomable Baba Yagas," focuses on the historical development of tales about witches such as Baba Yaga. Numerous feminist anthropologists and literacy critics have studied how the witches in folk and fairy tales were actually patriarchal reutilizations of ancient goddesses. I revisit their theories to understand how witches are related to fairies, how witches have been demonized, and how tales have been disseminated and adapted to reinforce dominant stereotypes about women.

Chapter 5, "The Tales of Innocent Persecuted Heroines and Their Neglected Female Storytellers and Collectors," deals with a significant, but obfuscated category of nineteenth-century folk and fairy tales that deserves greater attention: tales told, collected, and written by women. Hardly anyone—and this includes folklorists and fairy-tale scholars—knows anything about the tales of Laura Gonzenbach, Božena Němcová, Nannette Lévesque, and Rachel Busk, despite the great advances made in feminist studies that led to the rediscovery of important women European writers of fairy tales from the seventeenth century to the present. Not only are the tales by Gonzenbach, Němcová, Lévesque, and Busk pertinent for what they reveal about the beliefs and customs of specific communities in the nineteenth century and about the role of women, but they are also valuable in the study of folklore for elucidating the problematic aspects of orality and literacy, and the interpretation of particular tale types such as the innocent persecuted heroine.

"Giuseppe Pitrè and the Great Collectors of Folk Tales in the Nineteenth Century," chapter 6, continues the examination of neglected stories and collectors of folk tales. It explores the significance of collections in Germany, France, Italy, and other European countries that led to a greater cultural interest in folklore. Among the remarkable folklorists of the latter part of the nineteenth century, I have selected Pitrè's collection for a longer discussion because it is representative of the general work of folklorists and reveals the profundity of the oral tradition and why middle-class professionals turned to examining tales that stemmed from common people.

Chapter 7, "Fairy-Tale Collisions or the Explosion of a Genre," extends the discussion about women's contribution to the fairy-tale genre by focusing on contemporary fairy-tale drawings, paintings, sculptures, and photographs that all reveal how the genre of the fairy tale has expanded to include other art forms. What is interesting about fairy-tale artworks is that they offer a metacritique of canonical print versions. It is not by chance that fairy tales were reignited by the rise of feminism in the 1970s—a fervor for change that continues through the present. Of course, change always leads to conflicts, and fairy tales have become embroiled in all kinds of battles.

Interpretations and debates about fairy tales have always been based on ideological differences along with the vested interests of intellectuals and their pursuits. History, as we know, is always written by the victors and rulers who allow for a certain amount of dissent, or what Herbert Marcuse called "repressive tolerance." In the distant past those people who learned to read and write served the victors and rulers, taking little interest in the culture of the common people, whose tales and social relations were largely ignored or dismissed. We know little, and probably never will know more than we do now, about the assortment of wonder tales that people told throughout the world from pagan times to the present. But one must assume that they did tell millions of tales and continued to tell tales even after the invention of print, as the numerous nineteenth- and twentieth-century collections have revealed. If scholars do not deign to look at and listen to the common practices of the majority of people, it will appear in history as if the people were mute and did not actively tell their own stories, which included miraculous and magical motifs that formed the basis of oral wonder tales and literary fairy tales. Fortunately, the pioneer folklorists of the nineteenth century opened their eyes and ears and began preserving the rich narrative traditions of the folk.

I should like to stress here that I do not intend to romanticize the folk. As Alan Dundes, the great American folklorist once said to an audience of middle-class students, "We are the folk. We are all part of the folk." Class formation does not preclude class exchange and the transmission of cultural artifacts through orality and other modes of communication. Cultural and social patterns depend on various, complex sorts of class participation that must be studied carefully. Orality—that is, the oral transmission of tales— has always bound us to one another and continues to be effective in the mass media, our homes and schools, and the public sphere. Fairy tales have some-how staked out a privileged place in the cultural and civilizing processes of societies throughout the world. They have become second nature in our daily lives. How and why have they accomplished this? What makes fairy tales so irresistible? How do they function memetically in cultural evolution? These are some of the relevant questions I shall address by offering working hypotheses that take social life and theory into account and by refusing to provide definitive explanations about the fairy tale's history.

Acknowledgments

Over the past fifteen years I have collaborated with Cristina Bachilegga, Anne Duggan, and Donald Haase, who have transformed *Marvels and Tales* into the foremost journal of fairy-tale studies in North America and Europe and have always been ready to assist me. Their advice and criticism have been constant, and they were particularly helpful for my work on this present book. I have also benefited greatly from discussions and correspondence with Dan Ben-Amos, Michael Drout, Mark Scala, Tok Thompson, Francisco Vaz da Silva, and Jan Ziolkowski, who read some of the chapter drafts. They tempered the book's polemics and corrected some of its misconceptions, as did the three anonymous reviewers of my original manuscript. Graham Anderson, Pauline Greenhill, Donatella Izzo, Sadhana Nathanai, and Hans-Jörg Uther graciously helped me and stimulated me in different ways while I was doing my research. In addition, I cannot say enough to express my gratitude for the generosity of Dina Goldstein, Claire Prussian, Paula Rego, Sharon Singer, Kiki Smith, and Rima Staines. It is an honor to include their wonderful artworks in this book.

If it were not for Hanne Winarsky, my enterprising former editor at Princeton University Press, this book would not have reached fruition. I am most appreciative of her support. Another former editor, Christopher Chung, also played a major role in convincing me to revamp my manuscript at an early stage, while Kelly Malloy, who recently joined Princeton, did crucial and effective work in tying together the loose ends of the manuscript. As I worked on the images for the book, Dimitri Karetnikov went out of his way to advise me wisely about the technical reproduction of the illustrations. In addition Brigitta van Rheinberg provided invaluable advice and assistance during the final stages of my work, and Sara Lerner, the fairy godmother of this project, once again did a marvelous job of supervising the entire production of the book. Last but not least, I want to thank Cindy Milstein for her careful and thorough copyediting, which, I believe, has improved the quality of my writing.

The Irresistible Fairy Tale

1

The Cultural Evolution of Storytelling and Fairy Tales: Human Communication and Memetics

Even the simplest and most static of human cultures is an engine of inventive mutual influence and change. Furthermore, at least orally, human cultures preserve *historical* record, imaginative or real, couched in a human language. The past pervades human consciousness to some degree even in the simplest societies, and discussions of past events—narrating, sometimes dramatically, commenting on the narration, challenging points of fact or logic, and co-constructing a suite of stories—occupied many an evening for perhaps 300,000 years, but not for millions of years before that. And while our ancestors were arguing, many ape communities not far away in the forest were making their—yes, traditional—nests and drifting off to sleep. The only modern apes that have learned language learned it from human teachers, and none of their wild counterparts has anything like it. Even if their individual minds preserve some private history, it is difficult to see how they could have a collective one without being able to tell it to each other and to their young. All human cultures can, do, and probably must.

—Melvin Konner, *The Evolution of Childhood* (2010)

Stories may not actually breathe, but they can animate. The breath imputed by this book's title is the breath of a god in creation stories, as that god gives life to the lump that will become human. Stories animate human life; that is their work. Stories work with people, for people, and always stories work *on* people, affecting what people are able to see as real, as possible, and as worth doing or best avoided. What is it about stories—what are their particularities—that enables them to work as they do? More than mere curiosity is at stake in this question, because human life depends on the stories we tell: the sense of self that those stories

impart, the relationships constructed around shared stories, and the sense
of purpose that stories both propose and foreclose
—Arthur Frank, *Letting Stories Breathe* (2010)

Though it is impossible to trace the historical origins and evolution of fairy tales to a particular time and place, we do know that humans began telling tales as soon as they developed the capacity of speech. They may have even used sign language before speech originated to communicate vital information for adapting to their environment.[1] Units of this information gradually formed the basis of narratives that enabled humans to learn about themselves and the worlds that they inhabited. Informative tales were not given titles. They were simply told to mark an occasion, set an example, warn about danger, procure food, or explain what seemed inexplicable. People told stories to communicate knowledge and experience in social contexts.

Though many ancient tales might seem magical, miraculous, fanciful, superstitious, or unreal to us, people believed them, and these people were and are not much different from people today who believe in religions, miracles, cults, nations, and notions such as "free" democracies that have little basis in reality. In fact, religious and patriotic stories have more in common with fairy tales than we realize, except that fairy tales tend to be secular and are not based on a prescriptive belief system or religious codes. Fairy tales are informed by a human disposition to action—to transform the world and make it more adaptable to human needs, while we also try to change and make ourselves fit for the world. Therefore, the focus of fairy tales, whether oral, written, or cinematic, has always been on finding magical instruments, extraordinary technologies, or powerful people and animals that will enable protagonists to transform themselves along with their environment, making it more suitable for living in peace and contentment. Fairy tales begin with conflict because we all begin our lives with conflict. We are all misfit for the world, and somehow we must fit in, fit in with other people, and thus we must invent or find the means through communication to satisfy as well as resolve conflicting desires and instincts.

Fairy tales are rooted in oral traditions and, as I mentioned above, were never given titles, nor did they exist in the forms in which they are told, printed, painted, recorded, performed, filmed, and manufactured today. Folklorists generally make a distinction between wonder folk tales, which originated in oral traditions throughout the world and still exist, and literary fairy tales, which emanated from the oral traditions through the mediation of manuscripts and print, and continue to be created today in various mediated forms around the world. In both the oral and literary traditions, the tale types influenced by cultural patterns are so numerous and diverse that it is almost impossible to define a wonder folk or fairy tale, or explain the relationship between the two modes of communication. There are helpful catalogs of tale types along with encyclopedias of fairy tales such as Antti Aarne and Stith Thompson's *The Types of the Folktale* (1928), revised by Hans-Jörg Uther in 2004, my *Oxford Companion to Fairy Tales* (2000), William Hansen's *Ariadne's Thread: A Guide to International Tales Found in Classical Literature* (2002), Donald Haase's *Greenwood Encyclopedia of Folktales and Fairy Tales* (2007), and the worthwhile ongoing project *Enzyklopädie des Märchens*, begun in 1958 and still not finished. Yet despite the value of these books, the intricate relationship and evolution of folk and fairy tales are difficult to comprehend and define. In fact, together, oral and literary tales form one immense and complex genre because they are inextricably dependent on one another.

It is for this reason that I use the modern term "fairy tale" in this book to encompass the oral tradition as the genre's vital progenitor and try to explain the inexplicable fairy tale, including its evolution and dissemination. In other words, my use of the term fairy tale here refers to the symbiotic relationship of oral and literary currents, even if I occasionally make historical distinctions concerning the mediation and reception of different tale types. In focusing on the interaction between various mediations of the fairy tale, I want to refute the useless dichotomies such as print versus oral that some scholars are still promoting to paint a misinformed history of the fairy tale.[2] I also want to explore the more sophisticated and innovative theories of storytelling, cultural evolution, human communication, and memetics to see how they might enable us to understand why we are disposed toward fairy tales, and how they breathe life into our daily undertakings.

In his most recent book, *Letting Stories Breathe*, Frank notes that stories embody capacities we need to consider in order to articulate and discuss problematic issues in our lives. Frank maintains that he does not want to interpret stories. Rather, he uses several different types of narratives to explain the claims and operating premises of socio-narratology. He is not interested in interpreting stories because critics tend to use heuristics and critical methodologies to foreclose the meanings of stories. Frank wants to analyze how stories work by focusing on how they are in dialogue with one another, people's experiences, and societies.[3] The source for Frank's ideas on dialogic narratology is the Russian critic Mikhail Bakhtin, who elaborated principles of dialogic philosophy in his many works.[4] Key for Frank is the notion that all utterances are essentially dialogic because they depend on the interplay of varied, and at times opposed, meanings. At the same time, it is important to bear in mind that all language usage is a product of conflicting social forces that engender constant reinterpretation.

Given the dialogic nature of language and how we use it to form narratives that inform us, Frank's basic premises are these:

1. Stories do not belong to storytellers and story listeners because all stories are "reassemblies of fragments on loan" and "depend on shared narrative sources."[5]
2. Stories not only contribute to the making of our narrative selves but also weave the threads of social relationships and make life social.
3. Stories have certain distinct capacities that enable them to do what they do best and can be understood as narrative types or genres. Though distinct, genres of stories depend on one another, for there is no such thing as a pure genre, and all tale types have a symbiotic relationship to one another.
4. Socio-narratology encourages a dialogic mode of interpretation so that all voices can be heard, and open up a story for various interpretations and possible uses.
5. "Socio-narratology, although always relational in recognizing that all parties act, pays most attention to stories acting. It analyzes how stories breathe as they animate, assemble, entertain, and enlighten, and also deceive and divide people."[6]
6. Analysis demands that we learn from storytellers. "The primary lesson from storytellers is that they learn to work with stories that are not *theirs* but *there*, as realities. Master storytellers know that stories breathe."[7]

Among the stories that breathe, fairy tales are unique but not independent, just as most genres are unique in some way but are interdependent. To understand the uniqueness and impact of fairy tales on our lives, we need first to discuss the origins of language and its evolution, for once a plethora of stories began to circulate in societies throughout the world, they contained the seeds of fairy tales, ironically tales at first *without* fairies formed by metaphor and metamorphosis and by a human disposition to communicate relevant experiences. These primary tales enabled humans to invent and reinvent their lives—and create and re-create gods, divine powers, fairies, demons, fates, monsters, witches, and other supernatural characters and forces. An *other world* is very much alive in fairy tales, thanks to our capacity as storytellers.

Human Communication and the Origins of Fairy Tales and Other Genres

It is impossible to locate and study the history of stories and the evolution of genres because people began speaking and told stories thousands of years before they learned to read, write, and keep records. And even when they learned how to write, only a tiny minority of humans was capable of reading and writing, and these elite groups were preoccupied with their own interests, which had little bearing on the general or popular modes of communication. Nevertheless, there are certain grounded assumptions that we can make about the evolution of communication and storytelling as well as the origins of fairy tales. It is also possible to demonstrate how all stories are linked to one another, yet distinct in their personal and social functions.

In his recent, significant study, *A History of Communications: Media and Society from the Evolution of Speech to the Internet*, Marshall Poe maintains that the media, communicative networks, and culture have their own type-specific attributes that are related to each other. If we regard a medium as a tool for sending, receiving, storing, and retrieving information, there are eight media attributes that we must consider if we are to understand the evolution of speech as a medium of communication up to the Internet's invention: accessibility, privacy, fidelity, volume, velocity, range, persistence, and search ability. Poe divides the history of communication into six historical phases that began about three hundred thousand years ago: speech, manuscript, print, audiovisual, Internet, and digital. Throughout the development of communication in the course of these approximately three hundred thousand years, speech was and has remained the primary constant up to the present day. Communication developed in the first place, according to Poe, because we talk to be relevant. "Evolutionarily speaking, we talk because we were the only primates who gained social status and therewith fitness by talking. . . . Psychologically speaking, we talk because we must be heard."[8]

Building on the theory of Jean-Louis Desalles in *Why We Talk: The Evolutionary Origins of Language*, Poe points out that different social practices dependent on speech and human communication emerged, and that these social practices gave rise, and still do, to commensurate values. He argues that "the formation of allies and coalitions that cooperated with one another to live in groups that became societies was dependent on communication. Proto-humans had to look for a characteristic in allies that would be mutually beneficial. Desalles proposes that this criterion was relevance. Relevance here means utterances that will profit a listener and thereby recommend the speaker as an ally." Poe goes on to assert that "speech is not so much a form of cooperation as a contest between speakers for the approbation of listeners."[9]

Of course, speech has many other functions, but the point about relevance is significant, because almost all storytellers strive to make themselves and their stories relevant, and if they succeed, those stories will stick in the minds of their listeners, who may tell these stories later and contribute to the replication of stories that form cultural patterns.[10] Telling stories—that is, command of the word—was vital if one wanted to become a leader, shaman, priest, priestess, king, queen, medicine man, healer, minister, and so on, in a particular family, clan, tribe, or small society. Desalles maintains that language was a product of not only information sharing but also argumentation and verification. It was in conversation or dialogue that the communication of information could be assessed and verified. Desalles explains that

> the behaviors underlying conversation obey unconscious mechanisms. Speakers drawing attention to salient situations, hearers trying to trivialize them, others expressing doubts about the internal consistency of what they are hearing are all behaving instinctively. . . . At stake in these conversations is something of vital importance to each of the speakers: who is going to have a close relationship with whom, who will rise in the estimation of others, who will gain the benefits and the influence that come with status. What we are unconsciously exercising in our conversations is part of our biological programming. Behind the immediate stimulus of exchanging relevant information, what we are doing is assessing others' ability to decide what is good for the set of people who will choose to ally with them. Language can thus be seen more as a means than as an end. Just as phonology makes for the construction of an extended lexicon, so our use of language makes for the construction of coalitions.[11]

Telling effective, relevant stories became a vital quality for anyone who wanted power to determine and influence social practices. In the specific case of fairy tales, we shall see that they assumed salient aspects in conflict with other stories and became memetically and culturally relevant as a linguistic means to communicate alternative social practices. In the process fairy tales came to be contested and marked as pagan, irrelevant, and unreal. Poe traces how access and control over the changing media from antiquity to the present have defined which voices will be articulated and heard, and which stories will become part of a cultural network and tradition that people with different dispositions will either maintain or subvert.

Throughout human history, there has always been a tension between groups wanting to control speech and the way individuals have used speech to know themselves and the world. In his book *The Cultural Origins of Human Cognition*, Tomasello makes the point that

> language is a form of cognition; it is packaged for the purposes of interpersonal communication. Human beings want to share experience with one another and so, over time, they have created symbolic conventions for doing that. . . . Given that the major function of language is to manipulate the attention of other persons—that is, to induce them to take a certain perspective on a phenomenon—we can think of linguistic symbols and constructions as nothing other than symbolic artifacts that a child's forbears have bequeathed to her for this purpose. In learning to use these symbolic artifacts, and thus internalizing the

perspectives behind them, the child comes to conceptualize the world in the way that the creators of the artifacts did.[12]

Indeed, stories emanated in prehistory from shared experiences, and this is still the case. It is through oral transmission that stories of different kinds form the textures of our lives. Tomasello demonstrates that children learn early in social contexts by becoming aware of the intentions of other human beings through imitation, instruction, and collaboration, and he contends that learning is dialectical, plus involves understanding metaphor and different perspectives. Knowing the world is determined by culture and genetics. Therefore, words must somehow fit the world if they are to be continuously transmitted. Children are born into a particular cultural niche that will influence how they begin to know the world and benefit from the cumulative heritage of culture. They learn how language and narratives provide access to power, or deny access to it.

If it is through language and story that cognition is fostered, it is all that much more important that we see the connections between ancient stories and how as well as why we continue to repeat them in innovative ways. Though we do not have printed records of how people told stories thousands of years ago, we do have enough archaeological evidence through cave paintings, vases, tombs, carvings, codices, and other artifacts to enable us to grasp what kinds of stories were told in ancient pagan cultures. In *Structure and History in Greek Mythology and Ritual*, Walter Burkert makes some pertinent remarks about the origins and evolution of storytelling:

> A tale becomes traditional not by virtue of being created, but by being retold and accepted; transmission means interaction, and this process is not explained by isolating just one side. A tale "created"—that is, invented by an individual author—may somehow become "myth" if it becomes traditional, to be used as a means of communication in subsequent generations, usually with some distortions and reelaborations. At any rate, it is a fact that there are traditional tales in most primitive and even in advanced societies, handed down in a continuous chain of transmission, suffering from omissions and misinterpretations but still maintaining a certain identity and some power of regeneration. The fundamental questions thus would be: How, and to what extent, can traditional tales retain their identity through many stages of telling and retelling, especially in oral transmission, and what, if any, is the role and function of such tales in the evolution of human civilization?[13]

Using Vladimir Propp's classic study *Morphology of the Folktale* (1928; translated into English in 1958), in which Propp developed his theory about the thirty-one functions of the Russian wonder tale, or what the American folklorist Alan Dundes calls the "motifemes" of a tale, Burkert maintains that one can find a similar sequence or pattern of functions/motifemes in most fairy tales, myths, and other oral tales that involve the protagonist's departure/banishment from home to fulfill a lack.[14] This departure is also a quest to acquire qualities, properties, and capabilities that will help him/her in conflict with an antagonist. Frequently there is a rescue of an oppressed or persecuted person, or a tentative accomplishment of a goal followed by tribulation, recuperation, and salvation. Depending on how one interprets and uses Propp's theorems, Burkert believes that they generally hold true in most traditional tales, and therefore he defines a tale as a "sequence of motifemes; in linguistic terms: a syntagmatic chain with 'paradigmatic' variants; in more human terms: a program of actions—taking 'action' in a large sense, including plans, reactions, and passive experience in the sequence of the plot."[15]

Tales as programs of actions are derived, according to Burkert, from biological and cultural dispositions. That is, they emanate from social and biological practices that precede a communication. The various tale types are dependent on actions taken and conflicts that humans have experienced, and continue to experience, through biological and social behavior. Such basic actions as, for example, mating, procreation, child abandonment or abuse, hunting, planting, killing, exchanging gifts or people, violating women, and casting spells with words or signs involved programs of action and were structured in tales for effective communication. Burkert remarks that "the tale often is the first and fundamental verbalization of complex reality, the primary way to speak about many-sided problems, just as telling a tale was seen to be quite an elementary way of communication. Language is linear, and linear narrative is thus a way prescribed by language to map reality."[16]

Genres of storytelling and tale types originated from the application of storytelling and stories to social as well as biological life—that is, daily occurrences. Those tales that became relevant for families, clans, tribes, villages, and cities were retained through memory and passed on as traditional verbalizations of actions and behaviors. Different cultures throughout the world employed many of the same sequences of events or patterns in the communication of stories, but the application of the verbalization that included specific references to specific realities, customs, rituals, and beliefs led to various tale types, variants, and differences. For instance, almost all cultures have cannibalistic ogres and giants or dragons and monsters that threaten a community. Almost all cultures have tales in which a protagonist goes on a quest to combat a ferocious savage. The quest or combat tale is undertaken in the name of civilization or humanity against the forces of voracity or uncontrolled appetite. As a tale names characters, and makes distinctions among motifs, setting, and behavior, and as certain new stylistic and social applications are introduced or older ones are abandoned, the tale breathes differently— namely, it breathes new, meaningful life into the community of listeners, who often become carriers or tellers themselves. It defines itself differently while adhering to a tradition of tales that may be indecipherable, but is inherent in the telling as well as the writing of a story.

Burkert states that

> there is no denying that in any good tale, many additional structures may be discerned beyond the fundamental sequences of motifemes, disregarding still further stabilizing structures of individual languages, such as meter, assonance, and rhyme. What makes a tale specific, effective, unforgettable, as it seems, may be the interplay of multiple structures. I call this the crystallization of a tale. Its elements may thus be heavily overdetermined on account of superimposed structures, so that every change of detail results in deterioration; this is the mark of art. The question remains, however, whether a traditional tale is transmitted as an elaborate work of art, or in some more basic form.[17]

In the fairy tale's case, we can see that it has crystallized or evolved into both an elaborate and simple narrative. If we take any of the classical fairy tales such as "Little Red Riding Hood," "Cinderella," or "Beauty and the Beast," we can trace them as best as we can to tales of antiquity, perhaps even prehistory, that concern rape, sibling rivalry, and mating. The applied verbalization of social actions not only contributed to the formation of one particular tale type and genre such as the fairy tale but other genres as well that continue to interact with one another. In fact, the formation of the fairy tale as a genre can only be understood if we grasp its hybrid nature, and how it continues to borrow from, exploit, and thrive on storytelling innovations based on other simple genres. I shall discuss these innovations in the other chapters, but first it is necessary to understand how simple stories or genres contributed to the formation of the fairy-tale genre.

Simple Genres and Their Complex Interaction

Once upon a time—that is, about eighty years ago—a Dutch scholar by the name of André Jolles wrote an important yet nearly forgotten book about the interrelationship of short forms of narrative. The title of the book is *Einfache Formen: Legende/ Sage/Mythe/Rätsel/Spruch/Kasus/Memorabile/Märchen/Witz* (Simple forms: Legend/ rumor/myth/riddle/proverb/memoir/case reports/fairy tale/ joke), and the subtitle indicates what Jolles means by simple forms. He believes that these forms of telling were the building blocks of more complex literary narratives, and that they were related to one another but separate because their functions, what he calls *Geistesbeschäftigungen*, were different.

The word *Geistesbeschäftigung*, which can be defined as "preoccupation," needs some explanation since Jolles uses it to make distinctions between the simple forms of narrative. In English, the German word *Geist* can mean "mind," and the word *Beschäftigung* can mean "occupation." Together they can be interpreted to mean that the mind is occupied by a concern with something. In the case of storytelling, the mind is actually preoccupied by a concern with an action or behavior that needs to be verbalized, or calls for verbalization.

So, for instance, in the stone age if a man returned safely from an expedition into the forest where he had encountered a monstrous beast and killed it, his mind would have been preoccupied or already occupied by this clash, and he would have wanted to relate his experience to others in his clan as a warning or heroic deed. Undoubtedly, he would have used a particular simple form of narration to recount the salient aspects of his encounter, such as an anecdote, fable, exemplum, proverb, or fairy tale. Or he might have combined the forms to tell his story. What was and is crucial for this storyteller (and all storytellers) is shaping a tale so that it becomes alive, effective, and relevant. Indeed, he sought and seeks to make himself relevant.

While Jolles manages to make some critical distinctions among simple forms using this notion of preoccupation, his definitions of narrative genres lack historical substantiation and tend to be too abstract. Moreover, he overlooks other highly significant simple forms such as the anecdote, fable, ballad, and exemplum. Jolles's work nevertheless is important because it opens an approach to short narratives and verbalizations that allows us to understand their singular developments, and also the way that they are both related and interrelated to one another. Let us briefly consider the fable, for instance, and how it may have evolved to relate to the fairy tale, exemplum, animal tale, and warning narrative.

Most histories of the fable associate its beginnings with Aesop in 600 BC. Despite Aesop's significance, however, he did not invent the fable, which probably originated in Sumer and Mesopotamia sometime in 800 BC, and we are not even certain that he existed. But we are sure that archaeologists discovered didactic narrative works on clay tablets and in scripts that resemble the fable in form as well as subject matter, and these Sumerian and Babylonian texts were probably transmitted orally and through manuscripts to the ancient Greeks. The stories, although not called fables at that time, were short and primarily featured animals, which were anthropomorphized and exemplified a moral. As the fables were spread and transformed by different cultures, inanimate objects, mythical creatures, and even humans were often added to the cast of characters. Still, for the most part, animals dominated the stories and were involved in "human" conflicts that they had to resolve. The conflicts had to be adjudicated in such a way as to potentially establish ethical guidelines or principles of fair play. In this regard, fables contributed to the civilizing process of all societies and the constitution of the humanities. All the simple forms of narrative in fact weave themselves in and out of civilizing processes.

The development of the fable as genre is curious because most of these short, provocative stories were first part of a longer didactic literature such as *The Wisdom of Šur* (ca. 2500 BC) and were considered *exempla*—that is, fictional stories that provide a truth applicable in the real world as a moral.

Moreover, they were disseminated by word of mouth and script. In his significant study *The Ancient Fable*, Niklas Holzberg remarks:

> It would, after all, be safe to say, that the narrative texts brought from Mesopotamia only circulated in very rare cases as actual reading material, because the books of wisdom were written in a foreign language. It is much more reasonable to assume that, between the eighth and fifth centuries B.C., Greek familiarity with originally Babylonian fable literature was based almost exclusively on oral tradition. And who better to tell such fables than natives of the Near East living in Greece, for example, educated citizens from the towns of Asia Minor who had been carried off as slaves? Perhaps in the end there really is some historical truth behind the legendary Aesop who lived in bondage on Samos?[18]

Whether there actually was a slave named Aesop who played a major role in creating and cultivating fables is a moot point. What is significant is that the Sumerian and Babylonian fables gradually became more widespread in Greece in 600 BC, and in some instances, Aesop was the alleged storyteller, but he never wrote down his tales that were not "his" tales. They survived by word of mouth along with many other Sumerian and Babylonian fables, and when free speech was established in the Greek city-states, rhetoricians began using the fable to teach style and rules of grammar to scholars, and discuss morals and ethics in debates. Yet the Aesopian tales had already become part of Greek popular culture, and as Leslie Kurke demonstrates in *Aesopic Conversations: Popular Tradition, Cultural Dialogue, and the Invention of Greek Prose*, their importance, along with the anonymous *Life of Aesop*, reveals the profound depth and breadth of storytelling that contested the hegemonic rule of elite classes. Indeed, there are good reasons why the fables spread and have been spread memetically throughout the world. Kurke writes:

> We might say that Aesop, like folktale tricksters in many different cultures, enables the articulation in public of elements of what the political theorist James Scott calls the "hidden transcript," the counterideology and worldview developed by the oppressed when they are "offstage"— that is, free from the public world whose performances are largely scripted by the dominant. For the Aesop tradition exhibits simultaneously two characteristic forms of "political disguise" Scott identifies as enabling the speaking of opposition or resistance from the hidden transcript in the public world: anonymity of the messenger and indirection or obliquity of the message.[19]

As a reflection of the popularity of Aesop and his fables, there are many references to both in the works of Aristophanes, Plato, Aristotle, and other Greek writers. By 300 BC Demetrius Phalereus, a distinguished Athenian statesmen and orator, founded the Alexandria Library and collected two hundred fables in Greek prose under the title *Assemblies of Aesopic Tales*. Since

Alexandrian grammarians and scribes often used these fables in their teachings, the stories became known throughout the Mediterranean region, and at the beginning of the Christian era, Phaedrus, a Greek slave who was freed by Augustus, imitated them in Latin iambics. In the meantime, fables from India, associated with another legendary storyteller named Kasyapa, formed the basis of the Libyan fables of "Kybises" and were combined with Aesopian fables by a rhetorician named Nicostratus in the court of Marcus Aurelius. Then, in AD 230, Valerius Babrius turned three hundred of the Aesopian and Libyan fables into Greek verse with Latin meters. Rhetoricians and philosophers became accustomed to using the fables in exercises for their students and disciples, asking them to discuss and interpret the fables' morals. Rules of style and grammar were to be learned through the fables, and the young scholars were encouraged to create new fables, which can be found in isolated works during the early years of the Roman Empire. Later, about AD 400, the Roman Avianus wrote forty-two fables in Latin verse, based primarily on Babrius's work.

The spread of fables throughout the world is similar to the manner in which the so-called Aesopian tradition became established in Greece and then most of Europe. That is, fables became known through oral and literary cultivation. In India, for instance, Vishnu Sarma's famous collection of tales, the *Panchatantra* (ca. 200 BC), contained animal fables in verse and prose in Sanskrit and Pali written by Bidpai. These stories stemmed from an oral tradition, as did the fables in Sintipas's *The Story of the Seven Wise Masters* (ca. 100 BC). In most of the major countries and regions of the world, including China, Japan, Africa, South America, Australia, and North America, anthropologists and folklorists have discovered fable traditions of various kinds that are frequently related to one another. Moreover, in the Western tradition, many great authors have produced intriguing literary fables—Jean de La Fontaine, Jonathan Swift, John Gay, Benjamin Franklin, Gotthold Ephraim Lessing, Tomas de Yriarte, Ivan Andreyevich Kriloff, Ralph Waldo Emerson, Ambrose Bierce, Robert Louis Stevenson, and James Thurber, to name but a few.

In discussing the popularity of the fable, Thomas Noel observes,

> Certain collections, particularly the fables attributed to the legendary Greek sage Aesop, continue to hold their own on the list of recommended children's literature. Everyone knows the formula—a pithy narrative using animals to act out human foibles and a consequent moral, either explicit or implicit—and most people remain familiar with a handful of traditional fables, even though that familiarity might be hidden away in the dim recesses of the mind along with other pre-puberty remembrances.[20]

These remembrances have always been part of the human disposition toward storytelling and the fable's historical texture that originated in oral traditions several centuries before Aesop supposedly began telling his tales. Aesop's own fables were appropriated and modified by other great and not-so-great storytellers and artists as well as the common people. Notwithstanding the fact that adapters of Aesop's fables have used great poetic license, they have always been compelled to respect the genre's penetrating gaze into the dark side of human beings portrayed as animals in a dog-eat-dog world. Fables, inspired by Aesop, in this respect have generally posed a question that was at the heart of Aesop's tales: Can human beings rise above animals?

In her stimulating book *Fables of Power: Aesopian Writing and Political History*, Annabel Patterson argues that the fable must always be understood in its social-historical context and, at the same time, has universal appeal because of the way it functions. Interpreted by specific cultures yet relevant throughout the ages, the fable speaks to unequal power relations and prompts those without power to speak in metaphoric codes that can emancipate both the teller and listener.[21] Fables do not always end happily even when there is a resolution or moral. They move readers and listeners to contemplate how they might act if they were in a similar situation. They are simultaneously disturbing and enlightening. Fables are not preachy or moralistic in a strict sense because they expose the contradictions of human behavior more than they dictate principles of behavior. They explore the human condition rather than instruct how one must behave. They explain more than they sermonize. As exempla, fables warn and advise as opposed to prescribing behavior and manners. The listener and reader of a fable are always given a choice, and human agency is thus respected. Fables tell us that we all have choices to make.

As we can see, the preoccupation of the fable tends to be a short, metaphoric exploration of power relations that provides listeners with a moral or ethical example, and though the fable in its simple form is distinctly different from a fairy tale, the two genres also share a great deal because there is a certain overlap in their preoccupation. Jolles has some pertinent things to say about the fairy tale that reveal "universal" preoccupations, which account for similar stories throughout the world.

Influenced by Friedrich Schiller's treatise *On Naïve and Sentimental Poetry*, Jolles begins with the assumption that humans are all morally disposed and hence derive a naive moral pleasure in the natural world because of its sensuous truths. Nature reveals what we lack and also the possibility of discovering harmony. He distinguishes between the philosophical ethics of behavior based on Immanuel Kant's notion of duty, which must be taught and learned, and the ethics of incidents or happenings (*Geschehen*), which he calls naive morality based on natural disposition. For Jolles, in contrast to philosophical ethics, naive morality is *not* utilitarian, hedonistic, useful, or comfortable. Nor is it religious since it is tolerant, and not dictated by a specific divine order and socioreligious code. According to Jolles, naive morality is instinctual and prompts our pure ethical and absolute judgment.

If we now determine our form [of the fairy tale] from this perspective, then we can say that a form is present in the fairy tale in which incidents (*Geschehen*) are or the course of things is ordered in such a way that it fully corresponds to the demands of naïve morality, in other words, to our absolute instinctual judgment of what is good and just. As such the fairy tale stands in the sharpest contrast to what we in the world are accustomed to calling actual events. The course of things in reality corresponds extremely rarely to the demands of naïve morality, or it is mostly unjust. In opposition, the fairy tale confronts the world of "reality" because this world of reality is not the world which confers values on a general valid way of life. It is a world in which the incidents contradict the demands of naïve morality, a world which we naively experience as immoral. One can say that here the preoccupation [of the fairy tale] has a double effect: on the one hand, the preoccupation grasps and holds on to the world negating it as a reality which does not suit the ethics of the events. On the other hand, the preoccupation affirms another world in which all the demands of naïve morality are fulfilled.[22]

Indeed, the world of the fairy tale has always been created as a *counter-world* to the reality of the storyteller by the storyteller and listeners. Together, storytellers and listeners have collaborated through intuition as well as conscious conception to form worlds filled with naive morality. Fundamental to the feel of a fairy tale is its moral pulse. It tells us what we lack and how the world has to be organized differently so that we receive what we need. As types of fairy-tale telling evolved and became crystallized, the genre of the fairy tale borrowed and used motifs, themes, characters, expressions, and styles from other narrative forms and genres—and it still does. A good example is "Puss in Boots," which has a close connection to the fable and legend.

As is well known, the basic plot of this tale involves an anthropomorphized cat, who helps the destitute third son in a family of peasants impress a pompous king through flattery and tricks so that the king will believe that the young peasant is a rich lord. The peasant is often portrayed as an awkward dunce, while the supernatural cat—sometimes a fairy or fox in different European, Middle East, and Asian variants—is clever, and instructs the peasant how to speak and dress, for underlying the fairy tale is the proverb "clothes make the person."[23] Once the king believes that the peasant is a nobleman, the cat leads the king, his daughter, and the peasant to the large estate of an ogre. The cat rushes ahead of the party, outwits the ogre, and kills him. When the king, princess, and peasant arrive, the cat tells them that the castle and grand estate belong to the peasant, and the king, of course, gives his daughter to the peasant as his bride. They live happily ever after, and the cat is generally rewarded, for the animal is the actual hero/protagonist of the story.

Some critics interpret "Puss in Boots" as a "rise tale," in which the peasant is elevated and becomes a nobleman. But the peasant is not the driving force of the tale. The cat/fox moves the action, for he/she is often threatened with death by the peasant at the beginning of the tale, and must use his/her cunning to avoid death and find a rightful position. Quite frequently the cat/fox becomes a matchmaker, indicating a ritual role in marriage. As Hans-Jörg Uther notes, "The fox takes on an active role in contrast to the passive hero in various tales, particularly those that originate in Asia and are of the narrative type ATU 545B: *Puss in Boots.*"[24] Whether the hero is a cat or fox, this is a tale about the use of brains by cunning "people" in adapting to a difficult situation, and the active cat/fox exposes the contradictions and pretensions of the upper-class figures.

There are three major literary versions—crystallizations of oral folk tales, if you will—that have made this tale memetically traditional in the Western world: Giovan Francesco Straparola's "Constantino Fortunato" in *Le piacevoli notti* (*The Pleasant Nights*, 1550/1553), Giambattista Basile's "Cagliuso" in *Lo Cunto de li cunti* (*The Tale of Tales*, 1634), and Perrault's "The Master Cat, or Puss in Boots" in *Histoires ou Contes du temps passé* (*Stories or Tales of Time Past*, 1697). They are all unique and have specific cultural differences. For instance, in Straparola's tale, the cat is a fairy; in Basile's story, the cat is almost killed by the ungrateful peasant, while Perrault's cat becomes a royal messenger. But they all have some common features that reveal how they are closely bound to European, Middle Eastern, and Asian oral storytelling traditions about animal protagonists, and circulated hundreds of years before three educated writers shaped the tale in print. Nobody is certain when the first oral tale was created, and nobody will ever be able to determine the exact origins. Nevertheless, there are clues, fragments, and indications that this hybrid tale type involving motifs and themes such as an animal as helper, grateful recognition, the civilization of an uncouth lad, ruthless behavior for gain, and other popular themes was disseminated widely throughout the world. Ines Köhler-Zülch reports that hundreds of versions can be found in Europe, the Middle East, North and South Asia, North Africa, and North America.[25]

Dan Ben-Amos, an astute American folklorist, has made the following comment about Straparola's version:

> In this tale, European folk religion and folk literature converge and mutually influence each other, for the function of cats as agents of magical transformation in fairy tales builds upon supernatural associations, which are themselves distant reflections of cats in the mythology of the ancient world. In ancient Egypt, cats were an object of religious belief and ritual. . . . Bast, the cat goddess in Egypt, was a beneficent deity and a healer of disease. She was worshipped in ritual, festivities, and pilgrimages. And although the cult of Bast was not transferred to Rome, the related cult of Isis was. Mildred Kirk explains that Isis was "derived from Bast" and that she preserved Bast's association with the sacredness of cats. In European countries, cats were stripped from their position as objects of worship in religious cults and ritual, but they retained their

supernatural powers. Often they were considered the tangible representations of witches and fairies.[26]

In the three books of tales written by Straparola, Basile, and Perrault, which contain *mixed* genres, the authors make it clear that their stories do not belong to them but instead breathe through them. *They are to be told because they were told.* Straparola and Basile set frames in which characters from different social backgrounds tell tales, riddles, fables, anecdotes, and morals, while Perrault suggests that his tales were told to him by a nanny or mother goose figure. The tales that these authors heard were written to be told aloud because oral storytelling was the dominant mode of disseminating stories among all classes during the Renaissance.

Straparola is especially significant, not because he was an original storyteller or creator of the fairy tale, but because he wove all the simple forms of different genres into a master frame tale that celebrates storytelling, and in doing so, showed a great debt to a long history of Greco-Roman oral and literary storytelling that insightful scholars such as Burkert, Anderson, and Hansen, among others, have studied and documented. Among the seventy-four tales that Straparola recorded, fourteen can be designated as fairy tales.[27] All fourteen are remarkably different tale types with different plots and patterns, showing traces of Babylonian, Indian, Arabic, North African, and Hebrew oral storytelling and literary traditions that prefigured the artful cultivation of printed tales in the vernacular. Straparola's stories deal with basic human concerns such as incest ("Tebaldo"), mating ("The Pig Prince"), sibling rivalry and jealousy ("Ancilotto, King of Provino"), the master/slave relationship ("Maestro Lattantio and His Apprentice Magician"), and premarital sex and class struggle ("Pietro the Fool"). While many of the tales are related to Italian customs, laws, and rituals, others can be linked to tales from the medieval Arabic *Thousand and One Nights* and the Indian *The Ocean of Story* as well as the numerous adaptations of Apuleius's *The Golden Ass* of the second century. As Bartolomeo Rossetti indicates in his superb 1966 introduction to Straparola's *Le piacevoli notti,*

> The writers of Italian stories, beginning with the anonymous *Il Novellino* and [Giovanni] Boccaccio's *Decameron,* which is the acknowledged masterpiece of this most fertile genre, drew fully from the Oriental fairy tales, and we could also say, directly from the commercial and cultural exchanges with the Orient that had been conducted for centuries with the Italian coastal republics, above all with Venice. The continual flow of fairy-tale elements characteristic of the Orient and Arabic culture in particular fortuitously enriched the body of Italian story writing in this way. It was not the only factor. In the fervor generated by the study of the classics in the period of Humanism, there was also the rediscovery of ancient fairy-tale motifs such as the adventures and the amazing vicissitudes of the protagonist of *The Golden Ass* by Apuleius. All this continually

reinvigorated the fortune and richness of this narrative current, already fortunate and rich, that formed the literary arch from the fourteenth century to the seventeenth century, from Boccaccio to Basile.[28]

In the process of writing down literary and oral tales, Straparola selected and shaped those that he considered relevant, just as the tales themselves sought to be memetically relevant.

Memetics and Cultural Evolution

All tales want to be relevant, in the same way that we seek to make ourselves relevant through storytelling. Tales do not have agency. They are not alive, but they breathe and are vigorous, and as they are passed on to us through traditions of storytelling, they almost assume a life of their own. In my book *Why Fairy Tales Stick: The Evolution and Relevance of a Genre*, I sought to explain why certain fairy tales rise to the fore in our minds and Western culture, competing with other tales, and assume a specific status as classical or traditional. Some of these tales—such as "Cinderella," "Snow White," "Bluebeard," "Little Red Riding Hood," "Puss in Boots," and "Beauty and the Beast"—are so well known and have spread so widely in the world in all kinds of mediated forms that they appear to be universal memes, and I have tried to understand their significance as memes—a concept developed by Dawkins in his 1976 book, *The Selfish Gene*.

Dawkins maintains that there is one fundamental law of life that he believes is undeniable: "the law that all life evolves by the differential survival of replicating entities. The gene, the DNA molecule, happens to be the replicating entity that prevails on our own planet. There may be others. If there are, provided certain other conditions are met, they will almost inevitably tend to become the basis for an evolutionary planet." In fact, Dawkins argues that there is another replicator, which he calls a meme, a unit of cultural transmission.

> Examples of memes are tunes, ideas, catch-phrases, clothes fashions, ways of making pots or of building arches. Just as genes propagate themselves in the gene pool by leaping from body to body via sperms or eggs, so memes propagate themselves in the meme pool by leaping from brain to brain via a process which, in the broad sense can be called imitation. If a scientist hears, or reads about, a good idea, he passes it on to his colleagues and students. He mentions it in his articles and his lectures. If the idea catches on, it can be said to propagate itself, spreading from brain to brain. . . . [M]emes should be regarded as living structures, not just metaphorically but technically. When you plant a fertile meme in my mind you literally parasitize my brain, turning it into a vehicle for the meme's propagation in just the way that a virus

may parasitize the genetic mechanism of a host cell. And this isn't just a way of talking—the meme for, say, "belief in life after death" is actually realized physically, millions of times over, as a structure in the nervous systems of individual men the world over.[29]

In the years 2004–6, as I was writing *Why Fairy Tales Stick*, there were several serious books and essays about the meaning of memes, but the concept of a meme or memetics had not become popular and widespread. Yet within a short period of time—five years—the term "meme" has itself become somewhat memetic, and there are now over 441 million hits on Google to examine if one does a search for meme or memetics.[30] As we know, popularity can become dangerous for a person and term; it can cause the person and term to become trivial and meaningless. It can also bring about celebrity. To say the least, meme has suffered from its popularity and is now loosely used for anything and everything that becomes trendy and acts like a virus. The significance attached to it by Dawkins has largely been lost.

Nevertheless, there are numerous serious scholars who have endeavored carefully to explain the role that memetics plays in different cultural and scientific fields. Here I am thinking of Marion Blute's *Darwinian Sociocultural Evolution: Solutions to Dilemmas in Cultural and Social Theory* (2010), Distin's *The Selfish Meme* (2005) and *Cultural Evolution* (2011), Drout's *How Tradition Works: A Meme-Based Cultural Poetics of the Anglo-Saxon Tenth Century* (2006), Konner's *The Evolution of Childhood: Relationships, Emotion, Mind* (2010), Alex Mesoudi's *Cultural Evolution: How Darwinian Theory Can Explain Human Culture and Synthesize the Social Sciences* (2011), and Stephen Shennan's *Genes, Memes, and Human History: Darwinian Archaeology and Cultural Evolution* (2002). They all share a thoughtful approach to memetics, and while some of them have some doubts about the scientific validity of memetics, they have demonstrated why the term can be helpful in understanding cultural evolution.

Konner, for instance, views the meme as an elementary unit of cultural transmission, and contends, as do Distin and Blute, that

> the meme has proved useful in understanding cultural stability and change; at least four theories of cultural evolution have been based on it or some equivalent. As with genes, the faithfulness of replication and its associated repair mechanisms can ensure stability over time. And also as with genes the replication process is imperfect and errors have a creative function, serving as grist for the mill of cultural change, much as mutations offer the genetic variation that natural selection acts upon. But memes are largely independent of genes and enter a process of cultural evolution to some extent independent of its biological counterpart.[31]

He meticulously describes why and how memes function for children within a civilizing process, or what he calls acculturation. Memes, or cultural units of in-

formation such as stories, form meme or culture pools over time. Children's acculturation depends on memes, which do not always function smoothly. They
undergo change through innovation, the influence of chance events, the social
transmission between populations, the movement of carriers between populations, the natural selection of cultural variants, preservation through free decisions, and coerced preservation. Konner points out that "cultural constraints
include the limits imposed by technology, mental habit, and other inertial
factors that correspond to stabilizing cultural selection, the default condition
of cultural transmission. Values, imposition, and cultural constraints, among
other factors, affect the flow of memes, so that different ones have different de-
grees of likelihood of being transmitted to the next generation's culture pool."[32]

Drout's book, which is more concerned with oral and literary traditions
than it is with the evolution of childhood, complements Konner's work by
providing a thorough analysis of how memes as the simplest units of cultural
replication function to form oral traditions. He maintains that

> a tradition is an unbroken train of identical, non-instinctual behaviors
> that have been repeated after the same recurring antecedent conditions.
> The first time a behavior is enacted cannot be a tradition, but the sec-
> ond time can be, and the first enactment is then retrospectively defined
> as the origin of the tradition. . . . In memetic terms, a tradition is a com-
> bination of several smaller memes. The traditional behavior can be seen
> as one meme; let us call it *actio*. The response to the given antecedent
> condition that triggers the traditional behavior is another meme that
> enables the first meme; let us call it *recognitio*.[33]

Drout outlines a dialogic and dialectical process of action, recognition,
and justification, which is an explanation for the behavior, and this process
enables a specific cultural meme to develop into a universal one because it fits
general cultural views more than other cultural units of information. In other
words, the meme must be relevant if it is to be passed on. It must contain a
"word-to-world fit" that justifies its relevance; otherwise it will not be disseminated. The crucial elements in the evolution of the memetic process are
repetition and memory. Drout asserts that

> repetition creates patterns, and human brains, among their other tal-
> ents, are sublime pattern-recognizers. The combination of the patterns
> created by repetition with the human ability to recognize patterns
> means that in a culture that includes repeated traditions, information
> (memes) may be encoded and transmitted in significantly compressed
> form. Memes can also be retrieved from incomplete or noisy data, al-
> lowing traditionally encoded patterns to be transmitted and received in
> many different situations.[34]

In the case of fairy tales—and also such other simple forms or genres as the
fable, myth, and legend—memes help create and build traditions by creating

pools of stories, millions of stories, predicated on the human communication of shared experience. In human minds, we have made distinctions about which tales are more relevant than others and retain in memory the most relevant to retell and re-create. As programs of action, to recall Burkert's view of tales, fairy tales are preoccupied with removing listeners and readers from the world of reality to provide an alternative world of naive morality, and they have evolved by gathering fragments, bits of information, motifs, and characters from stories that have circulated around them. The fairy tale, as a memetic genre that retains its roots in oral traditions, has formed distinct patterns of action, employing other media such as print, electronics, drawing, photography, movies, and digital technology to create counterworlds and gain distance from our world of reality so that we can know it as well as ourselves. In the process fairy tales have been changed while changing the media. The salience and/or relevance of memetic fairy tales, which offer alternative patterns of action to real social behavior, is a cultural indication of what we have endeavored to communicate to help one another adapt to changing environments while preserving an instinctual morality. The memetic crystallization of certain fairy tales as classical does not make them static for they are constantly re-created and reformed, and yet remain memetic because of their relevant articulation of problematic issues in our lives. Fairy tales, like our own lives, were born out of conflict.

Fairy tales were not created or intended for children. Yet they resonate with them, and children recall them as they grow to confront the injustices and contradictions of so-called real worlds. We cannot explain why the origins of the fairy tale are so inexplicable and elusive. But we can elucidate why they continue to be irresistible and breathe memetically through us, offering hope that we can change ourselves while changing the world.

2

The Meaning of Fairy Tale
within the Evolution of Culture

Fairy Tale signifies belief in the supernatural, not the suspension of belief.
We all believe in the extra-ordinary of Once Upon a Time. We need to
believe. We all dream and breathe through our tales.

—Vincenzo di Kastiaux

Think of a gigantic whale soaring through the ocean, swallowing each and
every fish of any size that comes across its path. The marvelous, majestic
whale had once lived on land fifty-four million years ago and had been tiny.
Part of a group of marine mammals now known as cetaceans, the land whale
eventually came to depend on other fish for its subsistence and thrive on the
bountiful richness of the ocean. To grow and survive, it constantly adapted to
its changing environment. The fairy tale is no different.

The wondrous fairy tale emanated from a wide variety of tiny tales thousands of years ago that were widespread throughout the world and continue
to exist in unique ways under different environmental conditions. As I have
explained in chapter 1, the fairy tale's form and contents were not exactly what
they are today. To summarize my argument, the fairy tale was first a simple,
imaginative oral tale containing magical and miraculous elements and was related to the belief systems, values, rites, and experiences of pagan peoples. Also
known as the wonder or magic tale, the fairy tale underwent numerous transformations before the innovation of print led to the production of fixed texts
and conventions of telling and reading. But even then, the fairy tale refused to
be dominated by print and continued to be altered and diffused around the
world by word of mouth up to the present. That is, it shaped and was shaped
by the interaction of orality and print as well as other technological mediations
and innovations, such as painting, photography, radio, and film.

Technological inventions, in particular, enabled the fairy tale to expand in various cultural domains, even on the Internet. Like the whale, the fairy tale adapted itself and was transformed by both common nonliterate people and upper-class literate people from a simple, brief tale with vital information; it grew, became enormous, and disseminated information that contributed to the cultural evolution of specific groups. In fact it continues to grow—embracing, if not swallowing, all types of genres, art forms, and cultural institutions, and adjusting itself to new environments through the human disposition to re-create relevant narratives, and via technologies that make its diffusion easier and more effective. The only difference between the whale and fairy tale is that the tale is not alive and does not propel itself. It needs humans—and yet at times, it does seem as though a vibrant fairy tale can attract listeners and readers and latch on to their brains and become a living memetic force in cultural evolution.

Almost all endeavors by scholars to define the fairy tale as a genre have failed. Their failure is predictable because the genre is so volatile and fluid. As Haase remarks in one of the more cogent descriptions of the struggle by intellectuals to pin down the fairy tale,

> Despite its currency and apparent simplicity, the term "fairy tale" resists a universally accepted or universally satisfying definition. For some, the term denotes a specific narrative form with easily identified characteristics, but for others it suggests not a singular genre but an umbrella category under which a variety of other forms may be grouped. Definitions of "fairy tale" often tend to include a litany of characteristics to account for the fact the term has been applied to stories as diverse as "Cinderella," "Little Red Riding Hood," "Hansel and Gretel," "Jack and the Beanstalk," "Lucky Hans," "Bluebeard," and "Henny-Penny."[1]

The difficulty in defining the fairy tale stems from the fact that storytellers and writers never used the term "fairy tale" until d'Aulnoy coined it in 1697, when she published her first collection of tales. She never wrote a word about why she used the term. Yet it was and is highly significant that she chose to call her stories *contes des fées*, literally "tales about fairies."[2] The first English translation of d'Aulnoy's collection, *Les contes des fées* (1697–98), was published as *Tales of the Fairies* in 1707.[3] But it was not until 1750 that the term "fairy tale" came into common English usage.[4] Since this term—"fairy tale"/"conte de fée"—has become so troublesome for scholars and does not do justice in English to the "revolutionary" implications of its inventor, d'Aulnoy, I should like to explore its historical importance in greater depth by discussing the role of the fairies in d'Aulnoy's works, especially in "The Isle of Happiness," "The Ram," and "The Green Serpent." In the process, I shall also look at how fairies were part of a long oral and literary tradition in French culture, and how d'Aulnoy's employment of fairies in her tales owes a debt to Greek and Roman myths, the opera, theatrical spectacles, debates about the role of women in French society, and French folklore. At this chapter's conclusion, I shall examine how a cultural evolutionary approach to the rise of French fairy tales may help us understand how and why the elusive term "fairy tale" has spread as a meme and become so whalelike.

How the Term "Conte de Fée" Became Viral

The most striking feature of the most important foundational period of the literary fairy tale in Europe, 1690 to 1710, was the domination of fairies in the French texts. Up until this point, the literary fairy tale was not considered a genre and did not have a name. It was simply a *conte, cunto, cuento, skazka,* story, *Märchen,* and so on. No writer labeled his or her tale a fairy tale in print until d'Aulnoy created the term. If we recall, the title of Straparola's collection of stories, which contained a few fairy tales, was *The Pleasant Nights* or *Le piacevoli notti,* and Basile called his book, written in Neapolitan dialect, *The Tale of Tales* or *Lo Cunto de li cunti.* The Italians were among the early writers of vernacular fairy tales in print, and there were some fairies or *fate* in the Italian tales, but they were not singled out for attention, nor did they play the prominent role that they were assigned by the French seventeenth-century women writers, also known as *conteuses* and *salonnières.*[5] (And of course, some highly significant male writers such as Perrault and Philippe de Caylus also employed fairies in their tales.)

When d'Aulnoy included the fairy tale "The Isle of Happiness" in her novel *Histoire d'Hippolyte, comte de Duglas* in 1690, she was not aware that she was about to set a trend in France that became epidemic among her acquaintances and other readers of her social class. Though the nymphs in this tale were not called fairies, their resemblance was clear. Moreover, the princess whom they served was definitely a fairy, and the paradisiacal island represented an ideal fairy realm or utopia. (It should be noted that after Adolph, the protagonist, foolishly abandons this island, he is murdered by Father Time; happiness is lost forever. D'Aulnoy's tales thereafter mark what is lacking in the mundane world and depict how fairies must intervene to compensate for human foibles.) Within six years after the publication of "The Isle of Happiness," the *literary* fairy tale—heretofore a simple oral folk tale, or a printed conte, cunto, or *favola*—became the talk of the literary salons, or what had been the talk in these salons now came to print.

Orality was, as numerous French critics have recently demonstrated, inseparable from print fairy tales and defined in many diverse ways.[6] D'Aulnoy promoted the cause of fairy tales in the Parisian salons in which she recited them. Storytelling, riddles, and other parlor and salon games had been common in Italy, Spain, England, and France since the sixteenth century.[7]

D'Aulnoy's tales were part of a creative explosion that became contagious, featuring powerful and precocious fairies in Marie-Jeanne Lhéritier's *Oeuvres Meslées* (1696); Catherine Bernard's *Inès de Cordoue* (1696), a novel that includes "Les Enchantements de l'Eloquence" and "Riquet à la houppe"; Charlotte Rose Caumont de la Force's *Les Contes des Contes* (1698); Perrault's *Histoires ou contes du temps passé* (1697); d'Aulnoy's *Les Contes des fées* in four volumes (1697–98); Chevalier de Mailly's *Les Illustres Fées, contes galans* (1698); Henriette Julie de Murat's *Contes de fées* (1698); Nodot's *Histoire de Mélusine* (1698); Sieur de Prechac's *Contes moins contes que les autres* (1698); Catherine Durand's *La Comtesse de Mortane* (1699); Madame de Murat's *Histoires sublimes et allégoriques* (1699); Eustache Le Noble's *Le Gage touché* (1700); Louise de Bossigny, Comtesse d'Auneuil's *La Tyrannie des fées détruite* (1702); and Madame Durand's *Les Petits Soupers de l'été de l'année 1699* (1702).

It was only after d'Aulnoy introduced the title "contes des fées" in 1697 or before in the salons that other writers began using the term that signified much more than tales about fairies.[8] The term's usage was a declaration of difference and resistance. It can be objectively stated that there is no other period in Western literary history when so many fairies, like powerful goddesses, were the determining figures in most of the plots of tales written by women—and also by some men. These tales were programs of actions or social symbolic acts projecting moral and ethical conflicts in alternative worlds.

There are several reasons why marvelous tales became chock-full of omnipotent fairies and why so many writers labeled their tales "contes des fées"—a term that has stuck in French and English to the present day. These reasons also may help us understand why today we fail to recognize or understand the term's immense significance when we use or try to define fairy tale. To begin with, we must recall that the French women writers were all members of literary salons, where they told or read their tales before having them published. These private salons afforded them the opportunity to perform and demonstrate their unique prowess at a time when they had few privileges in the public sphere. The fairies in their tales signal their actual differences with male writers and resistance to the conditions under which they lived, especially regulations that governed manners and comportment in their daily routines within the French civilizing process.[9] It was only in a fairy-tale realm, not supervised by the church or subject to the dictates of King Louis XIV, that they could project alternatives stemming from their desires and needs. As Patricia Hannon observes,

> It is widely recognized that the seventeenth-century public demarcated fairy-tale writing as women's domain, inseparable from the feminocentric salons that nurtured it. Both modernist advocates of women's tales such as the *Mercure*, and detractors such as the clergymen Villiers, understood the fairy tale to be a female genre. . . . Thought to have

been transmitted by grandmothers and governesses, the fairy tale was an eminently female genre in the seventeenth-century consciousness. Yet, the era expanded its delineation of women's role to encompass the composing of tales in addition to their mere recitation.[10]

Other scholars such as Anne Duggan and Holly Tucker have also emphasized how important salon conditions were for stimulating the female writers of fairy tales.[11] It was in the salons that they shared their tales, forged alliances, exchanged ideas, and came to look on themselves as fairies. For a short period in their lives, they delighted in embracing a fairy cult without establishing a specific code. Their tales spelled out new diverse standards of behavior that were intended to transform the relationships between men and women, primarily of the upper classes.

In short, French women writers wanted to live their tales as specially gifted artists, and created and called on the fairies they created to arbitrate on their behalf. But their fairies were not always just. Rather, they could also be witchlike and had supernatural powers that they used to test or contest ordinary mortals. In the case of d'Aulnoy, Jacques Barchilon comments:

> Madame d'Aulnoy loved to tell tales, and imagination was what she lacked the least. She qualified her characters in terms not only evocative of their appearances, but even more with a picturesque sonority. Here are some examples. First, the evil fairies: Stiff Neck (Torticolis), Thick-Set (Ragotte), Grumbler (Grognette), Runt (Trognon), and Dirty One (Sousio), which means squalid in Spanish (soucio). Let us not forget the ogres Ravage (Ravagio) and Torment (Tourmentine). And now the more "sympathetic" fairies: Cod Fish (Merluche), Flower of Love (Fleur d'Amour), and Beauty of the Night (Belle de Nuit).[12]

In general, the awesome fairies with their kind and nasty personalities stood in opposition to the court of Louis XIV and the Catholic church, and they were the antithesis of the pietistic Madame de Maintenon, Louis's morganatic wife, who insisted on introducing a reign of strict piety in the court and preached against secularism and worldliness. As Lewis Seifert and Domna Stanton write:

> Nonetheless, in the context of a pietistic *fin de siècle*, the fairy tale constituted a defense of fashionable secular society. Its portrayal of earthly luxury and happiness and its reliance on the supernatural powers of fairies, sorcerers, and other "pagan" figures obviously run counter to a Christian world view. And yet, as a narrative form associated with children and the lower classes and championed largely by women writers, this defense of secular culture appeared largely innocuous, at least if the lack of extended critiques is taken as any indication. Still, the unsettled political and social climate of the time partially explains the appeal of the genre.[13]

Opera and *Féerie*

The fairy worlds conceived by the French women writers were spectacular, absurd, and naively moral. As Duggan points out, d'Aulnoy "especially celebrates the privileged *mondain* spectacle of the late seventeenth-century France, opera, by incorporating and mimicking aspects of it in her tales."[14] Duggan emphasizes correctly that the impact of the opera on the fairy-tale writers, especially the extravagant spectacles that were imported from Italy in the seventeenth century, has not received sufficient scholarly attention. This is especially true in light of the development of the unusual entertainment (divertissement) or melodramatic play/ballet called féerie. In his highly informative study *La Féerie*, Paul Ginsty states:

> The origin of the *féerie* can be found in the court ballets of the sixteenth and seventeenth centuries, inspired in their action by stories and the marvelous. The Italian ingénues, summoned by Catherine de Médici, were the first to introduce the *féerie*. These graceful people were the great disseminators of the marvels. The court of the grand duke of Florence had been the school of intricate machine makers and decorators, Timante Buonacorsi, Baldassare Lancia, Nicolo Tribolo—they excelled in the offering of complicated and luxurious entertainments. Catherine de Médici placed Baltazarini in charge of the ballets, and this man of imagination responded to the confidence placed in him by calling the king's painter, Jacques Patin, the musicians Beaulieu and Salmon, and the royal poet La Chesnaie to collaborate in producing the ballet *Circé*. He hardly had enough money, for the ballet cost two hundred thousand ecus.[15]

Ginsty forgets to mention that this *ballet comique de la reine* was five hours long, and danced by Queen Louise and the women of the court. Moreover, there were other developments in sixteenth-century Italy that may have influenced Médici's penchant for the arts, such as the reciting and enactment of fairy tales and myths in different courts.[16] In all the court entertainments in Italy and France during the baroque period, the spectacle was of utmost importance, consisting of magnificent displays based on myths and fairy tales that celebrated the glory as well as power of the court, which was likened to some kind of enchanted fairy realm. These ballets, masquerades, and operas were taken seriously in various European courts; they often were made up of ten to fifteen tableaux or scenes; the stories were danced and sung by gifted actors and acrobats; machines and traps were invented and used to create illusions; and characters such as fairies, witches, wizards, gnomes, gods, ghosts, devils, and noble protagonists were involved in plots that demanded the intervention of some good higher power, either a fairy, god, or goddess.

It should be noted that at the same time that these artful and serious spectacles were being cultivated, there were also comic representations that contained fairy-tale characters and themes and were influenced by the commedia dell'arte. By the time of Louis XIV's reign in the late seventeenth century, it became common for the court to hold gala spectacles that certainly could be called féeries, and for writers such as Pierre Corneille, Molière, and Jean-Baptiste Lully to write plays based on myths and fairy stories. As Duggan explains,

> Louis XIV grew up listening to fairy tales, a genre that later, as Mainil contends, would define the nature of royal fêtes, consisting of forms of entertainment like equestrian games, ballets, and theater, referred to as *divertissements*. . . . The spectacular/specular nature of the marvelous as performed in royal festivals would be integrated into opera, whose *divertissements*, the term also used for operatic interludes of song and dance, recall those of the royal fête. As its precursor, opera marks the tale of d'Aulnoy in very specific ways, including: 1) the use of supernatural means of movement borrowed from the opera's machinery; 2) the inclusion of choruses; 3) the incorporation of verse songs into her tales; and 4) inscriptions of Versailles or Versailles-like palaces.[17]

From the beginning, d'Aulnoy and the other salonnières saw the subversive potential of the fairy-tale operas along with the supernatural attributes of fairies that could be woven into their tales to comment on the narrow religiosity of Louis XIV's court and its misogynist tendencies.

Magical Midwives

In addition, there are two other profound reasons why fairies were so important to them. The first involves the role that midwives, nannies, and childbirth played in the lives of the women writers—a role that is more or less designated for fairies. As Tucker writes:

> In oral and literary *contes de fées*, fairies are also no strangers to the drama of royal births. Fairies do more than attend the birth scene; they also orchestrate every stage of reproduction. They predict conception and, if angry, cast spells of infertility. They determine the circumstances and outcome of pregnancy by providing—or withholding—aid to the mother-to-be. Following labor, they attend to the needs of the newborn and dictate the child's path in life through their gifts, beneficent or malevolent. And, in true fairy-tale fashion, woe to those who forget or refuse to offer adequate compensation to the fairies' contributions to these rites of childbirth.[18]

It is crucial to note that d'Aulnoy gave birth to four children when she was still a teenager, and depended greatly on the help of midwives and other women. Her husband was a depraved scoundrel, and with her mother's help, she participated in a scheme to have him executed for an offense against the king. It failed, and she spent some time in jail while she was pregnant. D'Aulnoy was thoroughly aware of the intrigues, corruption, and decadence of the nobility, courtiers, and priests in and around Louis XIV's court by the time she was twenty, and it is not by chance that she assigns the midwife or protector role to fairies in her tales.

It is not the Christian God or church that d'Aulnoy's queens and princesses call on to grant them a child or assist them in childbirth but rather the fairies. Though some of the fairies can be malevolent, as I have already indicated, there is a sense in her tales that only the fairies can clean house, so to speak—that is, put an end to deceit and abusive treatment. "The Green Serpent" begins this way: "Once upon a time there was a great queen who, having given birth to twin daughters, invited twelve fairies who lived nearby to come and bestow gifts upon them, as was the custom in those days. Indeed, it was a very useful custom, for the power of the fairies generally compensated for the deficiencies of nature. Sometimes, however, they also spoiled what nature had done its best to make perfect, as we shall soon see."[19] As midwives and godmothers, the fairies frequently cross swords with one another, just as the Greek and Roman goddesses did. They make their presence known in the French tales and orchestrate the plots. Endowed with supernatural power that harks back to Greco-Roman and Egyptian mythology as well as French customs and beliefs in regard to childbirth and rearing, the fairies in the tales of the conteuses had real relevance for the women writers, as shown in the manner in which they represented them.

The Importance of the Morgan and Mélusine Fairies in d'Aulnoy's Tales

If d'Aulnoy and the other conteuses of the late seventeenth century chose the fairies over the Virgin Mary, Jesus, and Christian saints—and here we have the second reason why fairies were profoundly important to these writers—it was because they were steeped in the lore of fairies and appealed to them out of protest against the church and state. This is not to say that the cultivated writers believed in folklore along with the rites and superstitions of the common people. In fact, as Barchilon, Raymonde Robert, Nadine Jasmin, Jean Mainil, Constance Cagnat-Debœuf, and other scholars have demonstrated, their perspective on folk tales was ironic, and their complex tales often mocked folklore and were carnivalesque. Nevertheless, they fondly embraced fairy lore to veil their critiques of church and state, which are portrayed either as decadent or impotent in their tales.

It is impossible to overestimate the significance of d'Aulnoy's embrace of the Morgan and Mélusine fairy tradition and folklore in France, not to mention how this was welcomed by other French conteuses. In her magisterial study of all aspects of d'Aulnoy's works, Jasmin devotes an entire chapter to the author's knowledge and use of medieval materials and folklore. She notes:

"Remarkably eclectic, the conteuse (d'Aulnoy) did not in effect deny herself any source of inspiration. Her rejection of literary discrimination and bias led her quite naturally to borrow from the most diverse categories. Also she is coherently remarkable. Much less scattered than would appear at first view, the intertextual references form a notable *modern* literary constellation, characterized by the integration of the most recent forms and genres at the heart of a culture resolutely *mundane*, even better, *galant*."[20]

To grasp how profound and significant her amalgamation of diverse sources is for the defining movement of the conte de fée in 1690 as well as most of the fairy tales written between 1690 and 1710, I should like to summarize some of the major theses in Laurence Harf-Lancner's superb study *Les Fées au Moyen Âge: Morgane et Mélusine. Naissance des fées*. Like many other reliable scholars who have written on the origins of the fairies, such as Louis Ferdinand Alfred Maury, Harf-Lancner views the Greek and Roman myths about the Moirai (Greek fates) and Parcae (Roman fates) as forming the foundation of Western beliefs in fairies.[21] In the Greek tradition, their basic function was to prophesy the destiny of a newborn. Eventually the Romans endowed Fauna with some of these qualities as the goddess of fertility and prophecy, and tales circulated about her as the Bona Dea, or the good goddess, who had her own cult and came to be associated with wild nature and eroticism because she was deemed to be the force of life.[22] There is an informative historical synopsis of Fauna on the Web site for obscure goddesses:

> Fauna is an old Roman Goddess of Prophecy and Fruitfulness, with ties to the forest and fields and the animals found there. She is closely related to the God Faunus; she is variously his wife, sister, or daughter. Her name, like Faunus's, is from the Latin *faveo*, "to befriend, support, or back up," from which we get our "favor"; an alternate etymology is from *fari*, "to speak, talk, or say," referring to their powers of prophecy. Her name then could be variously translated as "She Who Favors," "the Friendly One," "the Speaker," or even "She Who Has Your Back." She was identified with the prophetic Goddess *Fatua*, again meaning, "the Speaker," but with additional meanings of "She Who Speaks Prophecy," or "the Oracle."[23]

Like many goddesses or divinities, Fauna had a split image, and was often associated with courtesans and free sex. At the same time, she was known to be a model of chastity and modesty, and rarely left her domain. John Scheid points out how many of the good characteristics of Fauna, as an antecedent of the fairy, were fused with the bad qualities of the witch.

According to the founding myth of the Bona Dea, the goddess herself was ambiguous. Bona Dea was supposedly the divine name of Fauna, wife of the archaic Faunus. In one version of the story, Fauna is beaten with myrtle branches and tortured for drinking undiluted wine. In another version she refuses, even though drunk and battered, to give in to the incessant advances of her father, Faunus, who has his way with her after assuming the form of a serpent. In short, all the sources portray the cult of Bona Dea as an upside-down world. But this world was not only upside-down. It was also, like the Roman view of feminine chastity, deeply ambiguous. The seemingly contradictory attitudes of Bona Dea and her matrons toward wine, sex, and men are somewhat reminiscent of the ambiguous status of the Vestals. The matrons both accept and reject undiluted wine and sex, signifying an ambivalence of masculine and feminine, active and passive. The role of women in the cult was portrayed in both ritual and exegesis as an exception. Women did what they did in secret, at night, in a private residence, and in disguise. . . . Note that the mythographers placed the origin of Bona Dea and her cult among the Fauna, legendary inhabitants of the woods surrounding what would become the city of Rome.[24]

During the early Middle Ages, the images of the Greek and Roman fates were changed by different groups of people in popular culture throughout Europe. The fates became fantastic or supernatural creatures, circulating in marvelous stories associated with the divine powers of prophecy and love. As other figures and divinities were created, such as sirens, nymphs, sylphs, mermaids, and nixies, they were given different names. Leslie Ellen Jones remarks that

> the names of fairies vary from locale to locale. Perhaps the most famous are the Irish Tuatha Dé Danann (Tribes of the Goddess Danu) or people of the *sidh*. In Wales they are the Tykwyth Teg (the Fair Tribe) or Plant Rhys Ddwfn (Children of Rhys the Deep). English fairies have more names than can be listed in one breath: boggarts, brownies, greenies, pixies, knockers, lobs, hobs, and lubberkins. The French call them *fées*, the Bretons *Korrigans*. In Sicily there are the *donas de fuera* (ladies from outside). In the Balkans the main word is *vila*; in Russia *rusalka*; in Greece the classical *nereid*, originally a water sprite, has expanded to cover all fairylike beings.[25]

Clearly, pagan divinities were the predecessors of fairies, and their roles and functions were transmitted memetically in different cultures over thousands of years to form the modern concept of the fairy or notions of feerié. One common function that can be traced throughout Europe is the pagan motif of the goddess and fairy as protector of children (associated with the midwife/nanny/Mother Goose figure). Laura Rangoni writes:

> This motif can be found frequently in the fairy tale, and if this narrative form can truly be considered the relic of pagan survival, then it is sufficiently evident that the fairies are in reality a symbol of pagan religiosity

in struggle with the unstoppable advance of Christianity. Moreover, despite everything, the fairy tale continues to conserve a ritual character that is typically pagan. In the vicissitudes of the fairy tale, there is, in fact, a pattern or plot of experiences that can easily be retraced in the variegated world of pre-Christian myths. Consequently, the theme of fairies springs with good probability from ancient lineages of pagan religiosity to take part in popular mythology through diverse routes.[26]

It is always a difficult task to trace a fairy tale's lineage, and the sociocultural context in a particular time period must always be considered when trying to grasp the symbolic function of a fairy and tales about fairies. What is striking in the changing image of the figure that eventually was called a fée in France is that she was depicted with just as many similarities in other cultures along with differences. As Harf-Lancner notes,

> the Middle Ages knew two types of fairies: the fates (parcae), whose classical image had been profoundly transformed by that of the popular tradition, and the ladies of the forest, whose path often crossed with that of mortals. The latter became the "fairies" upon their entrance into learned culture (*culture savante*) in the twelfth century with the gradual severing of the word "fairy" from the personage of the fate. Moreover, the two folkloric types, primitively distinct, continued in the thirteenth century to merge at the same time into a new figure, appropriately literary—an enamored goddess and a mistress of destiny. After the Middle Ages the fairies will no longer have any other visage but that, and the fairies of our popular tales often submitted to the influence of this creation of romantic literature.[27]

Harf-Lancner studies Latin and vernacular texts, romances, stories, and *lais* recorded by clerics and learned scholars to show how the transformation of stories about the classical Greek fates led to two types of plots that involved powerful fairies. The stability of the medieval plots indicates for Harf-Lancner the popularity of the tales about fairies and their oral dissemination among the common people during the early Middle Ages, and how the fairies more or less erupted into the literate culture, forming the basis of numerous romances and lais by the twelfth century. The first distinct tale type is based on the adventures of the famous fairy Mélusine and involves an enamored fairy who enters the world of mortals.[28] The second concerns the notorious fairy Morgan le Fay and a hero who enters into her realm.[29] The pattern of the Mélusine texts has three parts to it:

1. The encounter—a mortal discovers a fantastically beautiful fairy, generally in a forest, and falls in love with her.
2. The pact—the hero proposes to wed the fairy, and she accepts on the condition that he agrees to respect a prohibition.

3. The violation of the pact—the hero is either persuaded to break the prohibition by jealous siblings, or makes a wrong, fateful decision, thereby losing his wife and happiness.

In some of the romances and tales, there is a recovery or reconciliation. But the dominant tale types do not provide for a happy end.

The pattern of the Morgan le Fay texts has certain similarities to the Mélusine stories, but there are distinct differences. The plot of this tale type consists of the following:

1. Journey to another world—the hero seeks out a nymph or fairy in an enchanted world, separate from the world of mortals.
2. Long residence in a supernatural realm—the hero spends an indefinite amount of time in a state of bliss without realizing how fast time passes.
3. Permission and prohibition—the hero becomes bored or longs for a return to his home, and asks permission from the fairy to visit the world of mortals, and the fairy grants him permission providing that he respect a prohibition.
4. Violation of the prohibition—the hero breaks his promise or violates the prohibition in some way, and consequently, he is banished from the enchanted world of fairies and dies.

D'Aulnoy, Greco-Roman Myths, and Fairy Lore

Though there is no documentary evidence that d'Aulnoy knew tales about Mélusine and Morgan le Fay, there is sufficient proof in her fairy tales that she had some knowledge of either printed texts or oral tales. We must also bear in mind that she was born and raised in Normandy, where the Celtic tradition of fairies was strong.[30] There is a clear indication as well that d'Aulnoy was familiar with a wide array of Greco-Roman myths, which were also performed as ballets or plays in Louis XIV's court. Seifert and Stanton remark:

> Intent on affirming their own social status, the conteuses disguised and transformed whatever they borrowed from lower-class tales with an abundance of literary and cultural references. Indeed, the wide variety of intertexts woven into their *contes de fées* shows a sophistication that defies the stereotypical simplicity of the fairy-tale genre. Notwithstanding their modernist affiliations, allusions to Greek and Roman mythology recur throughout the texts of the conteuses, sometimes alongside more traditional folkloric characters. In many of d'Aulnoy's tales, for instance, Cupid makes an appearance as either an ally or an enemy of the fairies. More often mythology is used as a conventional rhetorical trope. The stories in Ovid's *Metamorphoses*, extremely popular throughout early modern Europe, were particularly useful to the

conteuses, especially for the concept of metamorphosis and the plot situations it could generate. However, their tales also evoke motifs and characters reminiscent of medieval romance, with such figures as the fairy and such topoi as the maiden imprisoned in a tower.[31]

A good example of the manner in which the women writers worked is d'Aulnoy's first tale, "The Isle of Happiness." It weaves elements and motifs of French folklore, medieval romance, and Greco-Roman mythology into a plot that fits Harf-Lancner's "Morgan le Fay pattern": journey to another world; long residence in a supernatural realm; permission and prohibition; and violation of prohibition. D'Aulnoy "disguises" her borrowing and use of intertextual references by setting the story in Russia. The hero, Prince Adolph, loses his way in the woods while hunting a bear and then encounters the mother of the Greek four winds in a cave. When all the winds return to the cave, Zephir, the west wind, talks about the fairy Princess Felicity living on the Isle of Happiness, and Adolph becomes so enchanted by Zephir's description of the princess that he asks Zephir to carry him there. Zephir agrees and gives him a cloak that makes Adolph invisible to protect him from the island's guards, who are monsters.

When Adolph arrives, he is stunned by the magnificence of the isle and its grottos. At one point he comes across Cupid's grotto, with its inscription: "Love is the greatest of all blessings. Love alone is able to fulfill our desires. All other sweet things of life become dull if they are not mixed with love's attractive charms."[32] When he accidentally exposes himself before Princess Felicity, whose beauty is so perfect that she seems to be a daughter of the heavens, she believes that he is the bird Phoenix because she has never seen a human before. Then he tells her the truth: that he has come to admire her divine beauty. They fall in love and stay young by drinking from the fountain of youth.

Adolph spends three hundred happy years with Princess Felicity without realizing it. Once he learns how long he has been on the island, he complains that he has neglected his duties, and thus lost glory and honor. He consequently wants to return to his kingdom. Princess Felicity is upset with and disappointed in him, especially because he places his honor and ambition over their love. So she regretfully gives him a magnificent horse named Bichar and marvelous weapons, telling him that the horse "will take you wherever you must go to do battle and triumph. But don't place your foot on the ground no matter what happens in your country, for the fairy spirit that the gods have given me enable me to prophesy that if you neglect my advice, Bichar will not be able to extricate you from your trouble."[33] After Adolph promises to obey her and departs, but Father Time tricks him into touching the ground, whereupon he is smothered to death. When Princess Felicity learns about his fate, she closes her palace doors forever, and this is also why human beings will never find perfect happiness.

D'Aulnoy's first fairy tale begins the "modernist" re-creation of oral folklore, French medieval literature, and Greco-Roman mythology to celebrate fairies along with their high standards of love and secular morality. Her tale is indeed about fairies first and foremost—their beauty, generosity, and glorious realm, which harbors eternal youth and true love. D'Aulnoy reassembles motifs from folklore (a hero lost in the woods, helpers, an invisible cloak, the fountain of youth, a magic horse, and Father Time), Greco-Roman myths (the four winds and Cupid), and Torquato Tasso's *Jerusalem Delivered* (reference to the sorceress Armida) to create her own version of a Morgan le Fay tale. It is a jarring dystopian narrative because the gift of a fairy is unappreciated and a prince pays with his life for violating a promise. From this point on in her writing about fairies, d'Aulnoy imbues her tales with a protofeminist spirit and endeavors to articulate and maintain the mundane or secular position that educated, upper-class women took against the pietistic restrictions as well as outdated manners and social codes of the ancien régime. Her aim was to rewrite the civilizing process through the representation of modern fairies, who strived to introduce new customs and moral behavior into narratives, while also reutilizing the stuff of Greco-Roman mythology, folklore, and medieval romances.

Two other d'Aulnoy tales, "The Green Serpent" and "The Ram"—strongly influenced by Apuleius's "Cupid and Psyche" in *The Golden Ass*, Jean de La Fontaine's version, *Les Amours de Psiché et de Cupidon* (*The Loves of Cupid and Psyche*, 1669), and the Mélusine cycle of romances and tales—demonstrate how experimental and sophisticated her fairy tales were. In the Mélusine tradition, there is generally an encounter with a supernatural creature in a forest, a pact that entails a promise and prohibition, and a violation of the promise/prohibition. In these two tales there is a gender reversal too. That is, normally the hero meets the extraordinary Mélusine or a supernatural creature in a forest. D'Aulnoy's tales, however, depict a young princess who encounters a male transformed into a supernatural beast, who leads her to an idyllic realm.

In the beginning of "The Green Serpent," Laidronette is cursed to be ugly by a malicious and powerful fairy, Magotine, at birth, and is troubled by her ugliness during her youth. At one point she meets the Green Serpent, a king, who has also been cursed by Magotine and transformed into a serpent. He wants to help Laidronette, but she is frightened of him. Later, when stranded on the magnificent island of Pagodia, she is impressed by the splendor and culture of the pagods, tiny elflike creatures, who serve an invisible king, the Green Serpent. Eventually she agrees to marry the invisible king, who makes her promise never to look at him until he has completed the seven-year curse. But curiosity gets the better of her. She breaks her promise and is punished by Magotine. With the help of the Fairy Protectrice, however, Laidronette completes three difficult tasks and is changed into Queen Discrete. Her transformation causes Magotine to have a change of heart and allow Laidronette to join the Green Snake, transformed into a handsome king, and live on the utopian island of Pagodia.

"The Ram," which has echoes of the King Lear story, concerns a princess named Merveilleuse, condemned to death by her father because she allegedly insulted him. But a captain of the guards lets her escape into the forest, where she meets a talking ram, who was once a handsome prince. Unfortunately, the prince has been cursed because he did not return the affection of the ugly fairy Ragotte, who punished him by making him live as a ram for five years. This king of the rams takes Merveilleuse through a cave to his magnificent underground realm, where all the animals, former humans, can talk and act with great civility and culture. She is impressed by what she sees and experiences. After some time, however, she asks permission from the ram to return to her father's kingdom to participate in the marriage of one of her sisters. The ram, desperately in love with her, sadly complies, providing that she promises to return or otherwise he will die. She agrees and returns, but another sister has a wedding, and she asks again to attend the marriage. This time, she reconciles herself with her father and forgets about the ram king, who searches for her in her father's royal palace. Denied entry, the ram king dies outside the palace gates.

Together, these tales form a critical dialogue or meditation about proper behavior and the responsibilities that love entails. In both tales, each containing allusions to other idyllic worlds with naive morals, the fairies set the conditions under which the protagonists—princesses and princes—interact. With references to "Cupid and Psyche" in both tales, d'Aulnoy places great emphasis on love within the courtly civilizing process. It is through love filled with empathy that men become gallant, and women become virtuous and precocious. When Laidronette arrives on the island of the pagods, for instance, she hears a voice singing to her:

> Let Cupid make you now his own.
> Here he rules with gentle tone.
> Love with pleasure will be sown.
> On this isle no grief is known.[34]

When Laidronette breaks her promise to the Green Serpent, she is exiled from the island and must prove herself by acquiring the qualities that will distinguish her with the name Queen Discrete. She is assisted along the way by the Fairy Protectrice, and it is through love that she becomes more diligent, trustworthy, and courageous. When Discrete/Laidronette must travel to Pluto's underworld to liberate her lost husband, the Green Serpent, she calls on Cupid to help her. And it is Cupid who accompanies the reunited couple back to earth, where Magotine is so inspired by their love for one another that she restores the kingdom of Pagodia to them.

In contrast to the utopian ending of "The Green Serpent," "The Ram" is a tragic fairy tale because love is denied. When Princess Merveilleuse is given refuge in the king's sylvan court, she does not fall in love with the ram. Her neglect allows the malevolent fairy Ragotte to gain revenge. The ram dies when Merveilleuse breaks her promise, and d'Aulnoy comments sarcastically about the ram's fate in the moral to this tale:

> In truth he should have had a better fate,
> For spurning a sordid Hymen's chains;
> Honest his love—unmakes his hate—
> How different from our modern swains!
> Even his death may well surprise
> The lovers of the present day:
> Only a silly sheep now dies,
> Because his ewe has gone astray.[35]

Though all of d'Aulnoy's fairy tales take place in some unknown realm and at some indefinite time, they concern the contemporary sociopolitical conditions of her own day. The fairies are all power brokers, whether they are gentle or witchlike. (There is an unusual likeness to the great Russian witch Baba Yaga, who can be cruel or kind. And we shall see how closely related fairies and witches are in chapter 4, dealing with Baba Yaga.) D'Aulnoy consciously endowed fairies with unusual powers and also gave them the responsibility to uphold an alternative to the civilizing process of King Louis XIV's court. An interesting passage in "The Green Serpent" reveals d'Aulnoy's ideological concept of the fairies. In this case, a canary, who had once been a man who had loved too much, tells Queen Discrete:

> You should know, madam, that several fairies were distressed to see various persons fall into bad habits on their travels. At first they imagined that they needed merely to advise them to correct themselves, but their warnings were paid no need. Eventually the fairies became quite upset and imposed punishments on them. Those who talked too much were changed into parrots, magpies, and hens. Lovers and their mistresses were transformed into pigeons, canaries, and lapdogs. Those who ridiculed their friends became monkeys. Gourmands were made into pigs and hotheads into lions. In short, the number of persons they punished was so great that this grove has become filled with them. Thus, you'll find people with all sorts of qualities and dispositions here.[36]

The theme of transformation runs through all of d'Aulnoy's tales and most of the ones about fairies written by the other conteuses of her time. These storytellers were propelled to take and transform the cultural materials at their disposal—literature, opera, ballet, folklore, and mythology—to create new or modern "tales about fairies," as they designated them. Their personal identification with their fairies, which varied according to their dispositions, imbued their narratives with a depth that one does not encounter in the fairy tales written in France, Europe, and America from 1750 to the present. After this major wave of contes des fées, the narratives called fairy tales have tended to lack a passionate belief in and identification with fairies. It was not until the late 1960s and 1970s that women writers were motivated to re-create tales as well as identify with the extraordinary power of fairies and witches. What is interesting about all the changes and transformations of fairies and the term "fairy tale" from the Greco-Roman period to today is that they reflect key moments in cultural evolution and reveal the memetic power of the term "fairy tale" or "conte de fée."

The Cultural Evolution of the Fairy Tale

In his highly stimulating book, *Creation of the Sacred: Tracks of Biology in Early Religions*, deserving of more attention than it has received, Burkert, the renowned scholar of Greek mythology and cult, uses concepts and hypotheses from sociobiology to explain the origins of religion and its persistence up to the present. Unlike many orthodox Darwinians, Burkert's notions about the historical and cultural evolution of religion are based on interdisciplinary methods coupled with judicious historical analysis. In a long passage worth quoting, he stakes out his position:

> The process of *semeiosis*, the use of signs and symbols, operates within the whole sphere of living organisms and was evidently invented long before the advent of man. This does not mean that genes prescribe culture—clearly, they do not. But it could be said that they give recommendations that become manifest in the repetition of like patterns, "the kinds of memories most easily recalled, the emotions they are most likely to evoke." The biological makeup forms preconditions or "attractors" to produce phenomena in a consistent fashion, even if these patterns are created and recreated afresh in each case. Scientific proof of such connections by means of statistics or experiment will remain impossible; what can be shown is the near-universality and persistence of patterns through place and time, and the existence of certain analogies or even homologies in structure and function in animal behavior. This suggests that details and sequences in rituals, tales, works of art, and fantasies hark back to more original processes in the evolution of life; they become understandable not in isolation nor within their different cultural contexts, but in relation to this background.[37]

His emphasis on studying patterns in cultural artifacts to understand the evolution of a particular "strand" or "strain" of culture has great implications for the study of folklore and fairy tales. At one point, he dedicates an entire chapter, "The Core of a Tale," to examining how tales can be related to basic human needs, rituals, customs, and the resolution of problems in human adaptation to changing environments.[38] He interprets Propp's structural analysis of the folk tale in an original way by indicating how the sequence of functions in Propp's morphology is related to biological necessities. "The organizing principle of a tale, the soul of the plot, is found to operate at the level of biology. The tale is created as a necessary sequence of 'motifemes,' and it has the pragmatic function of solving a problem. In other words, the quest is established as the means for problem-solving, and it is represented and communicated through the tale."[39] Aside from discussing the significance of the quest tale, he also elaborates on the shaman's tale and other tale types.

Most important are his remarks about the initiation tale, which he subtitles "the maiden's tragedy," and relates to Apuleius's "Cupid and Psyche." According to Burkert, this tale type differs from the Proppian pattern of the quest tale. The key functions that set a pattern related to female experiences are:

1. An eruption in a young girl's life that causes her to separate from family and home.
2. Seclusion for a certain period in an idyllic setting such as an island, forest, or temple.
3. A catastrophe that drives the young girl from the idyllic setting due to her violation of a promise or her being violated.
4. A period of wandering in which she suffers and must atone for her mistakes.
5. The accomplishment of a set of tasks or a rescue that brings about a happy ending.

Burkert cites how popular "Cupid and Psyche" became—and of course, we have seen how d'Aulnoy and other writers re-created this tale in diverse ways—and he takes issue with Detlev Fehling's study that purports to prove that all the known variants of "Cupid and Psyche" are dependent on Apuleius's literary text, not on oral tradition. "Fehling's thesis leaves us with the problem of where Apuleius got his tale from; that he simply invented his story is hardly an answer. It is quite difficult to invent a tale; even a new creation will inevitably merge with the stream of tales heard before, and thus become a variant of what has already been around."[40]

As we have seen, d'Aulnoy's tales about fairies merge with a long, profound stream of tales, heard and read, that stem from Greco-Roman myths and may even have more ancient, pagan roots. We must remember that a supernatural creature like a fairy may have been called something else and may have existed in people's minds, ritual practices, and stories for thousands of years. D'Aulnoy's invention or coinage of the term "conte de fée" only indicated a pronounced emphasis on the significance of fairies that informed the tales she wrote and told as well as many other tales by the conteuses and male writers of her time. She was using information about fairies with which she was familiar in a particular French sociocultural context.

In her most recent book, *Cultural Evolution*, Distin remarks: "Cultural evolution has taken off precisely because of this unique human ability to extract information from one context and manipulate it in another, which brings with it the possibility of new species emerging from the convergence of old ones. We can see this in the evolution of languages, of genres in literature and music, and in any other cultural area you care to mention."[41] The term "fairy" and "fairy tale" are units of cultural information otherwise known as "memes" that d'Aulnoy had inherited, and was passing on to other receivers of her tales with great innovation. Again Distin is most helpful in enabling us to grasp why d'Aulnoy's efforts were so relevant in developing the fairy-tale genre so that it attracted a large readership in France and beyond the cultural borders of France:

> Where humans do differ most strikingly from other creatures, however, is in the extent to which we are capable of acquiring information and the extent to which we are prone to sharing it. The motivation to share information with conspecifics is dependent not only on membership of an essentially cooperative species but also on the metarepresentational knowledge that one has information worth sharing. The ability to acquire information from conspecifics is dependent on the capacity to discretize information in the same form as that in which its originator is offering: only once a species has a steady supply of members that share the same method of representing information can that information be exchanged. And only once a species is able to reflect on the information that it is sharing, and on its method of representation, can there be evolution in both the information itself and its representational system or the metarepresentational ability to develop one, making humans unique in our ability to exchange cultural information with sufficiently persistent and differential heredity to support cultural evolution.[42]

In d'Aulnoy's case, she inherited information that she wanted to share discretely with her conspecifics (salonnières, male and female readers and writers of her social class, and eventually readers in the other languages into which her tales were translated). Once prompted by d'Aulnoy, they all shared in re-creating tales about fairies that informed the narrative tradition in unusual, extraordinary ways that expanded the meaning of fairy tale so that it grew and became more encompassing in the eighteenth century. D'Aulnoy wrote in an artefactual language that had to be learned and appreciated by her conspecific conteuses. Artefactual language must be distinguished from natural language that is biologically determined. Distin's observations are useful here too:

> The cultural evolution of natural language was accelerated by the biological advantages of enhanced communication among members of a cooperative species. As a consequence, natural languages are important markers of social identity, and they exclude outsiders from a social group as effectively as they define which individuals count as insiders and facilitate communication between them. Artefactual languages, on the other hand, evolved under adaptive pressure for more effective

representation, and one of their representational advantages over natural language is that they can be detached from their human originators. This enables information not only to be disseminated over much greater expanses of time and space than the content of speech but also to shed the social associations of its human originators.[43]

The terms "fairy tale," "conte de fée," and "fairy" are discrete units of information that emanate and depend on artefactual language. And thanks to artefactual language, fairy tale has successfully detached itself from its human originators and been spread by human receivers/producers throughout the world, often in the English language, but also in similar terms in other languages. Disseminated as a unit of information (meme), it has assumed so many different meanings and associations that it has almost become meaningless. Certainly, the conte de fée that had a profound cultural significance for the conteuses and other conspecifics in late seventeenth-century French society is not the same fairy tale as it is today.

Yet to say that it is meaningless would be to misunderstand the mechanics of cultural evolution. If anything, like the whale, fairy tale has grown immensely in importance and has "swallowed" and/or consumed other genres so that it has become more complex and more difficult to define. While the Disney Corporation has sought in the twentieth century to completely commercialize and dominate fairy tale with its latest banal filmic series of "Fairies" and its blundering and distorted adaptation of "Rapunzel" in the animated film appropriately titled *Tangled*, fairy tale has spurred numerous more innovative experiments in literature, opera, and the theater as well as on film, television, and the Internet that expose the frauds of corporate productions.[44] Like Herman Melville's White Whale, its essential truth will never be captured or defined. The irony of fairy tale's cultural evolution is that it originated out of human necessity, and we are still trying to determine why fairy tale is still so irresistible and necessary.

3

Remaking "Bluebeard," or Good-bye to Perrault

Figure 1.
Catherine Breillat, still from the film *Bluebeard*, 2008.

When I was a child this was my favourite fairy tale, but I was always astonished that this tale was actually told to little girls, because it's a fairy tale in which women are killed—Bluebeard is a real serial killer. In fairy tales, you often find a protagonist who is an ogre, like in *Little Red Riding Hood* for instance, who feels the urge to eat the victims in order to feed himself. But in the case of Bluebeard, you are talking about a human being who marries his victims, including this young woman. But in a way, he is as innocent as Marie-Catherine.

   If you look at my films, you will see that I am somewhat obsessed by the relationship between victims and their executioner, but as if the relationship was a rational thing in a physical sense, a relationship between two different forces that measure themselves. And therefore I've always wanted to make a movie about Bluebeard.

   —Catherine Breillat, interview, July 16, 2010

Little did Perrault know when he created the fairy tale about the serial killer Bluebeard that his villain would become a memetic icon in most Western societies by the twenty-first century. Moreover, if he were living today, Perrault would be surprised to learn that his ruthless scoundrel has undergone hundreds, if not thousands, of interpretations, operations, and transformations. He in fact might be puzzled, if not dazzled, by what he has wrought.

   Soon after it was printed in 1697, Perrault's tale was adapted in unusual ways through chapbooks and theatrical performances, translated into different European languages, and recast over the past four centuries through other artistic means and cultural institutions: opera, theater, broadsides, postcards, poetry, radio, novels, picture books, comics, cinema, photography, painting, television, and digital representations on the Internet. Furthermore, in the last ten years alone, four lengthy academic studies have appeared: Mererid Puew Davies, *The Tale of Bluebeard in German Literature: From the Eighteenth Century to the Present* (2001); Maria Tatar, *Secrets beyond the Door: The Story of Bluebeard and His Wives* (2004); Casie Hermansson, *Bluebeard: A Reader's Guide to the English Tradition* (2009); and Shuli Barzilai, *Tales of Bluebeard and His Wives from Late Antiquity to Postmodern Times* (2009). All attest to widespread stories about serial killers in Western and Middle Eastern cultures, from antiquity to today, and how Perrault's "Bluebeard" became the master narrative. Interestingly, though killed by Perrault, Bluebeard did not die. He instead has been resurrected thousands of times and has assumed many different forms, while Perrault's status as the author of "Bluebeard" has waned and is generally neglected. Despite the great attention paid to Perrault by academics, his name has been more or less effaced in popular memory, while Bluebeard's name lives on.

There is something uncanny at work in the adaptation and dissemination process of oral stories and literary fairy tales, for it appears that once a narrative becomes so relevant and memorable in particular societies, it is memetically appropriated by large sectors of the populace that neglect the author to make the tale their own or honor the tale in its own right. Here Drout, whose work I briefly discussed in chapter 1, is helpful again in understanding what is at work when we talk about appropriation and adaptation. He points out that "a meme is the simplest unit of cultural replication; it is whatever is transmitted when one person imitates, consciously or unconsciously, another."[1] Drout demonstrates how memes form oral and literary traditions through imitation and repetition. "A *proto-tradition* [of memes] could easily arise in a culture from trial and error, and spread widely due to the general tendencies of humans to repeat actions that appear to lead to successful outcomes, to imitate others who are successful, and to teach valuable information to members of a younger generation."[2]

Although we do not know whether Perrault was aware of a particular oral tale with the title "Bluebeard"—actually storytellers rarely gave titles to their tales in Perrault's time—he certainly knew tales about notorious serial killers such as Gilles de Rais through hearing or reading about them. He certainly was familiar with the biblical story of Adam and Eve, and how Eve's curiosity drove the pair from Eden. He was acquainted with Pandora and how her curiosity led her to open the dreaded box of ills. Perrault may have even known about King Minos of Crete, who brought about fatal endings to the women with whom he had sexual relations.[3] It is impossible to say how many tales figured in his memory—tales that were part of his upbringing and culture, and thus repeated. But such tales doubtless marked Perrault in some way, for they played a role in the French cultural tradition.

Once he began writing and composed his narrative about a ruthless murderer with a strange beard, who might have been a caricature of his archenemy, Nicolas Boileau, it attracted readers and listeners, who recorded elements of his tale in their minds. In turn, some republished their impression of Perrault's tale in different texts and contexts. Others simply retold it, retained it, and referred to it at times. In this way, Perrault's "Bluebeard" also entered into oral traditions or complemented similar tales about serial killers in circulation. While Perrault's name has generally been associated with the text in printed editions, this is not the case in many translations and picture books or other forms of media, particularly film. Almost all the "Bluebeard" films, which I have analyzed in my book *The Enchanted Screen*, from Georges Méliès's comic and bizarre *Bluebeard* of 1904 to Breillat's scintillating *Bluebeard* of 2009, barely refer to Perrault, if they do so at all. The author is replaced by the notorious villain of his work, just as Hans Christian Andersen demonstrated how his protagonist, a poet, was effaced by his own insidious creation in his famous tale "The Shadow." Bluebeard overshadows Perrault.

Overshadowing, transformation, and remaking are key functional components in a memetic process that enable a particular fairy tale to become popular and classical in Western culture—and in the case of "Bluebeard," especially in French culture. For instance, Pierre Saintyves traces the origins of the tale as part of an initiation ritual and examines how it was transformed over centuries.[4] In this regard, Breillat's appropriation of Perrault's "Bluebeard" is exceedingly significant for what it reveals about the historical evolution of the fairy tale from the oral tradition through print to our present-day cinematic-digital representation. The effacement of Perrault—and eventually Breillat's name will be effaced too—indicates how the tales themselves along with storytelling depend greatly on the resonance they find in large groups of people and their cultural processes. Bluebeard tales and their variants in other fields of cultural production such as film act as memes with supernormal stimuli and are part of a singular discursive process of remakings within the larger genre of the fairy tale. I want to analyze Breillat's *Bluebeard* as a filmic remake with an eye toward understanding how oral and literary tales have interacted with new media in a long historical tradition to form a fairy-tale discourse that addresses changes in manners, attitudes, and values.

Understanding the Remake

First, a word about the definition of remake, which has generally been used as a technical term in the field of cinema studies to indicate and categorize a film based on another film, with the intention to interpret, improve, or criticize it in some novel way. There can also be remakes of remakes or partial remakes with intertextual references. What is important here is that the notion of remaking is not limited simply to the field of film and cinema studies, for practically every story ever told or written is some sort of remake. There is no such thing as a pure, original text or urtext, even when a tale merely recounts a person's experience that seems unique or significant enough to be communicated in narrative form. People have never told or repeated the same story without remaking their experience or a narrative form in some way, nor have they written stories without remaking other stories, referring to other stories, reliving experiences and dreams, and reconfiguring a genre.

Perrault, for example, was an erudite writer, and when he conceived and wrote down his tales, sometimes twice or more, he referenced classical Latin literature, myths, the Bible, sixteenth- and seventeenth-century tales, contemporary French poetry, fables, novellas, and oral tales that he had heard in his childhood and retold to his own children; fairy tales written by many gifted French ladies, such as his niece Lhéritier and acquaintance d'Aulnoy, who often performed and discussed them in salons; and the literary and political disputes that he had with Boileau and other French intellectuals of his time. They all formed his narrative habitus—a concept that Frank, influenced by Pierre Bourdieu, has defined as a "disposition to hear some stories as those that one ought to listen to, ought to repeat on some appropriate occasions, and ought to be guided by. . . . [N]arrative habitus involves a *repertoire* of stories that a person at least recognizes and that a group shares. These stories are known against an unseen background of all the stories that person does not know and stories that do not circulate within any particular group."[5] Indeed, Perrault ingested the cultural goods around him, and his ulterior motive was to re-create and celebrate the glory of a "modern" French literature that included a putative minor genre, the fairy tale.

As I have shown in the previous chapter, d'Aulnoy designated this genre conte de fée, which had its genesis in the oral wonder tale and medieval literature. All the talented fairy-tale writers of the 1690s and early part of the eighteenth century were in the "business" of remaking, and their "industriousness" and "operations" have had profound consequences for how films are remade. In turn, the cinematic fairy-tale remakes of the twentieth and twenty-first centuries indicate how the genre of the fairy tale has expanded since the seventeenth century, flourished in surprising ways, and reflected back on the cultural processes that informed the genre.

Numerous essays and books have been written about the filmic adaptation of novels and stories, and they are all illuminating in one way or another. For my purposes, the most useful and comprehensive one is Constantine Verevis's *Film Remakes* (2006). In his preface, he states, "Drawing upon recent theories of genre and intertextuality, *Film Remakes* describes remaking as both an elastic and a complex situation, one enabled and limited by the interrelated roles and practices of industry, critics, and audiences." Industry consists of issues of production, including commerce and authors; the subject of critics involves an analysis of genres, plots, and structures; the topic of audiences consists of questions of reception and institutions. As Verevis notes, "The film remake emerges from this discussion as a particular case of repetition, a function of cinematic and discursive fields that is maintained by historically specific practices, such as copyright law and authorship, canon formation and media literacy, film criticism and re-viewing."[6]

Although Verevis focuses primarily on filmic remakes, he basically outlines the cultural process that led to the formation of many different literary/ artistic genres. In the fairy tale's case, he exposes the weaknesses of the formalist textual and structuralist approaches that are beholden to close readings of texts and intertexts, for they ignore the extratextual factors that contribute to the making of a genre and its remakes.

> Like all critical constructs (genre included), remaking—quotation, allusion, adaptation—is created and sustained through the repeated use of terminology. The suggestion that the very limited direct intertextual referentiality between the remake and its original is organised according to an extratextual referentiality, located in historically specific discursive formations—especially film criticism and reviewing, but also copyright law and authorship, canon formation and film literacy—has

consequences for purely textual descriptions of the remake, particularly those which seek to ground the category in a rigid distinction between an original story and its new discursive incarnation. Aside from the questionable move of assuming that the unchanging essence of a film's story can somehow be abstracted from the mutable disposition of its expression, demarcation along the lines of story and discourse is evidently frustrated by those remakes which repeat not only the narrative invention of an original property but seek, for instance, to recreate the expressive design of an early film.[7]

Verevis's theory of the remake breaks down the barriers between orality, literacy, and the visual arts and technologies of representation to show that every cultural genre is fluid and undergoes changes due to the interaction of intertextual and extratextual conditions at specific times and places. The meaning or meanings of a tale cannot be derived solely by focusing on textual and intertextual matters but also must include an analysis of personal, social, and cultural factors of production and reception. The printed text consists simply of letters impressed on some kind of paper asking to be deciphered, and it has no meaning unless acted on by actual readers, and also readers not complicit in its production and anticipated reception.

The genre of what has come to be known as the fairy tale is a historical, memetic, discursive process constituted by orality and media technologies, such as print, radio, cinema, and the Internet. To understand the genre of the fairy tale and the relationship of Perrault's text to Breillat's film, we might first benefit by exploring the tale's genericity.

Genericity

In their recent book *Textualité et intertextualité des contes: Perrault, Apulée, La Fontaine, Lhéritier*, Ute Heidmann and Jean-Michel Adam have significantly expanded their dynamic notion of genericity (*génericité*) in an endeavor to deepen the notion of genre as well as transcend the limitations of a textual and intertextual approach to fairy tales. They propose to replace the category "genre" with the more discursive "genericity"—a term that I have already discussed in *Why Fairy Tales Stick*. In their most recent elaboration of genericity, they state:

> This concept denotes the process of inscription of an articulation (*énoncé*) in one or more genres of discourses practiced in a given discursive community. It permits the "avoidance of the essentialist stumbling block," which makes any interlingustic and intercultural comparison impossible. Genericity effectively takes the side of "fluidity, instability, and constant re-categorization"; it is inseparable from the

variation of the *system of genres* of an epoch or a social group. From this viewpoint, it is less a question of classifying a text within a genre such as "folk tale" (*conte*) than to show the evidence of "generic tensions" that cut across it.[8]

Heidmann and Adam seek to separate themselves from the literary formalists who primarily perform close readings of texts without considering contexts, and they also criticize folklorists who rely on the study of tale types and "universalize" the meanings of tales without considering their specific sociocultural context and intertextual meanings. They want to grasp how elements of a text are in dialogue with other texts, sometimes from different cultures and time periods, and how elements of a text are in dialogue with cultural discourses and factors that influence the production of the text. In short, the text is to be understood in its context.

I have no quarrel with their critique of formalism and structuralism, but I fear that they do an injustice to folklorists as well as themselves by excluding the study of oral influences and folklore in their study of Perrault's tales along with those written by fairy-tale writers of the ancien régime.[9] In expanding the notion of genericity, Heidmann and Adam emphasize the significance of the concept of reconfiguration, which designates how the configuration of a genre like the fairy tale undergoes transformations.

> This concept permits the inclusion of the inscription of articulations (*énoncés*) in the systems of existing genres as an endeavor to inflect the generic conventions, to make them better adapted to the sociocultural and discursive contexts that change from one epoch and from one cultural and linguistic sphere to another. In connection to the concept of genericity to which we return to designate more generally the dynamics and fluctuations which reveal each inscription (authorial, editorial, and lectorial) of an articulation in a system of genres, the concept of re-configuration should permit more precise distinctions to be made in the general fluctuations of the phases and contours.[10]

All this is well and good, but Heidmann and Adam exclude any reference to oral discourses and possible sources in social storytelling practices that may have contributed to Perrault's reconfigured texts. They play down written and pictorial evidence that indicate clearly how nannies or lower-class storytellers might have influenced Perrault. They discard the significance of the cover design of Perrault's book, featuring an old spinster telling stories to upper-class children. Most important, they do not seem to realize that some of their own key intertextual discoveries are rooted in the oral tradition of the Bible along with Greek and Roman myths. In Heidmann and Adam's tour de force interpretation of Perrault's "Little Red Riding Hood" and "Bluebeard," they demonstrate how strongly Perrault may have relied on Lucius Apuleius's second-century Latin novel, *The Golden Ass*, and La Fontaine's *contes galantes* in his endeavor to reconfigure his tales that were not called fairy tales at that time but have been designated as fairy tales ever since.

It is largely on the basis of highly sophisticated, specialized intertextual analysis that Heidmann and Adam determine meanings. By privileging print and literature, they establish a hierarchy of influences and sources that contribute to the production as well as reception of a text. No thought is given to the fact that Perrault was also reconfiguring oral stories that were part of his narrative habitus, and he was using a male Cartesian rational style to break with classical literature and popular narrative modes of telling stories. There is no appreciation for the deep oral currents of the literary myths that Heidmann and Adam cite that were disseminated over hundreds of years in theaters, oral retellings, salons, schools, and other public places. We must remember that the Greeks and Romans lived their myths. In particular, the tale of "Cupid and Psyche," though its oral roots have been questioned, stems from the oral rituals of the Greeks and Romans.[11] One could even make a case for including "the tale of the snake charmer's wife" in *Genesis Rabbah* and the "Prometheus myth," including Pandora's box, as providing elements for Perrault's writing of "Bluebeard," and certainly most of the Greek and Roman myths were disseminated just as much in oral traditions as they were in print up through the 1690s in Paris.[12]

My point in discussing Heidmann and Adam's notion of genericity is not to prove them "wrong" but instead to question why they have refused to include historical folklore studies in their analyses, do not explore Perrault's narrative habitus, and have refused to distinguish among folklorists, who, they seem to believe, are all mostly universalists. Certainly, we owe a great debt to the careful philological and linguistic analyses of Heidmann and Adam, who basically want to reestablish Perrault's tales as literature—that is, complex literary texts that rely on intertextual references. But Verevis makes an apropos remark about scholars who paradoxically become limited when they focus too much on intertextuality to the detriment of extratextuality:

> While a general and cinematic competence enables the construction of an intratextually determined hierarchy of story descriptions, which range from the most succinct to the most detailed, the construction of a particular intertextual relation between a remake and its presumed original is *an act of interpretation*, one which is "limited and relative— not to a [viewing] subject but to the interpretative grid (the regime of reading) through which both the subject position and the textual relations are constituted." Finally, and as [John] Frow argues generally in relation to the concept of intertextuality, what is important to an account of the remake is not the detailed "identification of particular . . . intertextual source[s]," which function retrospectively as designated

points of origin, but the determination of "a more general discursive structure—*the genre of re-viewing labelled 'remake.'*"[13]

Though their theory of genericity and reconfiguration claims to be inter-disciplinary and embrace sociocultural conditions, Heidmann and Adam study the evolution of the fairy tale as genre basically within *literary* move-ments of intertextuality and interculturality that surge and resurge, configure and reconfigure, to bring about literary innovation. In this respect, Verevis's theory of the remake augments their work and can enable us to appreciate the significance of Breillat's film within the discursive tradition of "Bluebeard" as well as study how the sociocultural conditions under which Breillat remade "Bluebeard" reflect on the cultural tradition of the fairy tale and storytelling that induced Perrault to create his tale. In fact, his comprehensive notion of remake, which includes notions of genericity and memetics without making explicit reference to them, is crucial for understanding why Breillat's film has attracted so much attention, why it may signal a turning point in how Per-rault's tale is viewed today, and why it contributes to the fairy-tale representa-tion and broader cultural discourse about serial killers and female curiosity.

Breillat's Remake of "Bluebeard"

Just as the women writers of fairy tales in the 1690s were part of a protofemi-nist movement of their times (and Perrault was influenced by these writers), Breillat was influenced by and played a significant role in the second wave of contemporary feminism in France, and consequently, her reconfiguration of Perrault's "Bluebeard" must be placed within the French feminist movement that began in the late 1960s, and has continued to alter cultural and social practices within France. Indeed, her film must be understood within the con-text of the cinematic culture industry in the West. Breillat's remake of "Blue-beard" must also be studied as part of a wave of fairy-tale films produced in the last five years. Part of that wave includes the American Catherine Hard-wicke's *Red Riding Hood* (2011), another remake of a Perrault tale, which is a trivial commercial film filled with a father/werewolf as a serial killer, ri-diculous peasants and religious fanatics, a juvenile love triangle, and an inane happy end. Breillat is "guilty" of commercialism and pretentiousness, too, in her most recent remake film, *The Sleeping Beauty* (*La Belle endormie*, 2010), a pastiche of Perrault's "Sleeping Beauty" and Andersen's "The Snow Queen." In this film, there is a touch of feminism as Breillat seeks to transform Perrault's and Andersen's fairy tales into a coming-of-age story, with Sleeping Beauty moving in and out of predictable experiences mimicking Andersen's tale and throwing in some juicy sex scenes in a film that leads nowhere. It is a film that reduces feminism to platitudes. Be that as it may, Breillat must be taken seriously as a feminist filmmaker.

Born in 1948, Breillat was a feminist avant la lettre. She came to Paris from a provincial town in western France when she was sixteen years old with the hope of becoming a film director. Yet she was not admitted to the Institut des Hautes Études Cinématographiques and had to settle for minor acting jobs. At the same time, she began writing stories, poems, and essays, and in 1968 published her first novel, *L'Homme facile* (*A Man for the Asking*), which brought her immediate notoriety because of her frank depiction of sex. Whether she wrote, acted, or directed films, Breillat became known as a *provocatrice*, exploring women's sexuality and the shame that they have been compelled to feel under the male gaze. Almost all her major novels and films are unabashed portrayals of sexual relations that can best be described as intense entanglements and struggles in which women seek to gain a sense of self by discovering as well as claiming their sexual desires. Moreover, some of her films such as *À ma soeur* (*Fat Girl*, 2001) deal with sibling rivalry or competition between girls or women that involves free sexual expression.

It does not seem that Breillat took a great interest in the radical feminist transformation of the fairy tale during the latter part of the twentieth century, although most of the important Anglo-American tales by Margaret Atwood, Angela Carter, A. S. Byatt, and many others were well known in France. There also were several key French writers who turned Perrault's tales inside out, like Pierrette Fleutiaux in her significant collection of tales *Métamorphoses de la reine* (1985). Breillat was more influenced by the writings of Marguerite Duras and Hélène Cixous. And as Douglas Keesey points out, "Breillat can be seen as part of a growing group of women writers who are most unladylike in their sexually explicit confrontations with some of the darker aspects of passion. These authors include Virginie Despentes (*Baise-moi*, 1994), Marie Darrieussecq (*Truismes*, 1996), Catherine Cusset (*Jouir*, 1997), Christine Angot (*L'Inceste*, 1999), Camille Laurens (*Dans ses bras-là*, 2000), and Catherine Millet (*La Vie sexuelle de Catherine M.*, 2001)."[14] The works by these authors, her childhood readings, the films she viewed and produced, and many discussions of tales and her own storytelling all formed Breillat's narrative habitus.

Despite the fact that Breillat had shown no artistic interest in fairy tales until 2005, when she began work on adapting Perrault's "Bluebeard," she has stated in different interviews that the tale had always been a favorite of hers and her older sister in their youth, and that the idea for a filmic adaptation of "Bluebeard" had been percolating in her head for at least twelve years before she set out to realize the film.[15] Here it is crucial to note that Breillat is the *first* female filmmaker ever to adapt "Bluebeard" for the screen—in this case, first for television—not only in France but also in all of Europe. Since 1945, approximately twenty films worldwide have been based on Perrault's "Bluebeard"; Christian-Jaque, Claude Chabrol, Alexandre Bubnov, and Pierre Boutron directed the most important French versions.[16] But none of the directors of the twenty-odd films, including Charlie Chaplin, whose *Monsieur Verdoux* (1947) is an extraordinary remake with grave political allegations, has remade the tale with such exquisite photography and such a profound focus on a young woman's passionate desire to assert herself than Breillat.

To a certain extent, it is because Breillat lives and breathes through all her stories and films that she has managed to transform Perrault's "Bluebeard" into a film that explores a young woman's rebellion rather than her victimization. Breillat conceived the idea for the film, wrote the screenplay, chose the film's setting in northern France, auditioned the actors, many of whom were amateurs, designed some of the sets and costumes, and edited the final version. Explicit autobiographical elements dealing with the sibling rivalry between her and her sister mark the film. The monstrous serial killer Bluebeard is ironically depicted as an intellectual loner. He almost becomes incidental because the two young protagonists, Catherine, the six-year-old storyteller, and Marie-Catherine, the young woman who marries Bluebeard, dominate the action as they take charge of the narratives of their own lives.

At first the film does not appear to be about a female narrator contesting the dominant male narrative, the female versus male gaze, or Breillat versus Perrault. But it is about all these conflicts and more. Unlike Perrault's fairy tale, Breillat's fairy-tale film begins on an unhappy note. The first scene takes place in a cold, prisonlike convent school somewhere in northern France. Two sisters, Marie-Catherine (about seventeen) and Anne (about nineteen), are summoned by the severe mother superior and informed that their father has died in a carriage accident. The mother superior also literally kicks them out of the private Catholic school because they cannot afford to pay. Once we, the audience, are faced with the plight of these two girls in the seventeenth century, Breillat ushers us without any transition to an old country house in France during the 1950s; two girls are climbing stairs to an attic in the barn, and there they begin exploring the wonderful, stored items. From this point on, Breillat switches back and forth as she films parallel stories from the past, the 1690s and 1950s, to reflect on problems faced by young girls in the present, for serial killers have not disappeared. Nor has sibling rivalry. Some critics have referred to Breillat's film narrative as a story within a story, but this is not the case. Breillat mirrors two different but similar narratives and uses doubling to create an estrangement effect, stimulating the audience to compare and contrast the two stories. There is really no frame tale, unless one takes into account that Breillat films the stories within the frame of a "Bluebeard" discourse that has deep roots in an oral and literary tradition in France and elsewhere. The oral and literary tradition memetically provide the film's frame.

The plots of the stories are separate. In the case of the seventeenth-century sisters, the younger sister, Marie-Catherine, vows to take revenge on the heartless mother superior, for she intends to marry well, become rich, and live in a castle similar to the one inhabited by Bluebeard. She refuses to accept her impoverished condition. Despite the fact that she hears that Bluebeard is dangerous, she soon gains his trust, marries him, and controls him. A gentle giant of a man, Bluebeard remarks that Marie-Catherine has the innocence of a dove and pride of an eagle. It is the eagle in her that eventually brings about the villian's beheading.

In the case of the twentieth-century sisters, the tiny assertive Catherine finds a book of Perrault's fairy tales in the attic and begins reading the tale of Bluebeard to her older sister, who is sensitive and frightened by the story. The story that Catherine reads is far from a faithful rendition of Perrault's tale, nor are her imaginative projections of different scenes accurate. What is significant about her reading of the tale is the manner in which she appropriates it and makes the tale and its incidents her own. In fact, we have a remake within a remake. Clearly she identifies with the Marie-Catherine in her creative retelling. Catherine also takes a sadistic delight in scaring her older sister and accidentally causes her death by driving her backward as she reads the tale so that the sister falls through a trapdoor in the attic.

The doubling of the characters throughout the film enables Breillat to shift the perspective of Perrault's ironic third-person narrative and question it. Just as the two young "protagonists" assume control over the narratives of their lives, for better or worse, Breillat radicalizes Perrault's tale to comment on the oppression of young women and her own past experiences with her sister. The camera's eye probes aspects of Perrault's narrative from unusual angles that focus more on women's choices than on the mystery behind Bluebeard's murderous acts. Breillat connects the mirroring tales about two sets of sisters only once when tiny Catherine is pictured entering into the bloody room where three of Bluebeard's murdered wives are dangling from a wall. Otherwise, Breillat's filmic version does not weave the tales together, and the sets of sisters are very different. One plot concerns the deep desire of a young girl, who wants to avoid poverty and live in a fairy-tale world. In the process she learns from Bluebeard, shares his loneliness, and strangely strokes his decapitated head after he is killed. The fairy-tale world is not as happy and dreamlike as girls would wish it to be. Yet in the end, Catherine has attained what she sought and resembles the strong, chaste Judith in the great oil paintings by Lucas Cranach the Elder and Fede Galizi, who portray her after she has slain the Assyrian general Holfernes—his head on a table of plate. The second tale is more about sibling rivalry and how a self-assertive younger girl "twists" Perrault's tale, so that she dominates and accidentally kills her older sister. Perhaps, she, too, has unconsciously attained what she sought.

Unlike Perrault's "Bluebeard," both of Breillat's "Bluebeard" tales end tragically and yet open up further stories. We have no idea what Marie-Catherine, pictured with Bluebeard's head on a platter, as if in some oil painting, will undertake. We have no idea what will happen to little Catherine, who stands with her mother as they overlook her sister, who has fallen to her death through the trapdoor. But we do know that Breillat's remake of Perrault's tale revolutionizes the memetic tradition of Bluebeard tales in a manner consistent with changed attitudes about women's roles in the late twentieth and early twenty-first centuries.

Interrogating Serial Killers, the Role of Women, and the Bluebeard Discourse

It is virtually impossible to say when the oral and literary discourse about serial killers and the curiosity of women began. In his significant study *Fairytale in the Ancient World*, Anderson notes: "It often requires the assembly of a good many hybrid outlines before we are in a position to see that most of the features now known in a tale already exist in antiquity in some sort of stable relationship to one another. Seldom, too, are we able to make any progress towards constructing an archetype of any given tale. The variants encountered in surviving literature are at least as varied and confused as their modern counterparts, suggesting that the tales themselves are already old."[17] In the case of "Bluebeard," I have already indicated that there are "old" motifs and elements that Perrault wove into his text from Bible tales such as "Adam and Eve" as well as the Midrash commentary on the Book of Genesis, and tales of antiquity such as "Pandora's Box" and "Minos of Crete." One could even include the frame tale of *Thousand and One Nights* as a forerunner of the hybrid fairy tale "Bluebeard." After all, King Shahryar, who marries virgins daily and kills them after sleeping with them, is the most notorious serial killer of all humankind.

In the evolution of stories that contributed to the formation of the literary fairy-tale genre and a Bluebeard discourse in particular, narratives had lives of their own, circulating through humans and their social relations with one another. Indeed, they still do. In Frank's remarkable study *Letting Stories Breathe*, he stresses that "stories work with people, for people, and always stories work *on* people, affecting what people are able to see as real as possible, and as worth doing or best avoided.... Stories breathe life not only into individuals, but also into groups that assemble around telling and believing certain stories."[18]

It is not inconceivable that people told numerous tales about serial killers thousands of years ago to alert others about these murderers. It is not inconceivable that they also told tales about women's curiosity, indicating that they might endanger themselves if they were too curious and disobeyed an autocratic husband. As Barzilai observes, the plot of the tales that contributed to the development of the Bluebeard discourse involves the stages of prohibition, transgression, and punishment.[19] These stages can be found in the patterns of many types of tales, but what is distinctive about the Bluebeard discourse is that it stemmed from a misogynist strain of storytelling within patriarchal cultures. "Bluebeard" is a tale about power, among other things, and who is in control of power, and why power should always be in the hands of men.[20] As Barzilai notes:

> If fear of women's unruly sexuality is factored into this sociopolitical context, as suggestively imaged by Pandora's breaking the seal or lifting the lid of a vessel, it is indeed issues of power and control that generate the successive stories of texts designed to represent the humiliation of women and vindicate the hegemony of men. The affirmation of male dominion is dialectically dependent on female fallibility. In terms borrowed from Jacques Lacan, the husband is constantly compelled to seek reassurance about the whereabouts of the phallus.[21]

The significance and popularity of Perrault's "Bluebeard" can be attributed to Perrault's subtle, artistic composition of various motifs and themes that focus on male power and women's curiosity, and his invention of the iconic character Bluebeard. Perrault lived and breathed this tale. He breathed life into this tale through his consummate skill as storyteller and writer, so that the story became memorable and memetic. Moreover, in his *remaking* of other stories that he assembled in his tale, he poignantly shaped his own narrative to open up the question about the validity of male hegemony and stimulated further thinking through his two *moralités* about women's curiosity and the changing relationship between men and women. Ironically, as mentioned earlier, he created the name of a discursive tale type that was to eliminate his own name, for "Bluebeard," a tale that still breathes, has become more important than Perrault's name and his life.

Breilllat has breathed new life into the Bluebeard discourse by remaking Perrault's tale through the writing of her screenplay and directing of the film *Bluebeard*. It is a radical remaking because she complicates the plot of prohibition, transgression, and punishment, and focuses on women's assertion of their power as opposed to their curiosity. There is not an iota of misogyny in her film, nor does she vent her rage against female oppression by depicting Bluebeard as a cruel killer. As I have already noted, Bluebeard is more an intellectual loner than a monster.

At the film's end, Marie-Catherine caresses his head lovingly as if she pitied Bluebeard. The time of arbitrary male domination appears to have ended. But as Breillat knows, this is not the case. Her story is certainly a rupture in the Bluebeard discourse, and part of a vigorous feminist cultural movement of retelling and remaking the tale that began in the 1970s, and will continue well into the twenty-first century. As long as serial killings continue and patriarchy demands women's subservience, we shall have Bluebeard remakes that embody a culture's conflicts and possibilities for resolutions. Breillat's film indicates that it may be time to say good-bye to Perrault's proposals, but Breillat will undoubtedly not have the last word.

4

Witch as Fairy/Fairy as Witch: Unfathomable Baba Yagas

Figure 2.
Rima Staines, *The Old Woman as Baba Yaga*, 2009.
Charcoal and pencil drawing. Courtesy of Rima Staines.

It is . . . very remarkable that in Italy there are two very distinct and contradictory currents of Witch-lore. One is the true old Latin-Etruscan legend,
in which the witch is merely a sorceress or enchantress, generally benevolent and kind. She is really a *fata*, like the French *fée*, who is always a
lady, loving children and helping poor men. There is in this witchcraft
nothing to speak of, of selling souls to the devil, and all the loathsome
abominations of living only for evil. There are good witches and bad,
the old Canidia of Horace still exists, but though she lames donkeys and
blasts vines, she does not make a specialty of getting people to hell. The
Italians seem to have believed that men could do that abundantly well for
themselves, without help.

The other current is of the diabolical sort, and it is due almost entirely
to the Church and the priests. This is the kind which caused witch mania,
with its tortures and burnings. It is very curious that despite all the efforts of
Saint Barbato, and an army of theologians after him, the old genial classic associations still survive, and witches of Benevento are still believed to
be a beautiful, gay and festive society, whose queen is Diana—with very
little of Hecate-Hexe in her.

—Charles Leland, *Etruscan Roman Remains in Popular Tradition* (1892)

Magic is an area where popular culture meets with learned culture. Popular notions of magic got taken up and interpreted by "intellectuals"—a
term here used for those with philosophical or theological education—
and their ideas about magic, demons, and kindred topics were in turn
spread throughout the land by preachers. One of the most important tasks
in cultural history is working out these lines of transmission. . . . [M]agic
represents a particularly interesting crossroads between fiction and reality.
The fictional literature of medieval Europe sometimes reflected the realities
of medieval life, sometimes distorted them, sometimes provided escapist
release from them, and sometimes held up ideals for reality to imitate.
When this literature featured sorcerers, fairies, and other works of magic,
it may not have been meant to be taken as totally realistic. Even so, the
magic of medieval literature did resemble the magical practices of medieval life in ways that are difficult but interesting to entangle.

—Richard Kieckhefer, *Magic in the Middle Ages* (2000)

Notes on Goddesses, Witches, and Fairies

Witch is memetically loaded. We use the word "naturally" in all Western
countries as if we all know what a witch is. We don't. Nevertheless, we assume
we do. Witches are replicated in our minds through all modes of communication, and we employ the concept of witch in various ways, often changing the

witch's meaning, in information or stories, especially fairy tales. We do this without realizing that the memetic staying power of the word and concept "witch" are rooted in pagan cultural traditions that hark back to the Neolithic period, if not before. Witch is a word/concept/image that has undergone a process of "demonization" that is still potent today.

We are not certain of the witch's origins because we do not have written records of early pagan periods, only artifacts such as amulets, gravestones, vases, statues, scrolls, inscriptions, and names of forests, woods, and caves that indicate women were often depicted as goddesses and were worshipped because they had extraordinary powers that allowed them to perform miraculous acts such as making people and environments fertile, or destroying people and environments. As goddesses and divinities in pagan times who were later associated with witches and fairies, they were powerful helpers or enablers who had a command of some kind of magic and were praised for the qualities that they were assumed to possess. They could bring about any kind of extraordinary transformation, guide young girls and boys through initiation rituals, protect people from calamities, change infertile couples so that they could reproduce, provide propitious conditions for hunting and farming, grant wishes, predict the future, make prophecies, and determine the destinies of newly born children. They knew the source of the fountain of youth and immortality, could guide people to the land of the dead, and could bring about reincarnation of the dead. For the most part, they performed good deeds, but when wronged, could wreak revenge and destroy. Their kindness and vehemence knew no bounds. They were embodied in the rituals and customs of pagan people. We embrace and embody them today in our superstitions and religions without even realizing it.[1]

Witches as ancient divinities are intriguing because the pagan goddesses in the Western world eventually gave birth to the Greco-Roman goddesses and fates, who, as I discussed in chapter 2, engendered fairies, nymphs, mermaids, sirens, pixies, and other supernatural creatures.[2] That is, not only were the goddesses transformed into witches, they were also precursors of the fairies and their kin. All this means that the irresistible and inexplicable fairy tale cannot even be partially explained unless we endeavor to draw connections to ancient rituals and customs pertaining to magical transformation, witches, and fairies. The fairy tale's evolution can only be understood if we study explicit and implicit references to goddesses, witches, fates, and fairies of the pagan world, for their symbolic significance is still with us today.

Laura Verdi argues that "we cannot recognize solutions to the breaks in the continuity of the venerated ancient mother goddesses in all of the Middle East and Eastern Europe from the Neolithic period and of that particular re-elaboration of the feminine divinities of the pagan pantheon that gave us the fates, indisputable protagonists of all fairy literature, until we grasp how this literature took shape at the beginning of the eleventh century in Europe."[3] This is absolutely true, but the witches, too, were involved in the same processes of transformation and reelaboration, and their destinies up to the present day are inextricably connected to those of the fairies. Jones makes this clear:

> While fairies are the secular complement to the angels and demons of the religious sphere, fairies can also be seen as the supernatural complement to the witches of the mundane realms. As several scholars of early modern witch beliefs have pointed out, fairies and witches are both blamed for causing sudden and otherwise inexplicable illnesses in humans and animals (a stroke was originally a fairy stroke) or changes in the weather (whirlwinds are troops of fairies passing by), or affecting the fertility of fields and livestock, and for having particular interest in human children, whom they may kidnap or otherwise harm. Both fairies and witches are believed to be predominantly female, and congruent with their association with matters of fertility, many stories deal with the consequences of a man marrying a woman who turns out to be a fairy (positive) or a witch (negative). In some cases in early modern Europe it appears that human women may have formed groups that were believed to mirror in the mundane realm, the groups of trooping fairies believed to inhabit the supernatural realm. These trooping fairies are headed by a figure known as Herodias, Herodiana, Perhta, or Holda, suggesting continuity with classical and northern goddess figures.[4]

Many of these classical and northern goddesses also became associated with names of witches throughout Europe in the early and late Middle Ages, and their stories, whether oral or literary, formed part of the evolution of the fairy tale as a simple genre according to Jolles's theories, which I discussed in chapter 1. In her important book *Märchen und mittelalterliche Literaturtradition* (Fairy tales and medieval literary tradition), Maren Clausen-Stolzenburg remarks:

> The "sorceress," who can be found in ancient literature, was succeeded on her behalf in a certain way in that she (a) was enlisted in the late middle ages explicitly to shape the Christian anti-figure of the "witch" and (b) penetrated right into the *Children's and Household Tales* [Grimm] as sorceress in some cases. The image of the witch in *Children's and Household Tales* (c) originated gradually from the literary portrayal of the sorceress and the shrilly witch documents from the fourteenth and sixteenth centuries. Thus the "fairies," who had originated from the ancient goddesses and the powerful sorceresses of the Greek and Roman literature, found their way into the popular fairy tales of the nineteenth century.[5]

Indeed, there are hardly any fairies in the Brothers Grimm's collection; rather, there are witches, who function as fairies or sorceresses. They all owe their existence to pagan goddesses.

Most scholars of witchcraft and fairy lore have recognized the debt that both the oral wonder tale and literary fairy tale owe to pagan beliefs and customs as well as Greco-Roman myths. Though we do not have massive written evidence showing a direct lineage of fairy tales from pagan periods to the early modern period in Europe because scribes, intellectuals, and priests were not prone to record tales of the common people, or even tales they themselves told, we do have immense proof that people of all classes believed in gods, goddesses, magic, and sorcery, and as I assert above, we still do. People from all classes also exchanged stories about them, and we still do that too. One need only read Ronald Hutton's significant study *The Triumph of the Moon: A History of Modern Pagan Witchcraft* to grasp the pervasiveness of the belief in witches. Explore any country in Europe or North and South America, and you will find a wide variety of witchlore.

For example, folklorist Monika Kropej published numerous tales—gathered in the Karst region of Slovenia in 1996—about witches and other supernatural creatures, and one of them reads as follows:

> Witches flew on different occasions. On Midsummer Eve, after the bonfire went out. Don't know why they need all those ashes. For their potions, I reckon. Us girls were curious if one would come, so we went nosing around towards Podgora, down from Hunter's cottage.
>
> I still see her! She was covered with a kerchief and had a real long nose and a tuckup skirt. She had bare feet, a broomstick and a tail made of cloth in the back. We knew her.
>
> "Look at her, she's off! Did her stuff around the bonfire!"
>
> But she couldn't help it. I was already foretold, she had been marked by the cradle.[6]

This report is not exceptional, and it is significant because it reveals just how strong a basic stereotype of a witch has been memetically disseminated from the Middle Ages to the present. What is not clear, however, is how this stereotype is the result of misogynist cultural processes that have transformed goddesses into witches and fairies.

In the past twenty years, scholars of the European medieval period and folklore have published a vast amount of essays and books based on new research along with interdisciplinary approaches demonstrating that most people believed in witches, fairies, wizards, and magic up through the Renaissance, if not through the nineteenth century.[7] Europeans of all classes also thought that animals could talk, had magical powers, and consciously committed crimes, so many animals were brought to trial.[8] In particular, pagan beliefs remained widespread up through the fifth century when Roman Catholicism began making a stronger effort to demonize pagan tales, rituals, and customs.[9] By the fifteenth century, it became dangerous in most parts of Europe to show allegiance to witches or fairies, for witchcraft/sorcery had become associated with the devil. Yet it would not be an exaggeration to assert that despite the danger of declaring a belief in witches and fairies, these supernatural creatures featured prominently in all kinds of oral storytelling and the nascent vernacular literature of the early and late Middle Ages. In *The Witch in History*, Diane Purkiss discusses the practices of witches in Scotand and northern England during the seventeenth century, pointing out that

> all these people [the witches] used the corpus of fairy stories in inventive ways to understand the practices of others or to legitimate their own. Such moves did not always work; the godly, at least, made no distinction between Robin Goodfellow and a demon, and a learned sceptic like Regindald Scot found both incredible. Fairy-beliefs were a sign of an outmoded structure of belief, always already on the point of disappearing, and hence associated, like folktales, with elderly, uneducated women. Consequently, courts and other interlocutors were more than likely to reinterpret a "fairy story" as a story about some more up-to-date bugbear: a demon, a witch. The result was that some stories originally told as "fairy stories" are re-presented as stories about witchcraft.[10]

In short, if we are to understand how fairy tales evolved and were shaped from ancient pagan beliefs in goddesses and gods, we must try to trace how fairies and witches were the seeds of these tales. We must also realize that despite the fact that hundreds, if not thousands, of different types of tales about witches and fairies were told and written in the early and late Middle Ages, including documents that contained stories of witches, fairies, accusations, and confessions during the diverse witch hunts, sermons, anecdotes, rumors, scholarly studies of sorcery, and so on, we cannot exactly define a witch, fairy, or fairy tale. There were enormous regional differences among peoples in Europe as to how they regarded pagan and Greco-Roman goddesses and gods, cultivated pagan and Greco-Roman beliefs and customs, and adapted them to Christian stories and prescriptions. It is worth exploring the inexplicable, though, for there are shards of history that can shed light on our present attitudes toward witches, fairies, and fairy tales.

In this chapter, I want to try to clarify the importance of the connections between witches and fairies coupled with their deep roots in pagan and Greco-Roman beliefs by moving away from western Europe to look at the great witch Baba Yaga of Slavic countries. There are several reasons why I want to concentrate on Baba Yaga and Slavic fairy tales.

The first one regards neglect. For the most part, the focus of folklore and fairy-tale studies in the United States and western Europe has been on the works of the Brothers Grimm and other notable western European writers and folklorists, even though the great Russian scholar Propp stamped the study of folk tales with his significant analysis, *Morphology of the Folktale*. Despite his influence and some other key studies by Slavic folklorists, and despite the notable recent scholarship of Jack Haney in the United States, the discussion of Russian and Slavic fairy tales, Propp's other more historical works, and even Baba Yaga have taken second place to studies of the western European tradition. This is unfortunate because there are numerous fruitful parallels that can be drawn between cultures of eastern and western Europe to help us understand how fairy tales originated, contained similar motifs, and were disseminated.

The second reason why a focus on Baba Yaga might help us understand the relationship between goddesses, witches, and fairies is that Christianity came later to eastern Europe, and thus pagan beliefs were stronger in eastern Europe in the nineteenth century than in the West. This development may illuminate why fairies are not as significant as witches in Slavic fairy tales, or why the word "fairy tale" is not used by Slavic people to denote what people in the West consider wonder folk tales and fairy tales. The Russian word for a fairy tale is *skazka*, which means "tale." Incidentally, this is the case in German. *Märchen* simply means "little tale" or "tale." The folk tales of Slavic and northern European countries are not notable for their fairies, but they do include various witch figures who have "fairy" virtues.

The third reason—and it is only appropriate that there are three reasons—is that a brief analysis of Baba Yaga tales with a focus on the neglected work *Russian Folk Tales* (1873), translated and edited by W.R.S. Ralston (1828–89), might assist us in grasping how oral and literary traditions work together to reinforce the memetic replication of fairy tales.

Baba Yaga

In *Baba Yaga: The Ambiguous Mother and Witch of the Russian Folktale*, the most thorough study of Baba Yaga to date, Andreas Johns demonstrates that Baba Yaga has appeared in hundreds, or perhaps thousands, of folk tales in Russia, Ukraine, and Belarus since the eighteenth century, if not earlier. She is not just a dangerous witch but also a maternal benefactress, probably related to a pagan goddess. Many other scholars of Russian culture and history, such as Johanna Hubbs in *Mother Russia: The Feminine Myth in Russian Culture*, Linda Ivanits in *Russian Folk Belief*, and Cherry Gilchrist in *Russian Magic: Living Folk Traditions of an Enchanted Landscape*, have confirmed this: Baba Yaga transcends definition because she is an amalgamation of deities mixed with a dose of sorcery, shamanism, and fairy lore. Though it is difficult to trace the historical evolution of this mysterious figure with exactitude, it is apparent that Baba Yaga was created by many voices and hands, starting in the pre-Christian era in eastern Europe up through the eighteenth century, when she finally became "fleshed out," so to speak, in abundant Russian and Slavic tales collected in the nineteenth century. These Russian and Slavic folk tales were the ones that formed an indelible, unfathomable image of what a Baba Yaga is. I say "a Baba Yaga" because in many tales there are three Baba Yagas, often sisters, and in some tales a Baba Yaga is killed only to rise again. And no Baba Yaga is exactly like another.

A Baba Yaga is inscrutable and so powerful that she does not owe allegiance to the devil, God, or even her storytellers. In fact, she opposes all

Judeo-Christian and Muslim deities and beliefs. She is her own woman, a parthogenetic mother, and she decides on a case-by-case basis whether she will help or kill the people who come to her hut, which rotates on chicken legs. She shows the characteristics and tendencies of Western witches, who were demonized by the Christian church and often tend to be beautiful and seductive, cruel and vicious. In time, however, the beauty of witches was downplayed in most European countries so that the witch was likened to an ugly hag. Baba Yaga sprawls herself out in her hut and has ghastly features—drooping breasts, a hideous long nose, and sharp iron teeth. In particular, she thrives on Russian blood and is cannibalistic. Her major prey consists of children and young women, but she will occasionally threaten to devour a man. She kidnaps in the form of a whirlwind or other guises. She murders at will. Though we never learn how she did it, she has conceived daughters, who generally do her bidding. She lives in the forest, which is her domain. Animals venerate her, and she protects the forest as a Mother Earth figure. The only time she leaves the woods, she travels in a mortar, wielding a pestle as a club or rudder along with a broom to sweep away the tracks behind her. At times, she can also be generous with her advice, yet her counsel and help do not come cheaply, for a Baba Yaga is always testing the people who come to her hut by chance or choice. A Baba Yaga may sometimes be killed, but there are others who take her place. She holds the secret to the water of life and may even be Mother Earth herself.

Baba Yaga plays a key role in Aleksandr Nikolaevich Afanasyev's *Russian Folk Tales* (1855–66) and Ivan Aleksandrovich Khudiakov's *Great Russian Tales* (1860–62)—two of the pioneer collections of Russian folk tales. As Jack Haney points out in his highly informative study *An Introduction to the Russian Folktale*, Afanasyev and Khudiakov were not alone during this period, since many writers and scholars began collecting folk tales, but their collections are generally considered the richest and most interesting, especially with regard to the oral wonder tales that feature Baba Yaga. Afanasyev did not collect most of his tales himself but instead relied on the archives of the Geographical Society in Moscow along with tales sent to him by friends and colleagues. Khudiakov, on the other hand, actually went into the countryside to collect his tales and had a keen eye for satirical stories.[11]

It was not easy for either Afanasyev or Khudiakov to publish their tales because of the Russian Empire's strict censorship during the nineteenth century, and any work that appeared to be anticlerical, politically questionable, or scatological was often denied publication permission. Even if they did obtain permission, the texts were often heavily edited and changed. In general, tales largely told by peasants, which might reinforce belief in ancient rituals, beliefs, witches, wizards, and supernatural animals, were looked on with great suspicion by the governmental authorities, church, and upper classes. Nevertheless, it had been impossible before—and still was in the nineteenth century—for the church and state to prevent the oral dissemination of wonder tales, which were deeply rooted in pagan traditions. By the nineteenth century their appeal to intellectuals grew. Indeed, the national and cultural interest in historical Russian folklore had grown stronger among the literate classes, so social conditions in the late nineteenth century favored the publication of all kinds of tales. Finally, we must bear in mind, as Haney suggests, that Russians, especially the peasants, continued to believe deeply in the tales' meanings for their lives, and in such figures as Baba Yaga, Russalka, Kolschei the Deathless, fierce dragons, and bears with magical powers. What may seem fiction and superstition to us today was mixed with fact and faith in the nineteenth century.

Various Baba Yagas functioned and figured in different tale types of the mid-nineteenth century and lent a distinct Russian aura to the stories. No matter what a tale type or how common it may be in the Indo-European tradition, a Baba Yaga will frequently emerge in the story as the decisive figure, turning the plot in favor of or against the protagonist. Moreover, I know of no other awe-inspiring witch/wise woman character in European folklore so amply described and given such unusual paraphernalia as Baba Yaga. Most important, she clearly announces how enmeshed she is with Russia whenever she senses Russian blood is near. No one has ever fully explained why she is always so eager to spill and devour Russian blood, rather than the blood of some other nation. One would think that as a protector of Russian soil, she might always be helpful when Russians appear at her hut. Yet she is most severe with Russians and strangely seems to be protecting Russian soil from the Russians, perhaps testing to see whether they deserve to exist on Russian soil. She also demands the most from Russians and shows no mercy if they fail to listen to her. A Baba Yaga is the ultimate tester and judge, the desacralized omnipotent goddess, who defends deep-rooted Russian pagan values and wisdom, and demands that young women and men demonstrate that they deserve her help.

But what Baba Yaga also defends in the nineteenth-century tales are qualities that the protagonists need in order to adapt and survive, such as perseverance, kindness, obedience, integrity, and courage. If we bear in mind that these tales reflect the actual living conditions of the Russian people in the mid-nineteenth century to a large degree, and that they were listened to and read at face value, they are profound "documents" about the struggles of ordinary Russians and their faith in extraordinary creatures to help them in times of need. They are also dreams of compensation for their helplessness— stories of resistance and hope. The tales are filled with sibling rivalry, bitter conflicts between stepchildren and stepmothers, incest, class struggle, disputes about true heirs, ritual initiations, the pursuit of immortality, and so forth. Although the tales may take place in another time and realm, they are always brought down to earth by the storyteller at the end, for what may happen metaphorically to the characters in the tales is close to the conditions experienced by the listeners. In all the tales Baba Yaga is compelling and dreaded because she forces the protagonists to test themselves while not deluding themselves that there is an easy way to reconcile conflicts. This is also why Baba Yaga transcends Russia and has become woven into the socio-cultural texture of other cultures in ways that are, to be sure, much different from the nineteenth-century Russian tales.

But before we consider how Baba Yaga is related to witches as well as fairies from other cultures, we must try to trace her origins in Russia and other Slavic countries, and here Propp's historical studies may help us.

Vladimir Propp

For many years now Propp has been famous in the West mainly for his innovative study *Morphology of the Folktale*, which I briefly discussed in chapter 2. His other major work, *The Historical Roots of the Wonder Tale* (1946), was partially translated into English in 1984 in *Theory and History of Folklore*, a crude pastiche with sundry articles and a misleading introduction by Anatoly Liberman.[12] It was suggested—and Liberman is not the only scholar to have done this—that Propp had yielded to Communist pressure and abandoned his "genuine" commitment to true scholarship to become a Marxist ideologue when he published *The Historical Roots of the Wonder Tale*. Furthermore, other Western scholars spread the same false rumors, arguing that Propp's so-called formalist approach to folklore had been considered heretical in the Soviet Union, Soviet folklorists were all obliged to follow a party line of orthodox historical materialism, and Propp was largely ignored as a folklorist in the Soviet Union. Nothing could be further from the truth, and thanks to Sibelan Forrester's forthcoming scrupulous and meticulous translation of *The Russian Folktale*, first published posthumously in 1984, it is now possible to gain a fuller understanding of Propp's development as a folklorist and the monumental contributions he made not only to Russian folklore but also to international folklore.[13]

The Russian Folktale is based on lectures that Propp delivered at Leningrad State University in the 1960s and represents the culmination of his thinking about the genesis, relevance, and structure of the Russian folk tale. Unfortunately, he died in 1970 as he was preparing the lectures for book publication and could not put the finishing touches on them. Thanks to notes by his former students, however, his lectures were eventually published as a book, and they complement *Morphology of the Folktale* and *The Historical Roots of the Wonder Tale*, so that we are now in a position to grasp Propp's comprehensive approach to folk tales and folklore in general.

In his insightful essay "V. Ya. Propp—Legend and Fact" (1986), Kirill Chistov, a former student of Propp, clarifies certain "myths" that had been spread about Russian folklore and Propp's status as a folklorist.[14] First, he explains that Propp was never regarded as a formalist in the Soviet Union but rather was considered a structuralist and an innovative folklorist. Without any training in folklore, Propp used a structuralist approach to analyze the Russian wonder tale long before structuralism became fashionable in the West during the 1960s. Second, Chistov shows that Propp's *Morphology of the Folktale* was well received in the Soviet Union when it appeared in 1928, and was discussed and cited by many scholars until and after his death in 1970. The Soviet academy or government in fact never censored Propp. Chistov demonstrates that Propp did not abandon his morphological approach to the folk tale under Communist pressure, nor was he forced to recant this approach. In contrast, it took the West thirty years to finally recognize the value of Propp's approach by bringing out the first translation of *Morphology of the Folktale* in 1958, when structuralism became popular within Western intellectual circles. Since many Soviet works in folklore had been published between 1930 and 1970, there had never been a linguistic barrier to publishing *Morphology of the Folktale*, only a lack of favorable conditions in the West. In short, Propp was ignored more in the West than he was in the Soviet Union. Once translated, however, Propp's work had a great impact, even though it was pegged as some kind of formalist study. Propp's early works consequently have never been fully understood in the West even when he endeavored to explain his attachment to history, ethnography, and anthropology in articles and essays.

The *Russian Folktale* rectifies some of the misleading impressions of Propp's work that various critics have disseminated. As Forrester points out in her introduction to the forthcoming English translation, Propp intended from the beginning of his career to work within a historical-anthropological framework, wanted to include a chapter on the historical origins of the wonder tale in *Morphology of the Folktale*, and would have preferred to use the term "wonder tale" in the title rather than just "folktale." Certainly, he could have been even more exact by using the term "Russian wonder tale," because his focus in *Morphology of the Folktale* was primarily on a hundred tales from the huge, groundbreaking collection of stories gathered by Afanasyev. The tales selected by Propp from this nineteenth-century collection all belong to the category of "wonder tales" (Aarne-Thompson-Uther tale types, 300–749) registered in *The Types of International Folktales: A Classification and Bibliography* (2004), which classifies hundreds of tale types with numbers according to similar motifs and plots.[15] In other words, there is an "organic" development in Propp's work on folk tales from the 1920s to 1970 that is made eminently clear in *The Russian Folktale*.

As Propp explains in *The Russian Folktale*, he believed that in order to establish what constituted a genre, one had to demonstrate that there was a constant repetition of functions in a large body of tales. (Incidentally, the repetition of functions enabled and enables the memetic dissemination of particular tales.) The purpose of his *Morphology of the Folktale* was to establish the thirty-one functions of the wonder tale, and then later in *The Historical Roots of the Wonder Tale* to trace the origins of the functions and genre to rituals and customs of primitive peoples. Propp, never a Marxist or Communist, was evidently strongly influenced by the British anthropological school of Edward Burnett Tylor (1832–1917), Andrew Lang (1844–1912), and James George Frazer (1854–1941), which he describes in the early chapters of *The Russian Folktale*. Indeed, *The Russian Folktale* is a book that brings together his structuralist leanings with his profound interest in the evolutionary process that brought about the genre of the wonder tale. But it is also more than just a summary of his own work and interests, for it was intended to provide a general history about the rise of folklore studies in Russia and Europe.

Though Propp was not a trained folklorist, he had a masterful command of the history of folklore by the time he began delivering his lectures that formed *The Russian Folktale*, and he provides important information about European folklore studies, debates, and collectors in the nineteenth and twentieth centuries, always with a focus on Russia. He then substantially reviews and supplements the theses that he had introduced in *Morphology of the Folktale*, distinguishing carefully between plots, motifs, and functions. His discussions of various tale types are illuminating. In writing about the genesis of the wonder tales along with their connections to rituals, customs, and myths, he is always cautious in making claims, but it is noteworthy that he neither idealizes the common people nor interprets the history of folk tales from an orthodox Marxist viewpoint. Certainly Propp was a historical materialist, but he was also a structuralist, and therefore was interested in belief systems and initiation rites that contributed to the formation of narrative structures, and that he tried to trace through history. Some of the parallels he draws cannot be substantiated, and many might not apply in particular cultures. But, as I have tried to stress, Propp was first and foremost interested in Russian cultural developments, and many of his discussions of initiations and characters such as Baba Yaga are highly stimulating. His propositions are convincing and can best be understood within the framework of Russian history.

Propp's Notions of Initiation

In all the studies that Propp published after 1928, he tried to develop a historical materialist explanation of why and how the Russian wonder tales functioned, and how one could trace the pagan remnants that undergirded them. Key to grasping their resonance and relevance, not only in the nineteenth century when most of the tales were first published, but also in our contemporary period, is their clear revelation of cultural patterns of ritual initiation and worship. Propp maintains that there are two sequences that form the functions and plots of the wonder tales: the initiation of a young man or woman that takes the form of a quest; and the visit to the land of the dead and regeneration. In the first sequence, the hero/ine of almost all wonder tales is an initiate who lacks something, must abandon or is banished from home, receives help in the form of advice or magical objects from a donor or donors (a witch, wise woman, or hermit), is tested, and either happily survives or dies. Another sequence in wonder tales involves the protagonist's allurement or mission, a journey to the otherworld, and encounters with death that are closely related to the initiation rites of fertility and a belief in reincarnation and regeneration. Propp claims that

> the compositional unity of the wondertale lies neither in the specific features of the human psyche nor the peculiarities or artistic creation; rather, it lies in the reality of the past. What is now recounted as a story was once enacted or represented, and what was not enacted was imagined. Of the two sequences, the first (the initiation rite) was lost earlier than the second. The ritual was no longer performed, but old ideas about death survived, developed, and changed even divorced from ritual. The disappearance of the ritual went hand in hand with the disappearance of hunting as the only, or main, source of livelihood. From that point the plot developed as a kernel that absorbed new details from later reality. On the other hand, new ways of life created new genres, like the novella, but their soil was different from the soil that produced the composition and plot of the wondertale. The development proceeded by adding new layers by changes, reinterpretations, and so on, as well as by innovations.[16]

What Propp describes is actually the memetic evolution of tales and their tradition as outlined by Drout in *How Tradition Works*. If we recall from chapter 1, Drout explains that a meme (in this case, a tale) is replicated through a process of *recognito*, *actio*, and *justifcatio*. A tale as meme must first be recognized as relevant, and repeated through action and behavior. Then this particular tale must continue to justify itself through an ongoing process of replication. Drout points out that the meme/tale keeps changing somewhat, and in order to be replicated and maintain its core relevance, it must fit the world that it is describing. He borrows this concept, "Word-to-World fit," from John Austin and John Searle. Drout states that

> Word-to-World fit is thus a key concept in our understanding of tradition and memetics, and it is worth taking a moment to examine it in more detail before proceeding with the development of the theory. First, the Word-to-World fit concept implies the existence of a world with which traditions interact. That world includes the physical world as well as social and cultural worlds, and it also must include the conception of the world, the *Weltanschauung*, held by individuals by means of whom the tradition meme is attempting to replicate itself. For example, a *justificatio* of "because you will be rewarded in the afterlife" would face a Word-to-World conflict if it attempted to replicate its associated tradition in the mind of someone who does not believe in an

afterlife. It is important to note, however, that Word-to-World conflict can also occur when the *Weltanschauung* is not incompatible with the *justificatio*, but some aspect of the physical world is. . . . Note that if a *justificatio* is sufficiently vague, it will more frequently fit the world than if it is precise.[17]

In the case of the Russian wonder tales, they often formed pools of stories (memeplexes) that had been part of initiation rituals in pagan times, and as the world changed, so did the sacred initiation tales that became myths and later "degenerated" into secular wonder tales. By degenerate, I do not mean that they became "worse" in some way or fell apart. Rather, I mean that the tales lost their initial relevance (word-to-world), and yet were transformed to fit new social and cultural conditions. One could say that a memetic tale must degenerate to a certain extent to be regenerated and maintain its relevance. Indeed, the degeneration and secularization of the sacred initiation tales led to a new genre in the early Middle Ages that Propp called a wonder tale, and that is generally accepted nowadays in English-speaking countries as a fairy tale.

At the same time that the initiation tales were being transformed and initially reshaped into myths, the functions of key characters changed so that divinities gradually became witches, fairies, mermaids, or some other supernatural creature in the Middle Ages. Propp describes Baba Yaga's function as follows:

> Yaga lives in a little hut. Yaga is a very complex, far from a monosemantic personage. In cases when the hero-seeker comes upon Baba-Yaga, she gives him a very unfriendly welcome. She recognizes him as an enemy by his smell. . . . Comparative study of this image shows that Yaga guards the boundary of the other world and the entrance to it. She lets only the worthy pass through. The hero is never disturbed by her welcome. . . . This is the benevolent type of Yaga, the gift-giver and advisor. She shows the hero the path. From now on he knows where to go. Sometimes she gives the hero a magical horse or eagle, which the hero rides to the thrice-tenth kingdom. This is the basic function of Yaga from the point of view of development of the action. She gives the hero magical objects or a magical helper, and the action moves to a new stage. Yaga belongs in the broad category of the folktale donor. Meeting with a donor is a canonical form of development of the action. He or she is always met by chance, and the hero earns or somehow otherwise obtains a magical object. Possession of the magical object defines success and the story's outcome. Yaga also behaves as a donor in cases where a stepdaughter finds her way to her. In those cases, however, there is always an extraordinarily stressed moment that can also be traced in "male" tales, but in forms that are less clear—the moment of testing. Yaga tests the hero or heroine. If the tale is "female," the test

has the character of domestic work: making up a bed, beating the feather-bed, hauling water, stoking the stove, etc. In this case the gifts do not bear a magical character, but represent material wealth. The tale ends with a reward. The stepdaughter returns home.[18]

Whereas Propp shows how Baba Yaga as witchlike figure has a crucial function within the wonder tale that furthers the initiation of a male or female protagonist, he does not examine how her role might be related to that of a pagan goddess or fairy. Thanks to Hubbs's *Mother Russia: The Feminine Myth in Russian Culture*, however, we can draw vital connections to archaic forms of female divinities. In particular, Hubbs focuses on the evolution of the Rusalki (nymphs, mermaids, and forest spirits) and Baba Yagas (wise women, cannibals, and witches), revealing how both figures are related to the great goddess Mother Earth as well as similar divinities that stemmed from Paleolithic and Neolithic cults and religions. Depending on the region and belief system, the Rusalki had various functions in Slavic lore: young and virginal, they lured men to their death through their singing; they were bringers of fertility; and they were mistresses of the forest and hunt. In some Slavic countries, they were beautiful flying creatures and wild Amazons, and performed magical and orgiastic dances in the forests, and in others they were large, hairy, and dangerous. They were both givers of life and destroyers. They also had the power to transform themselves into an animal, bird, or reptile. The Rusalki were the initiators of young girls about to be wed. Hubbs often suggests that they prefigured the Greco-Roman goddess Artemis/Diana:

> The *rusalki* personified the regeneration and rebirth of nature and suggested the cult of the maiden goddess Artemis. Their virginal or youthful attributes echoed the ancient belief in the parthenogenetic powers of nature herself, and their multitude seemed to underscore the critical role of the community of young women "priestesses" upon whose potential fertility the life of the village depended. But while the *rusalki* expressed "the force of life" in the form of fecund young women who dwelled outside the human and most particularly male control, the image of the ancient and all-seeing elder, once a mother and now past childbearing age, represented another and equally archaic form through which nature was embodied. The witch Baba Yaga dwells without a mate in the depths of the forest.[19]

What is interesting is that Baba Yaga appears to be an older and wiser Rusalka, with vast powers. Hubbs portrays her as follows:

> She is the expression of realized potential, the fulfillment of the cycle of life associated with woman. She has known all things: virginity (she has no consort), motherhood (her children in plant and animal form are legion), and old age (she gathers all things into her abode to die). In her the cycles of feminine life are brought to completion, and yet she

contains them all. The *rusalki* in their virginal nature and springtime appearances are the Artemis-Kore to her Demeter-Hekate, spring to her winter, sexual desire and love to her own iron rule over sexual union. The *rusalki* lure through their movements—spinning, dancing, and singing. Yaga cooks and eats and gathers all into her oven maw to create anew. They are connected with uterine waters; she with consuming fire.[20]

In the nineteenth-century Slavic wonder tales, the Rusalka and Baba Yaga figures frequently merge into one and resemble many types of fairies in western European oral and literary tales. That is, they exercise similar functions in initiation tales and other tale types and embody some of the same virtues. Though there is no absolute proof that all the witches and fairies in eastern and western Europe stem from pagan beliefs and rituals, there is strong evidence that Baba Yaga is an amalgamation of various pagan deities that underwent gradual transformation in the Greco-Roman period and early Middle Ages.

In Johns's thorough examination of the interpretations and history of Baba Yaga, he cautiously discusses the significance of pagan initiation rituals for explaining the origins of Baba Yaga or the wonder folk tale. Yet in the conclusion of his book, which includes a great amount of information, he remarks that "Baba Yaga emerges as a unique figure, but a comparison with other witch-like characters in European folklore shows that her image is a Slavic variation on an Indo-European (and wider) theme." Johns acknowledges that Baba Yaga might have been a cult or mythical figure, and that the ambiguous Russian Baba Yaga has forbears in Romanian, Hungarian, Slovakian, and other Slavic countries.[21] There is also good reason to believe that she is related to the ancient Germanic Perchta, who gave rise to the famous Frau Holle of the Brothers Grimm's and northern German tales. Her ambiguous quality of witch and fairy was actually a common trait by the late Middle Ages in Europe, for she had not only become a malevolent/benevolent figure that harked back to a great pagan mother goddess and initiation rites but a majestic, dangerous figure of resistance to Christianity that had demonized her virtues as well. In early nineteenth-century collections of Russian wonder tales, the demonization is clear to see, and I want to probe the first and most significant English translation, by Ralston, to study how she functioned despite demonization.

Ralston's *Russian Folk Tales*

Ralston, cofounder of the British Folklore Society in 1878, was one of the major pioneers of folklore studies in England.[22] He studied at Trinity College, Cambridge, and graduated with a degree in law in 1850, but never practiced law. Rather, he did church charity work and participated in the Working Men's College, eventually taking a position as librarian at the British Museum in

1853, until he resigned his post in 1875 due to ill health. His resignation actually was due to a conflict with the museum's management, and it enabled him to spend the latter part of his life producing invaluable studies of folklore. Indeed, Ralston became one of the most prolific and knowledgeable folklorists in England. He wrote numerous essays and reviews, translated Russian and German texts, and lectured on different aspects of folklore throughout England. Unfortunately, the loss of his library job and lack of money ultimately led him to commit suicide in 1889.

Like many of the early British folklorists, Ralston was an autodidact and brilliant intellectual with a great memory. Early in his career as a librarian, he took a profound interest in Russia and taught himself Russian. (Aside from Russian, he had a good command of German, French, and Italian.) In 1868 and 1870, he journeyed to Russia, where he made the acquaintance of the folklorist Afanasyev, the novelist Ivan Turgenev, and many other leading Russian intellectuals. He made his first important contributions to the study of Russian folklore with the publication of *Krilof and His Fables* in 1869 and *The Songs of the Russian People* in 1872 and was soon acknowledged as one of the foremost scholars and translators of Russian folklore and literature. Ralston had a great love for the Russian people and their customs, and thus it was not by chance that his next book was the first English translation of Russian folk tales.

Russian Folk Tales is not a traditional anthology, which normally consists of an introduction followed by tales and perhaps notes at the end. Ralston instead wove vast, detailed commentaries about Russian rituals and customs along with references to folk tales in Europe and America with the fifty-one major tales that he translated and included variants of his selected tales. His primary sources were Afanasyev's *Russian Popular Tales* (1860–63), Ivan Kudyakov's *Great Russian Tales* (1860), E. A. Chudiknsky's *Russian Popular Tales* (1864), A. A. Erlenvein's *Popular Tales* (1863), and I. Rudchenko's *South-Russian Popular Tales* (1869). In addition, he cited well over fifty other European collections and studies in endeavoring to draw parallels with characters and their functions as well as distinct customs and beliefs. Ralston's book is divided into six chapters that cover Russian life and customs, principal incarnations of evil, miscellaneous mythological impersonifications, magic and witchcraft, ghost stories, and legends about saints and demons. Among the fifty-one tales, there are six that deal directly with Baba Yaga or a witch: "Marya-Morevna," "The Baba Yaga," "Vasilissa the Fair," "The Blind Man and the Cripple," "The Witch," and "The Witch and the Sun's Sister."

What is interesting in Ralston's account of Baba Yaga's role in these tales is that although he regards her as the incarnation of evil, he distinguishes between Baba Yaga and the traditional witch figure:

> The supernatural being who, in folk-tales, sways the elements and preys upon mankind, is most inadequately designated by such names as *Vyed'ma*, *Hexe*, or *Witch*, suggestive as those now homely terms are of

merely human, though diabolically intensified malevolence. For more in keeping with the vastness of her powers, and the vagueness of her outline, are the titles of Baba Yaga, Lamia, Striga, Troll-Wife, Ogress, or Dragoness, under which she figures in various lands. And therefore it is in her capacity of Baba Yaga, rather than in that of *Vyed'ma*, that we desire to study the behaviour of the Russian equivalent for the terrible female form which figures in the Anglo-Saxon poems as the Mother of Grendel.[23]

While Ralston tends to see a Baba Yaga mainly as a supernatural embodiment of evil—a result of the Christian demonization of goddesses and sorceresses coupled with patriarchal prejudices—he also realizes that there is something extraordinary about a Baba Yaga that makes her role in the skazki different. She is terrifying and awesome because she is unpredictable, combining various divine powers that can be used for good or evil. In fact, Ralston cites many other Baba Yaga tales to show how she is often a benefactress and helps persecuted maidens, threatened by evil stepmothers or incestuous fathers and brothers. If Ralston had focused on patterns of initiation in the Russian tales, as Propp later did, he might have qualified his interpretation of Baba Yaga as the incarnation of evil.

In the four key Baba Yaga tales in his collection, for instance, the function of evil is *not* performed by Baba Yaga. In "Marya-Morevna," the evil is actually caused by the hero himself when he breaks Marya Morevna's prohibition and looks into the forbidden chamber, where he finds Koshchei the Deathless, who changes into a whirlwind and kidnaps Marya Morevna. It is only through the intervention of Baba Yaga, who provides the hero with a magic horse, that he is able to regain Marya Morvena. In "The Baba Yaga," the evil figure is the stepmother, who beats her stepdaughter and sends the young girl to Baba Yaga, knowing full well that Baba Yaga will devour her. Yet the girl demonstrates that she is kinder and smarter than Baba Yaga and receives aid from a cat and dogs, allowing her to escape to her home. Her father shoots the evil stepmother at the tale's end. In "Vasilissa the Fair," one of the most famous Russian fairy tales, which bears a strong similarity to "Cinderella" tales, Vasilissa is abused by her stepmother and stepsisters and sent to obtain light from Baba Yaga, who tests her and then sends her home, where her stepmother and stepsisters are burned to cinders. In "The Blind Man and the Cripple," Prince Ivan embarks on a quest to marry the most beautiful maiden he can find with his faithful tutor, Katoma. He weds the beautiful Princess Anna, who is just as evil as she is lovely. She causes Katoma to lose his feet and a blind man to lose his eyes so she can exploit the prince. Without their assistance, Prince Ivan is forced to become a cowherd by the evil princess. It is only with the help of a Baba Yaga, who knows the location of the fountain of healing and life-giving water, that the cripple and the blind man regain the ability, respectively, to walk and see. Since they don't trust the Baba Yaga, they kill her, return to the prince, expose the evil princess, and force her to be true to the prince.

Baba Yaga is not portrayed as malignant in any of these tales. Of course, she is dangerous and wary of anyone who enters her terrain. She has enormous powers and is inscrutable. Without her assistance, the protagonist, female or male, cannot overcome evil. It is clear in the tales I have described that she relentlessly initiates young maidens and tests young men, but she is not a force of evil. All four of the tales depict other worlds in which a naive morality and justice can somehow be realized in part due to the intercession of a Baba Yaga, who appears to be amoral. What is significant for the fairy-tale genre is that it counters the corrupt world in which the tellers of the tales exist. Certainly, Russian peasants and the educated classes were still experiencing wicked acts of princes and princesses as well as the abuse of non-biological parents, such as stepmothers and stepfathers. In all social classes, nineteenth-century Russians (not unlike contemporary ones) had to deal with incest, deceit, broken promises, the misogynist treatment of women, the exploitation of common people, brutal wars, and so on. And we shall see in the next chapter how women dealt with cruelty and persecution.

The tales told, collected, and published in Russia were like a breath of new life for the listeners and readers. This was one of the reasons they were frequently banned or censored. The tales were filled with Baba Yagas, who possessed just as many fairy virtues as witch powers. If the Baba Yagas lived in bizarre huts deep in forests, where they were revered by animals and caused humans to be fearful, it was with good reasons. The good reasons, in my opinion, can be found in the thousands of tales about witches and fairies that are desacralized stories, often fusing and confusing the functions and powers of witches and fairies, but still paying tribute to notions of some kind of a great goddess. While Ralston focuses on the diverse Russian traits that one can find in tales about Baba Yagas and witches, he also points constantly to the widespread appearance of these figures in other cultures, to which I shall now turn.

The Fusion and Confusion of Witches and Fairies

The intercultural weaving of witches and fairies is a fascinating aspect of all folklore worldwide. Indeed, when we begin to study the otherness of such characters as Baba Yaga, we learn a great deal about our own cultures by noting differences, while at the same time, we can make startling comparisons that show why the Baba Yaga image may be connected to other folk traditions of sorcery throughout the world, and why this figure continues to live today.

In an elucidating study of recorded stories of Sicilian fairies and witches from the sixteenth to nineteenth centuries, Gustav Henningsen writes:

Like southern Spain, Sicily was a region in which sorcery and black magic thrived, but where popular notions of witchcraft were absent. However, in contrast to Spain, Sicily could boast of a particular type of charismatic healer, who was a specialist in curing diseases caused by the fairies: these healers were women and sometimes men, too, who claimed to possess "sweet blood" (*sangre dulce*), and who therefore each Tuesday, Thursday, and Saturday night were obliged to rush out in spirit (*in espíritu*) and take part in the meetings and nocturnal journeyings of "the company."[24]

Henningsen explains that numerous Sicilian women during this same period asserted they were healers, *donas di fuora* ("ladies from the outside"), and that they often combined the qualities of a witch and fairy to perform healing acts to offset the evil of some other fairies, witches, or supernatural creatures. In other words, the donas di fuora were similar to the Baba Yagas of Russian tradition; they belonged to a dualistic system of widespread belief and could cause harm or perform good deeds. Even if fairy/witches caused harm, there were ways through offerings or expiation to repair the damage. "Everything considered," notes Henningsen, "we can see that Poor Sicilians talked endlessly among themselves about the fairies, and that those of them who were themselves *donas de fuera* gladly described their wonderful adventures, even when this might be dangerous." Henningsen believes that the fairy cult was, to a certain extent, compensation for the hopeless poverty of daily life throughout Sicily. More important, he explains that the Sicilian fairy cult is "a variant of a widely extended and therefore presumably old and deep-rooted Mediterranean and east European complex of shamanistic beliefs."[25] In Sicily, the belief in fairies and sorceresses led to the creation of a character called La Mamma-dràa (Mamma-draga the Ogress) by the nineteenth century. She appears in numerous Sicilian wonder tales and is connected to the ladies from the outside. Though this figure (sometimes a male) is never amply described in the tales, she functions like a Baba Yaga, dangerous and benevolent, a cannibal and wise counselor.

In another major study, *Ecstasies*, Carlo Ginzburg also demonstrates that there was a clear connection between fairies and witches in the belief system of the *benandanti* (people who go out to do good), mainly women, who confessed to flying to Sabbath gatherings in the Friuli region of northern Italy during the sixteenth and seventeenth centuries. According to Ginzburg, the ecstatic experience of these women and men had nothing to do with a belief in demons and devils. Rather, the people left their bodies in a sort of trance and were carried to the good goddess in the world of the dead. The goddess bestowed prosperity, wealth, and knowledge that the benandanti could carry with them back to the villages, where they were regenerated. In essence, the benandanti participated in some kind of shamanistic fertility ritual that involved a voyage to the world of the dead or an other world. There were numerous other shamanistic cults in Europe that celebrated the Sabbath in similar ways.[26] They were associated with witches and fairies, demonized by the church during the European Inquisition and witch hunts. In the particular case of benandanti, different cult groups preceded them in the thirteenth and fourteenth centuries, worshipping goddesses like Artemis/Diana and called good women who flew by night in companies. They were the *bonnes dames*, *bona gens*, good people, and good neighbors (fairies) in such countries as France, Ireland, Scotland, Spain, and Italy.

In an essay that reelaborates the theses of his book, Ginzburg writes that the benandanti were denounced by their fellow villagers in about 1570, and

> they told the inquisitors that during the year, when the Ember Days came round, they fell into a sort of trance. Some of them, mostly men, said that they then went fighting in far-off places, "in the spirit" or in a dream, armed with stalks of fennel; their adversaries were witches and wizards, armed with sorghum stalks, and they were fighting for the fertility of the fields. Others, mostly women, said that, either "in the spirit" or in a dream, they witnessed processions of the dead. All those questioned attributed their extraordinary powers to the fact that they were born within a caul. The inquisitors, having overcome their first astonishment, tried to make the benandanti confess that they were sorcerers and had taken part in a witches' sabbat. Under this pressure, the benandanti altered their story by degrees so that eventually—but more than fifty years later—it conformed to the stereotype of the sabbat, which had not previously figured in the proceedings of the Friulian Inquisition.[27]

The alteration of the stories about fairies and witches connected to good goddesses by inquisitors, clerics, authorities, intellectuals, and other "educated" prosecutors was common throughout Europe, from Ireland to Scandinavia, and from these northern countries to the Mediterranean region. Only by following the transformations of belief systems and the cultural evolution of storytelling can we begin to grasp how goddesses were changed into witches and fairies, among other supernatural creatures, and how the witches and fairies were denigrated and demonized. Ginzburg uses Propp's theses from *Morphology of the Folktale* to explain how ancient pagan rituals informed storytelling and folk tales. Noting that Propp focuses primarily on the structure of the wonder tale as related to initiation rituals, he seeks to complement Propp and maintains that his own research on the sabbat

> illustrates the decisive importance, traceable over a very large cultural area, of the image of the traveller, male or female, in a trance in the world of the dead, in relation to the genesis and transmission of the narrative structure—and perhaps more ancient and certainly more durable—elaborated by the human species. . . . Thus the stereotype of the sabbat represents a fusion of two distinct images. The first, a product of the learned culture (judges, inquisitors, demonologists) centred on the supposed existence of a hostile sect, inspired by the Devil,

members of which had to renounce their faith and profane the Cross and sacraments. The second image, rooted in folk culture, was based on belief in the extraordinary powers of particular men and women who—in a state of trance, and often in animal form or riding upon animals—travelled to the realm of the dead in order to bring prosperity to the community. As we have seen, the second image was much older than the first, and infinitely more widespread.[28]

Ginzburg has been criticized for drawing parallels between the rituals of the witches' sabbath, belief systems, and storytelling too wide and far without documenting his evidence. Yet in many cases there is no proof to document, only convincing hypotheses to be made. When there is collaborating evidence, it appears that Ginzburg's hypotheses have great validity. For instance, Éva Pócs has studied the Hungarian witch trial narratives, noting that

> witches with fairy attributes are mentioned several times in trial records. They brought glittering beauty to the houses in which they appeared, and they abducted their victims into their companies and their fairylike witches' sabbats by making music and dancing. Negative witch characteristics are totally absent from some of these source narratives, which depict an alternative world full of beauty and joy that contrasts with the miseries of the terrestrial world. So, fairylike witches' sabbats also belong in the world of desire.[29]

So it is not only compensation for poverty or lack that people sought in rituals and narratives about goddesses, witches, and fairies. They were not only initiation tales. There was a deep desire for another, more just and beautiful world that formed the moral basis of secular fairy tales. Pócs remarks that

> the fairy world of desire realized in dreams and apparitions was characteristic of the fairy beliefs of the central southeastern Europeans—it also has close parallels in the Celtic, Italian, and Scandinavian regions—and it lent particular fairy attributes to the witches' sabbat in many areas. Something fairylike is always closely linked with the archaic and demonic witches' world of the dead—so much so that at times the shiny, heavenly features are missing from the image of the feast, and a "black" fairy world of the dead appears before us.[30]

It is not necessary, I believe, to draw "exact" parallels between the European fairy/witch cults and shamanistic beliefs in Russia. There is enough evidence to indicate that there were strongly held beliefs in pagan goddesses throughout western and eastern Europe that were transformed into tales enabling peasants and also members of the elite classes in all regions to contend with their suffering while offering some hope for a better life. It is perhaps strange to conclude that Baba Yaga may be a symbol of hope because she is so ambiguous, just as frightening as she is benevolent. But hope may be best generated when a wise woman does not mince her words and instead resists people who invade her world, and a true Baba Yaga is never one to mince her words.

Coda: Untangling the Tangled Witch

I began this chapter by asserting that witches are still very much with us, and that we memetically pass on diverse images and stories of witches, who contain divine and fairylike features. In the late 1960s and 1970s, the feminist movement in Europe and North America made a major effort—and still does to some extent—to rectify the demonized, stereotypical image of the witch as bitch. That is, the "great accomplishment" of Christianity was its transformation of goddesses, sorceresses, and fairies into demonic and malevolent figures, whether real or fictitious. Some scholars have even argued that numerous goddesses and witches also became saints.[31] For the most part, however, witches have been depicted as cruel, exotic, devious, and evil figures in popular culture as well as the mass media.

Despite the demonization of witches in the popular imagination, the devout belief in sorcery and sorceresses as virtuous that began in pagan times has never abated, even though it has undergone transformations. As Berti observes,

> contemporary sorcery cannot be considered a rural phenomenon, nor can it be considered a product of culturally underdeveloped people. On the contrary, it has something to do with "ultra-developed" people who require continual innovations. But the traditional sorcery . . . has not come to an end. There still exists today, whether it be in the countryside or in the large cities (not only in Italy) particular individuals defined by diverse names from one region to another. . . . These personages have one or more "virtues" in common that have various origins: it could be an innate virtue, or some knowledge received in the course of simple rites of passage. It can also be the capacity that resulted from natural or psychological trauma (for example, an accident, the death of a beloved person, a revelatory dream, an apparition, a vision).[32]

"True" believers by the thousands, if not millions, around the world take witches (and yes, even fairies) seriously. At the same time, the culture industry continues to produce the stereotypical evil bitch/witch in all forms of the mass media. The latest banal version of the Disney Corporation, *Tangled* (2010), for instance, was a messy adaptation of the Brothers Grimm's "Rapunzel"—a tale that can be traced back to the period of witch hunts and probably even further in history. In the Brothers Grimm's version, the story concerns a pregnant woman who cannot control her desire for *rapunzel* ("cabbage"). Therefore, her husband trespasses in a witch's garden to fetch some rapunzel for his wife. Caught by the witch, the husband must promise to deliver their firstborn to the witch or be eaten. Of course, he and his wife deliver their baby daughter to the witch, who raises the child named Rapunzel in a tower in the woods. (She does not eat her.) Along comes a prince who also trespasses and climbs the tower to sleep with Rapunzel. Caught by the witch, he is thrown from the tower and becomes blind, while Rapunzel, who gives birth to twins, is banished from the witch's forest. In the end, after the prince wanders about, the couple is reunited by chance. The witch continues to live alone in her forest.

Now this is a fascinating tale that certainly can be interpreted in numerous ways. If we limit our explanation by focusing on the witch, however, we can see that she was the mistress of the garden and forest and punishes a couple because they trespassed on her territory (sacred ground) without asking permission. The witch raises Rapunzel with great care and desires to protect her from "male" intrusion. When a prince, who seduces Rapunzel, defies the witch, she justifiably punishes both the maiden and prince. In the end, there is an apparent mercy shown by the old woman/witch/mistress of the forest, who remains alive and powerful. Although not meant to be didactic, the tale concerns the initiation of a virgin, who must learn hard lessons when she defies her maternal protectress. And it contains a simple, if not naive, moral that can be seen in numerous European and Middle Eastern variants.[33] What is important is that the witch demonstrates divine and fairylike virtues.

Now, to return to the witch in the inane Disney film, we can see that the movie departs from the folk and literary tradition, and that the witch/bitch is portrayed as one-dimensionally evil. Following what Walt Disney did in his first animated feature film, *Snow White and the Seven Dwarfs* (1936), his "modern" corporation has followed suit by creating in *Tangled* an aging woman who will deceive and destroy just to remain beautiful. She is the pure incarnation of evil, and there is no just reason why she wants to kidnap Rapunzel except to further her narcissistic desire. Obsessed with beauty and her own desires, the Disney witches are stereotypical products of the Western male gaze and mass-mediated manipulation of the images of women that date back to the Christian church's demonization of women. There are connections to be drawn. All one has to do is to read a bit of history.

And this brings me finally to Linda Hults's fine study, *The Witch as Muse: Art, Gender, and Power in Early Modern Europe*. She approaches the witch from the perspective of art history and feminism, and links the sketches, drawings, and paintings of the late medieval period—that is, early modern Europe—to the witch hunts, in order to understand the practices and mentalities that led to the formation of stereotypical, misogynist images of the witch that became and are still generally associated with women up through today. As she explains,

> The formulation and perpetuation of witch-hunting, whether visual or verbal, and engagement in the debate surrounding witchcraft and its

appropriate punishment, were male prerogatives. Witchcraft was the most extreme expression of female deviance: a charge levied not against women in general but against women who were imagined as eluding or subverting patriarchal control. As such, the stereotype of the witch represents early modern Europe's profound fear of female deviance. It was the very banality of misogyny, its complete incorporation into binary patterns of thought so convincingly elucidated by [Stuart] Clark, and its intensification in the late fifteenth century that made the assertions of the demonologists plausible. Artistic images of witches fostered misogyny, often directly by engaging the debate about the reality of and the appropriate judicial and social response to witchcraft but always more subtly, I argue, by invoking ideas of artistic creativity as an exclusively male realm.[34]

Not all the images of witches produced in early modern Europe and contemporary Western culture are misogynist. There have always been contradictions and conflicts within fields of cultural production that reveal alternative images. Even the diverse drawings by the sixteenth-century Swiss artist Niklaus Manuel Deutsch show that he tangled the image of the witch as an old hag with the witch as a seductive, young flying fairy. But it is true that there is a difference when women produce their own art and tell their own stories. The resistance to violence and misogyny becomes clear, and we shall see in the next chapter how fairy tales told and collected by women offer us other worlds that question the dominant views of traditional patriarchy.

5

The Tales of Innocent Persecuted Heroines and
Their Neglected Female Storytellers and Collectors

Witches and fairies are not the only significant female characters in fairy tales. In fact, beautiful innocent maidens may be more important, but in the hands of male tellers, writers, and collectors, they tend to be depicted as helpless, if not passive. To be good, they must be obedient and industrious. The overwhelming number of oral and literary fairy tales up through the nineteenth century usually stereotype the young heroine, but this is not due to the demonization of women as deviants, as discussed in the last chapter. It is because of a more general patriarchal view of women as domestics and breeders, born to serve the interests of men. Yet as we have seen in early tales about women as witches and fairies, there were certainly thousands of stories that women told to one another, and that were never collected or written down, in which heroines were assertive, confident, and courageous—in short, nobody's slave.

It was only toward the end of the nineteenth century that we can find more of such heroines along with those wily, rebellious witches and fairies, and so I want to turn to four case studies to let the tales of these stories breathe—and they are stories that concern rape, incest, abuse, and violation, intolerable and unjust acts that continue today. Moreover, they continue to be major themes of many contemporary fairy tales. It is no wonder that fairy tales have not vanished from the cultural domains of our contemporary chaotic world. It is in the other moral world of fairy tales that women tend to find an iota of justice—and men as well, for there are numerous persecuted heroes. But in this chapter we shall focus on the more neglected women as storytellers, collectors, and figures in the tales.

The Persecuted Heroine

In the 1961 revised edition of Aarne and Thompson's standard category of folk tales, *The Types of the Folktale*, they assign the designation AT 510 to "Cinderella" and "Cap of the Rushes," describing this type as follows:

1. *The persecuted heroine.* (a) The heroine is abused by her stepmother and stepsisters, and (a1) stays on the hearth or in the ashes, and (a2) is dressed in rough clothing—such as a cap of rushes, wooden cloak, and so on; (b) flees in disguise from her father who wants to marry her; or (c) is cast out by him because she has said that she loved him like salt, or (d) is to be killed by a servant.
2. *Magic help.* While she is acting as servant (at home or among strangers) she is advised, provided for, and fed (a) by her dead mother, (b) a tree on the mother's grave, (c) a supernatural being, (d) birds, or (e) a goat, sheep, or cow. (f) When the goat (cow) is killed, a magic tree springs up from her remains.
3. *Meeting the prince.* (a) She dances in beautiful clothing several times with a prince, who seeks in vain to keep her, or the prince sees her in church. (b) She gives hints of the abuse she has endured as a servant girl, or (c) is seen in her beautiful clothing in her room or the church.
4. *Proof of identity.* (a) She is discovered through the slipper test or (b) a ring, which she throws into the prince's drink or bakes into his bread. (c) She alone is able to pluck the gold apple desired by the knight.
5. *Marriage with the prince.*
6. *Value of salt.* The father is served unsalted food and thus learns the meaning of the heroine's earlier answer.[1]

In a special 1993 issue of *Western Folklore* dedicated to "Perspectives on the Innocent Persecuted Heroine in Fairy Tales," Steven Swann Jones remarks,

> The persecution depicted in the acts of the Innocent Persecuted Heroine genre seems to be a metaphoric representation of the types of problems a young woman is likely to encounter and of her attitude, as well as society's, toward those problems. These basic and typical problems appear to concern her relationship to her parents, to her own sexuality, and to her mate. Ultimately, the tales are both psychological mirrors and socially framed registers, reflecting personal attitudes as well as reinforcing a code of beliefs and behavior to which the cultures and audience members are encouraged to subscribe.[2]

Although the type of persecuted innocent heroine type described by Aarne and Thompson, and elaborated by Jones, is helpful for scholars to trace and compare similar tales of persecution, there are many other tales of nineteenth-century innocent persecuted heroines that do not fit the parameters set by these folklorists and thus need careful examination, especially because they were told or collected in the nineteenth century by female storytellers and authors whose works have largely been neglected. For instance, what are we to make of the following Sicilian tale collected by Gonzenbach in 1868?

The Snake Who Bore Witness for a Maiden

Once upon a time there was a poor woman, so poor that she had to live in a very wild and desolate region. She had just one daughter, who was more beautiful than the sun. The mother gathered herbs and took them into the city where she sold them, while her daughter generally remained at home and cooked and washed.

One day, when the mother had gone into the city again with her herbs, the daughter remained all alone at home, and the king's son happened to enter into this wilderness. He had been hunting and had become separated from his entourage. When he caught sight of the little cottage, he got off his horse, knocked on the door, and asked for a glass of water because he was so thirsty. However, the maiden did not open the door. Instead, she opened the window and handed him the glass of water through the window. As soon as he saw how strikingly beautiful she was, he was overcome by a dark desire and impetuously demanded that she open the door for him. She refused, but he was driven by his wild desires and broke down the door. He forced his way into the house and overpowered the maiden. She yelled and cried, but nobody heard her. As she was looking around for some help, she noticed a snake crawling by. "Since nobody hears me in my need," she said, "I'm calling upon you, oh snake, to bear witness for me: prince, may you never marry anyone else other but me!" After she said this, she yielded to the prince's will. Then he left the cottage. She never told her mother anything about this.

Not long after this event a rumor spread that the prince was soon to marry a beautiful princess. One day, after the mother had gone to the city again to sell herbs, she returned in the evening, and the maiden asked her mother, "Tell me, dear mother, what's new in the city?"

"Oh, my child," her mother said, "I've heard such an unusual story, nobody believes it. Just think, the prince has a snake wrapped around his neck, and nobody can chase it away, and when anyone tries to pry it loose, the snake only tightens itself around the prince's neck so that he has almost been strangled to death."

As soon as the daughter heard this, she knew quite well what snake it was and set out early the next morning for the city without saying anything to her mother, and she went straight to the castle.

When the guards saw her and asked her what she wanted, she said, "Announce me to the king. I have a way to free the prince from the snake that's wrapped itself around his neck."

The guards began to laugh and said, "Many doctors and wise folk have already tried this, and nobody has succeeded. Now you want to try!"

But she responded, "Just announce me to the king."

When the king heard the noise, he asked what was happening.

"There's a maiden down below," his servants told him. "She boasts that she has a way to free the prince from the snake."

"Well, let her come up," the king said. "Even if she doesn't have a way, it won't harm to let her try."

So the beautiful maiden was led to the king, and the king conducted her into his son's room and left her there alone with his son. She stepped up to him and said, "Look at me. Do you recognize me?"

"No," the prince replied, but as he said this, the snake tightened itself around his neck.

"What?" she continued. "Have you forgotten how you charged into my house and forced me to do your will? Don't you recall how I called on the snake to bear witness so that you would not be able to marry anyone else but me?"

He would have liked to have responded with "no" again, but the snake tightened itself even more so that he finally said, "yes." Then the snake released its grip a little.

"And now you want to marry a princess and abandon me?" the maiden asked.

"Yes," he answered, and as soon as he said those words, the snaked wrapped itself more tightly around his neck until he finally promised that he would not marry the princess.

"Now swear to me that you'll marry me," the maiden said.

The prince swore, and just as he did, the snake released itself from his neck and disappeared. The prince rushed to the king and said, "Dear father, send my fiancée back to her father. This maiden over here has freed me from the evil snake, and she is the one who will be my bride."

Well, the prince married the beautiful maiden, and she also had her mother come to the castle. They lived happy and content, but we have nothing to pay the rent.[3]

What are we to make of the following French tale told by Lévesque in 1875?

Marion

There was a man who was a widower. Also the woman. They got married. The husband had a daughter who was called Marion. The wife had a daughter who was called Madeleine.

This aunt could not bear the sight of the daughter of her husband. She almost starved her to death; she gave her next to nothing to eat. However, the girl had to tend sheep in the field, even though she was dying from hunger.

Once she was in the field and starving, she could not even follow her sheep. She wept after her herd. She cried out of hunger.

One day a man came toward her, a man completely nude, completely tattered. He said to her:

"Why are you crying, my little shepherdess?"

"Ah, my friend, I'm crying because I'm hungry."

"Are you really hungry?"

"Yes, very hungry."

"Well, my child, I have bread. I have meat and some wine. If you want to eat some of this, I'll give it to you."

"Oh yes, I want to eat it. You'd be doing me a great favor by letting me eat all this. I'm very hungry."

"Well then, my child, eat and fill yourself," the man said to her.

The girl responded, "Yes, I'm done eating and I'm full. Thank you for your kindness."

"When tomorrow comes, I'll return and bring you something more to eat."

He went away, and Marion was very content. When the moment arrived to fence in the sheep, she returned home.

The next day her aunt gave her a bit of broth, but the broth was not good. The girl ate it, but she did not enjoy it. When she was in the field, she thought to herself, "My God, if only the man who came yesterday would come today, I'd eat something good."

As she was thinking about this, the poor man suddenly appeared, poorly clothed like the day before.

"Ah, my little shepherdess, you're still hungry?"

"Oh, my God, how hungry I am, my friend!"

"Well then, take this and eat and drink everything that seems good to you."

She said to him: "Oh my God, you are so good."

After she had eaten and drunk, this man turned to her and said, "Do not despair, my little one. I'll return tomorrow. As long as I live, I'll bring you something to eat and drink."

When the food was gone, she went and fenced in the sheep.

There was a woman who saw this man with Marion. This woman went to the home of the aunt and said to her, "Marion is leading a good life."

"Why?"

"Because a pilgrim comes to her every day."

The aunt spoke, "Don't say anything. Tomorrow I'll send my daughter Madeleine to keep an eye on her. Then I'll know whether or not she's living well."

"But yes, it's true. I saw a pilgrim with her, and he gave her something to eat and drink."

"Tomorrow I'm going to send Madeleine. Then I'll know if it's true."

When Marion was about to lead her sheep into the field the next day, the aunt said to her:

"Well now, Madeleine, go and see if there's a pilgrim with Marion. Hide yourself so that she doesn't see you."

Madeleine went and saw this tattered man bring Marion something to eat and drink. Madeleine did not let herself be seen and returned to the house.

"Yes, my mother," she said. "It's really true. I saw a man in rags who gave Marion something to eat and drink in the field."

"Oh," exclaimed her mother, "that woman who was here yesterday alerted me about this. But don't say anything when she returns from the field. I'll have her father kill her. This will teach her to lure pilgrims to her."

When Marion returned home after fencing in the sheep, the aunt said to her father,

"Well now, look at your wench who lures pilgrims to her in the field! You've got to kill your daughter. I don't want a bad girl like her in the house."

Marion responded, "It's not true. I haven't lured anyone to me. My father doesn't have to kill me."

"But your aunt," said the father, "she doesn't want you anymore. She was alerted by a woman who said that she saw you with a pilgrim. Also, Madeleine, she went to keep an eye on you and saw you with a pilgrim. Your aunt doesn't want you anymore. So I'm obliged to kill you, my child. I can't protect you."

"My father, don't kill me. I haven't lured anyone to me."

"Oh, my child, I'll have to kill you. Your aunt doesn't want you anymore. I'm forced to do this."

The father took his knife to kill her. His daughter began to run. Her father went after her, and Madeleine also ran to help him catch her.

When Marion arrived at a high rock, it opened for her and then closed in front of the father.

Every day God brought her something to eat. The rock opened and then closed after he left.

At the end of some days God led her to Heaven.[4]

And what about this tale, written in 1857 by the illustrious Czech author Němcová?

The Twelve Months

Once upon a time there lived a mother who had two daughters. One was her own child, the other her stepdaughter. She was very fond of her own daughter, but she would not so much as look at her stepdaughter. The only reason was that Maruša, the stepdaughter, was prettier than her own daughter, Holena. The gentle-hearted Maruša did not know how beautiful she was, and so she could never make out why her mother was so cross with her whenever she looked at her. She had to do all the housework, tidying up the cottage, cooking, washing, and sewing, and then she had to take the hay to the cow and look after her. She did all this work alone, while Holena spent the time adorning herself and lazing about. But Maruša liked work, for she was a patient girl, and when her mother scolded and rated her, she bore it like a lamb. It was no good, however, for they grew crueller and crueller every day, only because Maruša was growing prettier and Holena uglier every day.

At last the mother thought: "Why should I keep a pretty stepdaughter in my house? When the lads come courting here, they will fall in love with Maruša and they won't look at Holena."

From that moment the stepmother and her daughter were constantly scheming how to get rid of poor Maruša. They starved her and they beat her. But she bore it all, and in spite of all she kept on growing prettier every day. They invented torments that the cruellest of men would never have thought of.

One day—it was in the middle of January—Holena felt a longing for the scent of violets.

"Go, Maruša, and get me some violets from the forest; I want to wear them at my waist and to smell them," she said to her sister.

"Great heavens! sister. What a strange notion! Who ever heard of violets growing under the snow?" said poor Maruša.

"You wretched tatterdemalion! How dare you argue when I tell you to do something? Off you go at once, and if you don't bring me violets from the forest, I'll kill you!" said Holena threateningly.

The stepmother caught hold of Maruša, turned her out of the door, and slammed it too after her. She went into the forest weeping bitterly. The snow lay deep, and there wasn't a human footprint to be seen. Maruša wandered about for a long time, tortured by hunger and trembling with cold. She begged God to take her from the world.

At last she saw a light in the distance. She went towards the glow, and came at last to the top of a mountain. A big fire was burning there, and round the fire were twelve stones with twelve men sitting on them. Three of them had snow-white beards, three were not so old, and three were still younger. The three youngest were the handsomest of them all. They were not speaking, but all sitting silent. These twelve men were the twelve months. Great January sat highest of all; his hair and beard were as white as snow, and in his hand he held a club.

Maruša was frightened. She stood still for a time in terror, but, growing bolder, she went up to them and said: "Please, kind sirs, let me warm my hands at your fire. I am trembling with the cold."

Great January nodded, and asked her: "Why have you come here, my dear little girl? What are you looking for?"

"I am looking for violets," answered Maruša.

"This is no time to be looking for violets, for everything is covered with snow," answered Great January.

"Yes, I know; but my sister Holena and my stepmother said that I must bring them some violets from the forest. If I don't bring them, they'll kill me. Tell me, fathers, please tell me where I can find them."

Great January stood up and went to one of the younger months—it was March—and, giving him the club, he said: "Brother, take the high seat."

March took the high seat upon the stone and waved the club over the fire. The fire blazed up, the snow began to melt, the trees began to bud, and the ground under the young beech-trees was at once covered with grass and the crimson daisy buds began to peep through the grass. It was springtime. Under the bushes the violets were blooming among their little leaves, and before Maruša had time to think, so many of them had sprung up that they looked like a blue cloth spread out on the ground.

"Pick them quickly, Maruša!" commanded March.

Maruša picked them joyfully till she had a big bunch. Then she thanked the months with all her heart and scampered merrily home.

Holena and the stepmother wondered when they saw Maruša bringing the violets. They opened the door to her, and the scent of violets filled all the cottage.

"Where did you get them?" asked Holena sulkily.

"They are growing under the bushes in a forest on the high mountains."

Holena put them in her waistband. She let her mother smell them, but she did not say to her sister: "Smell them."

Another day she was lolling near the stove, and now she longed for some strawberries. So she called to her sister and said: "Go, Maruša, and get me some strawberries from the forest."

"Alas! dear sister, where could I find any strawberries? Whoever heard of strawberries growing under the snow?" said Maruša.

"You wretched little tatterdemalion, how dare you argue when I tell you to do a thing? Go at once and get me the strawberries, or I'll kill you!"

The stepmother caught hold of Maruša and pushed her out of the door and shut it after her. Maruša went to the forest weeping bitterly. The snow was lying deep, and there wasn't a human footprint to be seen anywhere. She wandered about for a long time, tortured by hunger and trembling with cold. At last she saw the light she had seen the other day. Overjoyed, she went towards it. She came to the great fire with the twelve months sitting round it.

"Please, kind sirs, let me warm my hands at the fire. I am trembling with cold."

Great January nodded, and asked her: "Why have you come again, and what are you looking for here?"

"I am looking for strawberries."

"But it is winter now, and strawberries don't grow on the snow," said January.

"Yes, I know," said Maruša sadly; "but my sister Holena and my step-mother bade me bring them some strawberries, and if I don't bring them, they will kill me. Tell me, fathers, tell me, please, where I can find them."

Great January arose. He went over to the month sitting opposite to him—it was June—and handed the club to him, saying: "Brother, take the high seat."

June took the high seat upon the stone and swung the club over the fire. The fire shot up, and its heat melted the snow in a moment. The ground was all green, the trees were covered with leaves, the birds began to sing, and the forest was filled with all kinds of flowers. It was summer. The ground under the bushes was covered with white starlets, the starry blossoms were turning into strawberries every minute. They ripened at once, and before Maruša had time to think, there were so many of them that it looked as though blood had been sprinkled on the ground.

"Pick them at once, Maruša!" commanded June.

Maruša picked them joyfully till she had filled her apron full. Then she thanked the months with all her heart and scampered merrily home.

Holena and the stepmother wondered when they saw Maruša bringing the strawberries. Her apron was full of them. They ran to open the door for her, and the scent of the strawberries filled the whole cottage.

"Where did you pick them?" asked Holena sulkily.

"There are plenty of them growing under the young beech-trees in the forest on the high mountains."

Holena took the strawberries, and went on eating them till she could eat no more. So did the stepmother too, but they didn't say to Maruša: "Here is one for you."

When Holena had enjoyed the strawberries, she grew greedy for other dainties, and so on the third day she longed for some red apples.

"Maruša, go into the forest and get me some red apples," she said to her sister.

"Alas! sister dear, how am I to get apples for you in winter?" protested Maruša.

"You wretched little tatterdemalion, how dare you argue when I tell you to do a thing? Go to the forest at once, and if you don't bring me the apples I will kill you!" threatened Holena.

The stepmother caught hold of Maruša and pushed her out of the door and shut it after her. Maruša went to the forest weeping bitterly. The snow was lying deep; there wasn't a human footprint to be seen anywhere. But she didn't wander about this time. She ran straight to the top of the mountain where the big fire was burning. The twelve months were sitting round the fire; yes, there they certainly were, and Great January was sitting on the high seat.

"Please, kind sirs, let me warm my hands at the fire. I am trembling with cold."

Great January nodded, and asked her: "Why have you come here, and what are you looking for?"

"I am looking for red apples."

"It is winter now, and red apples don't grow in winter," answered January.

"Yes, I know," said Maruša sadly; "but my sister and my stepmother, too, bade me bring them some red apples from the forest. If I don't bring them, they will kill me. Tell me, father, tell me, please, where I could find them."

Great January rose up. He went over to one of the older months—it was September. He handed the club to him and said: "Brother, take the high seat."

Month September took the high seat upon the stone and swung the club over the fire. The fire began to burn with a red flame, the snow began to melt. But the trees were not covered with leaves; the leaves were wavering down one after the other, and the cold wind was driving them to and fro over the yellowing ground. This time Maruša did not see so many flowers. Only red pinks were blooming on the hillside, and meadow saffrons were flowering in the valley. High fern and thick ivy were growing under the young beech-trees. But Maruša was only looking for red apples, and at last she saw an apple-tree with red apples hanging high among its branches.

"Shake the tree at once, Maruša!" commanded the month.

Right gladly Maruša shook the tree, and one apple fell down. She shook it a second time, and another apple fell down.

"Now, Maruša, run home quickly!" shouted the month.

Maruša obeyed at once. She picked up the apples, thanked the months with all her heart, and ran merrily home.

Holena and the stepmother wondered when they saw Maruša bringing the apples. They ran to open the door for her, and she gave them two apples.

"Where did you get them?" asked Holena.

"There are plenty of them in the forest on the high mountain."

"And why didn't you bring more? Or did you eat them on the way home?" said Holena harshly.

"Alas! sister dear, I didn't eat a single one. But when I had shaken the tree once, one apple fell down, and when I shook it a second time, another apple fell down, and they wouldn't let me shake it again. They shouted to me to go straight home," protested Maruša.

Holena began to curse her: "May you be struck to death by lightning!" and she was going to beat her.

Maruša began to cry bitterly, and she prayed to God to take her to Himself, or she would be killed by her wicked sister and her stepmother. She ran away into the kitchen.

Greedy Holena stopped cursing and began to eat the apple. It tasted so delicious that she told her mother she had never tasted anything so nice in all her life. The stepmother liked it too. When they had finished, they wanted some more.

"Mother, give me my fur coat. I'll go to the forest myself. That ragged little wretch would eat them all up again on her way home. I'll find the place all right, and I'll shake them all down, however they shout at me."

Her mother tried to dissuade her, but it was no good. She took her fur coat, wrapped a cloth round her head, and off she went to the forest. Her mother stood on the threshold, watching to see how Holena would manage to walk in the wintry weather.

The snow lay deep, and there wasn't a human footprint to be seen anywhere. Holena wandered about for a long time, but the desire of the sweet apple kept driving her on. At last she saw a light in the distance. She went towards it, and climbed to the top of the mountain where the big fire was burning, and round the fire on twelve stones the twelve months were sitting. She was terrified at first, but she soon recovered. She stepped up to the fire and stretched out her hands to warm them, but she didn't say as much as "By your leave" to the twelve months; no, she didn't say a single word to them.

"Why have you come here, and what are you looking for?" asked Great January crossly.

"Why do you want to know, you old fool? It's no business of yours," replied Holena angrily, and she turned away from the fire and went into the forest.

Great January frowned and swung the club over his head. The sky grew dark in a moment, the fire burned low, the snow began to fall as thick as if the feathers had been shaken out of a down quilt, and an icy wind began to blow through the forest. Holena couldn't see one step in front of her; she lost her way altogether, and several times she fell into snowdrifts. Then her limbs grew weak and began slowly to stiffen. The snow kept on falling and the icy wind blew more icily than ever. Holena began to curse Maruša and the Lord God. Her limbs began to freeze, despite her fur coat.

Her mother was waiting for Holena; she kept on looking out for her, first at the window, then outside the door, but all in vain.

"Does she like the apples so much that she can't leave them, or what is the matter? I must see for myself where she is," decided the stepmother at last. So she put on her fur coat, she wrapped a shawl round her head, and went out to look for Holena. The snow was lying deep; there wasn't a human footprint to be seen; the snow fell fast, and the icy wind was blowing through the forest.

Maruša had cooked the dinner, she had seen to the cow, and yet Holena and her mother did not come back. "Where are they staying so long?" thought Maruša, as she sat down to work at the distaff. The spindle was full already and it was quite dark in the room, and yet Holena and the stepmother had not come back.

"Alas, Lord! what has come to them?" cried Maruša, peering anxiously through the window. The sky was bright and the earth was all glittering, but there wasn't a human soul to be seen. . . . Sadly she shut the window; she crossed herself, and prayed for her sister and her mother. . . . In the morning she waited with breakfast, she waited with dinner; but however much she waited, it was no good. Neither her mother nor her sister ever came back. Both of them were frozen to death in the forest.

So good Maruša inherited the cottage, a piece of ploughland and the cow. She married a kind husband, and they both lived happily ever after.[5]

Finally, what are we to make of the Roman tale collected by Busk in 1877?

Maria Wood

They say, there was a king, whose wife, when she came to him, said to him,

"When I am dead, you will want to marry again; but take my advice: marry no woman but her whose foot my shoe fits."

But this she said because the shoe was under a spell, and would fit no one whom he could marry.

The king, however, caused the shoe to be tried on all manner of women; and when the answer always was that it would fit none of them, he grew quite bewildered and strange in his mind.

After some years had passed, his young daughter, having grown up to girl's estate, came to him one day, saying,

"Oh, papa; only think! Mamma's shoe just fits me!"

"Does it!" replied the simple king; "then I must marry you."

"Oh, that cannot be, papa," said the girl, and ran away.

But the simple king was so possessed with the idea that he must marry the woman whom his wife's shoe fitted, that he sent for her every day and said the same thing.

But the queen had not said that he should marry the woman whom her shoe fitted, but that he should not marry any whom it did not fit.

When the princess found that he persevered in his silly caprice, she said at last,

"Papa, if I am to do what you say, you must do something for me first."

"Agreed, my child," replied the king; "you have only to speak."

"Then, before I marry," said the girl, "I want a lot of things, but I will begin with one at a time. First, I want a dress of the colour of a beautiful noontide sky, but all covered with stars, like the sky at midnight, and furnished with a parure (jewels or jewelry that match) to suit it."

Such a dress the king had made, and brought to her.

"Next," said the princess, "I want a dress of the colour of the sea all covered with golden fishes, with a fitting parure."

Such a dress the king had made, and brought to her.

"Next," said the princess, "I want a dress of a dark blue, all covered with gold embroidery and spangled with silver bells, and with a parure to match."

Such a dress the king had made, and brought to her.

"These are all very good," said the princess; "but now you must send for the most cunning artificer in your whole kingdom, and let him make me a figure of an old woman just like life, fitted with all sorts of springs to make it move and walk when one gets inside, just like a real woman."

Such a figure the king had made, and brought it to the princess.

"That is just the sort of figure I wanted," said she; "and now I don't want anything more."

And the simple king went away quite happy.

As soon as she was alone, however, the princess packed all three dresses and many of her other dresses, and all her jewelry and a large sum of money, inside the figure of the wood woman, and then she got into it and walked away. No one seeing an old woman walking out of the palace thought she had anything to do with the princess, and thus she got far away without anyone thinking of stopping her.

On, on, on, she wandered till she came to the palace of a great king, and just at the time that the king's son was coming in from hunting.

"Have you a place in all this fine palace to take in a poor old body?" whined the princess inside the figure of the old woman.

"No, no! Get out of the way! How dare you come in the way of the prince!" said the servants, and drove her away.

But the prince took compassion on her, and called her to him.

"What's your name, good woman?" said the prince.

"Maria Wood is my name, your Highness," replied the princess.

"And what can you do, since you ask for a place?"

"Oh, I can do many things. First, I understand all about poultry, and then—"

"That'll do," replied the prince; "take her, and let her be the henwife, and let her have food and lodging, and all she wants."

So they gave her a little hut on the borders of the forest, and set her to tend the poultry.

But the prince as he went out hunting often passed by her hut, and when she saw him pass she never failed to come out and salute him, and now and then he would stop his horse and spend a few moments in gossip with her.

Before long it was Carneval time; and as the prince came by Maria Wood came out and wished him a "good Carneval." The prince stopped his horse and said, his young head full of the pleasure he expected,

"To-morrow, you know, we have the first day of the feast."

"To be sure I know it; and how I should like to be there: won't you take me?" answered Maria Wood.

"You shameless old woman," replied the prince, "to think of your wanting to go to a *festino* at your time of life!" and he gave her a cut with his whip.

The next day Maria put on her dress of the colour of the noontide sky, covered with stars like the sky at midnight, with the parure made to wear with it, and came to the feast. Every lady made place before her dazzling appearance, and the prince alone dared to ask her to dance. With her he danced all the evening, and fairly fell in love with her, nor could he leave her side; and as they sat together, he took the ring off his own finger and put it on to her hand. She appeared equally satisfied with his attentions, and seemed to desire no other partner. Only when he tried to gather from her whence she was, she would only say she came from the country of Whip-low, which set the prince wondering very much, as he had never heard of such a country. At the end of the ball, the prince sent his attendants to watch her so that he might learn where she lived, but she disappeared so swiftly that it was impossible for them to tell what had become of her.

When the prince came by Maria Wood's hut next day, she did not fail to wish him again a "good Carneval."

"To-morrow we have the second *festino*, you know," said the prince.

"Well I know it," replied Maria Wood; "shouldn't I like to go! Won't you take me?"

"You contemptible old woman to talk in that way!" exclaimed the prince. "You ought to know better!" and he struck her with his boot.

Next night Maria put on her dress of the colour of the sea, covered all over with gold fishes, and the parure made to wear with it, and went to the feast. The prince recognised her at once, and claimed her for his partner all the evening, nor did she seem to wish for any other, only when he tried to learn from her whence she was, she would only say she came from the country of Bootkick. The prince could not remember ever to have heard of the Bootkick country, and thought she meant to laugh at him; however, he ordered his attendants to make more haste this night in following her; but what diligence soever they used she was too swift for them.

The next time the prince came by Maria Wood's hut, she did not fail to wish him again a "good Carneval."

"To-morrow we have the last *festino*!" exclaimed he, with a touch of sadness, for he remembered it was the last of the happy evenings that he could feel sure of seeing his fair unknown.

"Ah! you must take me. But, what'll you say if I come to it in spite of you?" answered Maria Wood.

"You incorrigible old woman!" exclaimed the prince; "you provoke me so with your nonsense, I really cannot keep my hand off you"; and he gave her a slap.

The next night Maria Wood put on her dress of a dark blue, all covered with gold embroidery and spangled with silver bells, and the parure made to wear with it. The prince constituted her his partner for the evening as before, nor did she seem to wish for any other, only when he wanted to learn from her whence she was, all she would say was that she came from Slapland. This night the prince told his servants to make more haste following her, or he would discharge them all. But they answered, "It is useless to attempt the thing, as no mortal can equal her in swiftness."

After this, the prince fell ill of his disappointment, because he saw no hope of hearing any more of the fair domino with whom he had spent three happy evenings, nor could any doctor find any remedy for his sickness.

Then Maria Wood sent him word, saying, "Though the prince's physicians cannot help him, yet let him but take a cup of broth of my making, and he will immediately be healed."

"Nonsense! how can a cup of broth, or how can any medicament help me!" exclaimed the prince. "There is no cure for my ailment."

Again Maria Wood sent the same message; but the prince said angrily,

"Tell the silly old thing to hold her tongue; she doesn't know what she's talking about."

But again, the third time, Maria Wood sent to him, saying, "Let the prince but take a cup of broth of my making, and he will immediately be healed."

By this time the prince was so weary that he did not take the trouble to refuse. The servants, finding him so depressed, began to fear that he was sinking, and they called to Maria Wood to make her broth, because, though they had little faith in her promise, they knew not what else to try. So Maria Wood made ready the cup of broth she had promised, and they put it down beside the prince.

Presently the whole palace was roused; the prince had started up in bed, and was shouting,

"Bring hither Maria Wood! Quick! Bring hither Maria Wood!"

So they ran and fetched Maria Wood, wondering what could have happened to bring about so great a change in the prince. But the truth was, that Maria had put into the cup of broth the ring the prince had put on her finger the first night of the feast, and when he began to take the broth he found the ring with the spoon. When he saw the ring, he knew at once that Maria Wood could tell him where to find his fair partner.

"Wait a bit! There's plenty of time!" said Maria, when the servant came to fetch her in all haste; and she waited to put on her dress of the colour of the noontide sky. The prince was beside himself with joy when he saw her, and would have the betrothal celebrated that very day.[6]

Four different tales about innocent persecuted women collected by neglected female storytellers and writers—tales that do not fit neatly into the category AT 510 for they are tales about rape, starvation, attempted murder, physical and psychological abuse, and incest. They are not readily available in the classical fairy-tale collections of Perrault, the Brothers Grimm, and Andersen, to cite the most impressive canonical names in the nineteenth-century fairy-tale tradition. And even if Perrault, the Grimms, and Andersen do at times deal with abuse, incest, murder, and the persecution of innocent heroines, they do not depict them with such candor, nor indicate how cunning and resilient the heroines are, as do Gonzenbach, Lévesque, Němcová, and Busk. Nevertheless, our notion of female protagonists in fairy tales has been greatly informed by male collectors and writers who often domesticated the heroines and made them more passive than they actually were. This is not to say that all female protagonists in the classical fairy tales are always weak and helpless.[7] Clearly, though, there was a male perspective and bias about persecution in the tales of Perrault, the Grimms, Andersen, and other male writers and collectors.

On the other hand, there were much different persecuted innocent heroines in collections composed by women in the nineteenth century, and if I might exaggerate a bit, I would argue that they (the women and their collections) have been "persecuted" through thoughtless disregard. Hardly anyone—and this includes folklorists and other scholars with an interest in fairy tales—has taken the time to study the tales of Gonzenbach, Lévesque, Busk, and Němcová, despite the great advances made in recent feminist studies that led to the rediscovery of important European women fairy-tale writers from the seventeenth century to the present. Not only are the tales by Gonzenbach, Lévesque, Busk, and Němcová significant for what they reveal about the beliefs and customs of particular communities in the nineteenth century along with the role of women. They also are valuable in the study of folklore for understanding the problematic aspects of orality and literacy as well as the interpretation of specific tale types such as the innocent persecuted heroine.

Each of the tales I have presented, and each of the individual collections by Gonzenbach, Lévesque, Busk, and Němcová, presents a different challenge for researchers, and I shall comment briefly on the collections by Lévesque, Busk, and Němcová to illustrate just what makes them so unique. Then I shall focus in more detail on Gonzenbach's collection because I am most familiar with her work. The tales told, in all three cases, are part of memetic traditions of fairy tales, but the voices and information about these particular tales tend to be suppressed. Nonetheless, they are indicators of how unknown voices and tellers have always told tales relevant to their lives, and have spoken forcefully and fascinatingly, even when educated writers and folklorists were not in their presence to testify to the power of the oral tradition.

Nannette Lévesque

In 2000, two eminent French folklorists, Marie-Louise Tenèze and Georges Delarue, published a book with the full title *Nannette Lévesque, conteuse et chanteuse du pays des sources de la Loire. La collecte de Victor Smith 1871–1876.* After more than 125 years, Tenèze and Delarue unearthed a remarkable volume of tales and songs collected by Victor Smith (1826–82) that had been buried in the archives of l'Arsenal and the Bibliothèque de l'Institut Catholique in Paris. Smith, one of the most gifted nineteenth-century French folklorists, had gathered numerous tales and songs from a peasant woman named Lévesque (1803–80), who lived in the mountainous region of Fraisses near Firminy in central France. She was a weaver, married to a man who collected wood and sold wooden ladles in the region's towns. Lévesque was illiterate and regarded as one of the most resourceful of the storytellers in the vicinity. Between 1871 and 1876, Smith recorded numerous stories and songs that Lévesque told him in French and the local dialect, and he generally dated the recordings and provided some background information about the conditions under which he heard the tales. Most of the texts in Smith's manuscripts, which were not published until 2000, were in French because Smith, a judge, was not totally familiar with Lévesque's dialect.

Tenèze, who edited the manuscripts for publication, divides the texts into two broad categories: tales and Christian legends. The tales are subdivided into narratives that deal with eating, devouring, magical objects, kings and princess, animals, and fairies. In "Le Cycle de Marion," there are three variants, "Marion," "L'arbre merveilleux," and "Marion et Jeanne," about the persecuted heroine, Marion. There is also a dialect tale that repeats the story of "Marion and Jean." As the collector, Smith was meticulous in his recording of Lévesque's diction, tone, style, and grammar. There is no hint that he altered her tales, and her tales reveal the unhappy and desperate situation of young women confronted with uncaring stepmothers.

In two of the tales, the stepmother drives her husband to kill his own daughter, Marion, who only escapes murder through the hands of God. She does not marry. Even in the tale "Marion et Jeanne," in which Marion is saved and weds a young man, it is through the aid of the Virgin Mary and God that she survives. What is interesting in all three tales are the motifs of cruel treatment by the stepmother, attempted murder by the father, miraculous intervention of Christian figures such as Jesus or the Virgin Mary, the minor role played by a prince or marriage, and nonpunishment of the wicked characters. The emphasis in all three tales is on survival and the possibility that persecution will continue. In her commentary on the tales, Tenèze emphasizes that they all appear to signify a return to the dead mother, and through death (or salvation), the possibility for a new life.

Rachel Busk

The new life for the persecuted heroine in Busk's tales about Maria Wood is always through marriage, and this may be due to Busk's own more conservative religious attitudes and her editing of the oral tales she heard in Rome.[8]

Born 1831 in London, Busk grew up Protestant in a wealthy family. She benefited from private tutoring and often traveled to the Continent, thus becoming fluent in Spanish, Italian, French, and German. By 1858 she converted to Roman Catholicism, and in 1862 she moved to Rome, where she resided until her death in 1907.

Although not specifically trained in folklore studies, Busk became intrigued by the tales she heard during her numerous voyages. She began translating tales collected either through books or conversations with storytellers. In 1870 she published *Pantranas: Spanish Tales, Legendary and Traditional*, and in 1871 *Household Tales from the Land of Hofer*. Originally, Busk had intended to provide British travelers with background information about customs and settings with the reproduction of Spanish and German tales, but she was a scrupulous scholar and began a research project on European folklore, sending articles and stories to various British journals while also corresponding with all the leading folklorists in Europe. While she was living in Rome, she decided to produce a kind of Italian collection modeled on the *Children's and Household Tales* of the Brothers Grimm, especially because there was no such collection in existence at that time.

Thus in 1874, she published *The Folk-Lore of Rome, Collected by Word of Mouth from the People*. Her tales are based mainly on literary versions, which she harvested from secondhand books and stories that she actually collected from numerous inhabitants of Rome. She divided them into exempla (religious stories with a moral lesson); ghost stories along with local and family traditions; fairy tales; and *ciarpe*, or anecdotes that were similar to tall tales and gossip. All the sections have footnotes and commentaries, and thanks to Busk's vast knowledge of European tales, she was able to draw relevant parallels and provide crucial background information about the derivation of the Roman tales.

In her section on fairy tales, she presented three different variants of stories about incest all titled "Maria Wood." Busk was familiar with Perrault's "Donkey-Skin," and she notes the similarities; yet, all three of her versions of "Maria Wood" depict a young woman who is much more independent and courageous than the princess in Perrault's tale. Indeed, in each of the three Italian variants, clearly edited by Busk and written in a more elegant English than the Italian in which she heard the tale, the young woman takes destiny into her hands, overcoming the lascivious desires of the devil and her father.

In the first and long version, there are some interesting twists. A dead mother leaves her daughter with a ring, and she is only to marry the man whose finger will fit this ring. Her gullible old father arranges a marriage for her with the devil, not realizing what he has done. Fortunately, there is a fairy teacher, charged by the dead mother to look after Maria. As she tells Maria,

> The prince [devil] being what he is can have no power over you against your will. Your breaking from him must be your own act. Further, you

must understand the terms of the struggle. Power is given to him to deceive, and thus he has deceived your father. I have been sent by your mother to watch over you, and I can tell you what he is, but I have no power to undeceive your father. If I were to attempt it, it would do no good. He would not believe me, and it would break his heart to see you renounce so promising a union. On the other hand, you must understand that when the devil woos a maiden in this form he does not suddenly after appear with horns and hoofs and carry her off to brimstone and fire. For the term of your life he will behave with average kindness and affection, and he will abundantly supply you with the good things of this world. After that I need not say what the effect of his power over you will be. On the other hand, if you give him up you must be prepared to undergo many trials and privations. It is not merely going on with your present life such as it has been up till now. Those peaceful days are allowed for youthful strength to mature, but now the time has come that you have to make a life-choice. What do you say? Have you the courage to renounce the ease and enjoyment the prince has to offer you and face poverty, with the want and the insults which come in its train?[9]

Clearly, this is also a type of initiation tale as well as a story of persecution.

As in the two other versions, Maria is not afraid to abandon the comfort of a secure life. She steps into the wooden form of an old woman. This act—a stepping into a chest, an animal skin, and a coffin—is a stepping into a series of tests that lead to a new life. In two of the versions, Maria takes the initiative and transforms herself into a queen, who has complete autonomy at the end of the tales. In the third truncated version, her father orders her to be murdered because of her insolence. Yet his servants lock her in a great box and carry her into a field instead. A prince discovers and marries her, because she is not a common maiden. Indeed, many of Busk's stories are about extraordinary young women, whose tales are rarely told, and this leads me to Němcová's tales, which also deal with unusual heroines, whose lives of persecution are depicted in extraordinary ways with urgent voices.

Božena Němcová

Unlike Lévesque and Busk, Němcová (1820–62) is still well known in the former Czechoslovakia. Some scholars even consider her to be the mother of Czech prose. She was also among the first to collect and adapt Czech and Slovak folk tales, and her novel *The Grandmother* (*Babička*, 1855), which portrays a remarkable woman in an ideal peasant community, is regarded as a classic of Czech literature. Even her own life history has become a "classic" historical legend.[10]

Born in Vienna, her father, a German named Jan Pankl, was a coachman, and her mother, a Czech, named Terezie Novotná, was a maid for the aristocratic Raciborz family. Her birth is somewhat mysterious, however. It has generally been assumed that her biological father was a nobleman, and that Němcová was an illegitimate child, whom the duchess of Raciborz gave to Pankl and Novotná on their marriage to raise. Whatever the case may be, Němcová was under the care of lower-class parents, and given special attention and an education by the Raciborz family. Part of her youth was spent with her maternal grandmother in a village in northeastern Bohemia, where she learned Czech. By the time she was seventeen, her parents forced her into a marriage with Josef Němc, a custom official, who was fifteen years older. Within five years Němcová had four children and suffered abuse from an autocratic husband. It was an unhappy marriage. Due to his work they moved several times until 1842, when they settled in Prague.

At that time there was a strong Czech nationalist movement and vibrant cultural life. Under these conditions Němcová began to flower. She and her husband became involved with groups seeking Czech independence from the Austro-Hungarian Empire, and Němcová became acquainted with many of the leading Czech intellectuals, who encouraged her to write for newspapers and journals. One of her first poems, "To the Czech Women" (1843), was a nationalist call to women to become more engaged in politics. This poem, along with several other poems and stories, drew the attention of important cultural circles in Prague. The beautiful young woman especially intrigued people because of her mysterious past and talents as a writer, particularly because she had not received much formal education. Among her admirers was the great Czech folklorist Karel Erben, who urged her to write down stories she remembered from her childhood as well as collect tales from friends and other informants from different social classes. By 1845 she began publishing a series of pamphlets, *Folk Fairy Tales and Legends* (1845–48). Not only did she develop a special folk tone for the tales she gathered but she also transformed them into elaborate stories with a socialist slant and industrious girls.

Not all of her writing was accomplished in Prague because her husband was transferred to a village in Bohemia in 1845, probably because of insubordination. Němc had become so caught up in the Czech national revival that he found it difficult to serve the Austrian-Hungarian government and suffered from persecution for the remainder of his life, as did Němcová. In fact, most of Němcová's writings, especially her tales, are strongly influenced by her politics and stemmed from her desire to celebrate the folk culture of the Czechs and Slovaks.

After 1845, Němcová and her family had to move frequently, living in small towns in different parts of Bohemia. By 1850, her husband was sent to a small town in Hungary as punishment for his political activities, and Němcová took the children with her to Prague. A liberated woman, she had various love affairs while trying to raise the children and earn money through her writing. It was during the period of separation from her husband that she collected Slovak fairy tales and published them in Czech translation as *Slovak*

National Fairy Tales and Legends (1857–58). As Milada Součková remarks, this compilation of stories was "Němcová's major response to her stay in Slovakia. In the Slovak collection many things came together to produce a work of enduring value: her former experience, the colorful ethnographical milieu, and the excellent material at her disposal."[11]

Němcová made Prague her base during this period while she also joined her husband with their children whenever she could. By 1857, she was living with him and her children in Karnten, a small city in Austria, when he was summarily dismissed from his governmental job and given a miserly pension. She endeavored to support the family by writing stories and novels. In 1860 they moved back to Prague, where Němcová hoped to still support the family through her writing and a collected edition of her works. She also abandoned her family to work with her new publisher outside Prague. None of her plans came to fruition, however, and she exhausted herself while living in poverty. In 1861 her husband brought her back to Prague, where she died in 1862 from cancer. She was only forty-two years old.

Němcová's two large collections of Czech and Slovak tales and legends have been compared to the Brothers Grimm's *Children's and Household Tales*. Yet there is a major difference. Unlike the Grimms, she never claimed that the tales were "authentic" folk tales because she always strived to stylize them in keeping with the folk tradition. At the same time, it should be noted that she actually went to villages in Bohemia and Slovakia to collect them and also used major collections of Czech folklorists. Her early Czech stories are filled with local color and tend toward social utopianism, whereas her late Slovak tales are more brisk and unusual. She translated them into the Czech language, but kept the dialogues in the original Slovak and used many Slovak proverbs as well.

Similar to Busk and Lévesque, she depicted active heroines whether they were virtuous or malicious. For instance, in "Salt Is Worth More than Gold," the king banishes his youngest daughter from the kingdom because he believes that she has insulted him. Thanks to an old woman in the woods, however, she manages to overcome her father's fury and demonstrate (as in *King Lear*) that salt is indeed more valuable than gold. In "The Clever Maiden from the Mountains," a peasant girl helps her father obtain justice from a judge, who marries the maiden. Then the judge banishes her for interfering in his decisions, yet she cleverly outwits him, and he realizes that he cannot do without her. He not only brings her back to his home but also appoints her to judge in his place. In "The Witch Katrenka," a woman keeps house for a priest, although unknown to him, she is a witch. But the curious servant Janko suspects her of some mischief, and wants to find out where she goes off to every now and then. Katrenka allows Janko to fly with her on her broom to a witches' Sabbath, and frightened by the revelry, he breaks his promise and reveals himself to the other witches. Katrenka casts a spell, and he wanders seven years before he finds his way home and learns that Katrenka has disappeared forever.

Included in Němcová's collection are several tales that deal directly with a persecuted heroine. "The Twelve Months" is an interesting example of the tale type ATU 480, "The Kind and the Unkind Girls," and is one of the most widespread tales in Europe, with hundreds of variants. Součková remarks that the story was told to Němcová by an old maid named Marka and related to a story in Basile's *Lo Cunto de li cunti*:

> This *Pentameron* motif of "the Month" (as supernatural helper) is as gracefully stylized as in the Italian collection. It is difficult to say whether the stylization stems from Němcová or from her source. One is inclined to credit the interpreter with its stylistic ingenuity; especially in the allegorical panels of the seasons (spring with violets, summer with strawberrries, autumn with apples, and winter as the setting for the entire tale). . . . The effectiveness of the tale consists in its compound of different layers: the contemporary mid-century literary stylization, the oral tradition perhaps a century and a half old, and the remainder of Indo-European fire symbolism.[12]

The tale type generally involves disputes among women, especially in families with unprotected stepdaughters who must find their own way in the world. As we have already seen in stories that involve Baba Yaga, but also Mother Holle, the tale is related to some kind of ancient initiation ritual and concerns a maltreated beautiful maiden, sent into the forest by her nasty stepmother to perform a task. She generally meets an old woman, a hermit, an ogre, a supernatural being, or twelve men who personify twelve months. The kind maiden must comply with their commands and demands and is rewarded. After she completes her task three times, the ugly mean stepsister seeks the same reward, only to be punished or killed because of her greed and arrogance. "The Twelve Months" was more popular in eastern and southern Europe than in the West and was always recorded with different characters and motifs. Němcová's version emphasizes the perseverance and kindness of Maruša. The partiality of the tale reflects its naive morality. Maruša is simply good and bears her stepmother and stepsister no ill will. Němcová does not moralize. Rather, she matter-of-factly describes what happens to Maruša, who is thankful for the intercession of the helpful men. She is not vengeful, although as we shall see in Gonzenbach's tales, persecuted women are not afraid to seek revenge.

Laura Gonzenbach

Gonzenbach's *Sicilianische Märchen (Sicilian Folk Tales*, 1870), which I translated into English as *Beautiful Angiola: The Lost Sicilian Folk and Fairy Tales of Laura Gonzenbach* (2006), is the only volume of tales in the nineteenth century gathered by an upper-class woman from lower-middle-class and peasant women, straight from their mouths.[13] The gifted Gonzenbach translated them from the Sicilian dialect directly into high German, adding her own protofeminist convictions here and there. The tales are somewhat extraordinary because they extoll a set of morals counter to her own social class's stance with regard to women's proper behavior and expose unjust practices that were then the rule of the land. Almost all the tales in her collection call for women to challenge the oppression they experienced in their daily lives and take power into their own hands. If it had not been for Gonzenbach, the voices of these tales might never have been recorded.

The daughter of a wealthy Swiss merchant, Gonzenbach was born on December 26, 1842, in Messina on the island of Sicily. When her mother died in 1847, her older sister Magdalena, only sixteen, was placed in charge of her education. Cosmopolitan, trained in all the arts, classical literature, and the sciences, Magdalena took charge of the household. A young woman ahead of her times, she supported suffragette causes and had close connections to women's journals in Italy throughout her life. She also founded the first school for girls in Messina. Her influence on Laura was great. By the time she was a teenager Laura could speak four languages fluently, play different musical instruments, and was well versed in literature and the arts. She never attended a school of higher learning because it was not customary for young women at that time to study in a university. Yet she participated in the many cultural activities at her father's house and in the community and was regarded as a talented storyteller.

In 1868, when she was twenty-seven, a German historian named Hartwig asked her to send him some fairy tales for a history he was writing about Sicily. She complied by gathering numerous tales in the countryside near Mount Etna, in Catania, and Messina, and he published them in 1870 because he recognized their monumental significance as the first "authentic" collection of Sicilian tales. Meanwhile, she married the Italian colonel François Laurent Racine. After their marriage, Gonzenbach moved with her husband to Naples and had five children with him. Nothing is known about her life with Racine or the conditions under which she died in Messina in 1878 because an earthquake destroyed all the family papers in 1908. There is only a tombstone marking her young death at the age of thirty-six.

Though there are no papers that might inform us about the philosophy behind her method of collecting the folk tales, it is clear from the ninety-two texts that she managed to gain the trust of the Sicilian women storytellers and gave voice to their beliefs, superstitions, and dreams in a way that male collectors, often more pious and censorial, could not or did not want to do. Her tales cover topics such as rape, cruel incarceration, beatings, and murder, mostly perpetuated by men on women and children, and unlike the Brothers Grimm, she lets the sentiments of women be articulated and does not minimize the sufferings they endured. One need only compare "The Virgin Mary's Child" with two tales by the Grimms, "The Virgin Mary" and "All Fur," to see how they treat the same topic in completely different ways. In the first Grimms' tale, the Virgin Mary punishes an orphan girl for being disobedient, and in the second, the incestuous father is never punished. Rarely do the humble heroines in the Grimms' tales take destiny into their hands, and a patriarchal moral order is always upheld. It is just the opposite in the Gonzenbach collection.

There are few, if any, tales in European folklore that deal with incest in the manner that Gonzenbach's tale does, for it combines religious superstition with pagan beliefs, and the women are empowered to deal with the sins of men. The Virgin Mary is not your usual religious figure. She is more like a fairy, or as the Italians say, a fata, who is omnipotent, clever, compassionate, and stern. Since Sicilians believed in reincarnation, it is clear that the spirit of the girl's dead mother lives on through the Virgin Mary, who teaches and protects the girl and even opens up an inn with her. Perhaps Gonzenbach added this incident—we cannot be certain—but many of the tale's events, such as the bloody revenge of the priest, the unjust accusation and expulsion of the innocent queen, and the lesson of the three golden apples, were ancient Oriental and Occidental motifs woven together in this Sicilian tale to stress the "saintly" innocence of the heroine along with the sin of men in power, the priest and her husband.

Like many of the Italian tales written long ago by Boccaccio, Girolamo Morlini, Straparola, Basile, Pompeo Sarnelli, and others, the clerics were frequently seen as predatory and duplicitous. This is the case in this tale in which, from the beginning, the villagers want to expose the greediness of the priest. His sin is not just one of greed, though, but the abuse of power to serve his own lascivious ends. The priest therefore ingratiates himself with the powerful to destroy the life of an innocent, who is almost martyred like a saint. Whether the innocent can be considered a saint is another question. What is clear is that the saints in the Sicilian tales, many like the Virgin Mary, are always humanized and compassionate. They are earthy and do not represent a specific religious creed. They respond to the needs of the oppressed and are clearly wish fulfillments of miraculous intervention. That they are called on time and again in many of the Sicilian tales, whether as saints or fairies, reveals not so much religious devotion but rather a need to believe that sinners would receive their just due one day, even if the Sicilians and their storytellers might not really experience true retribution.

To collect, transcribe, and translate folklore is to recognize the values of common people and esteem their position in the world, even if one does not comprehend fully what the words of these people represent in the web of power and authority relations. There is always a struggle for appropriation, adaptation, and authenticity whenever tales are translated and printed. This is what makes them so interesting, especially if we admit to their conflicting and inexplicable nature. When Gonzenbach went to the peasant women in the Catania region and Messina in 1868 to collect their tales in Sicilian dialect, she did so as an upper-class authority figure who had, at best, a dim understanding of what it meant to lead the life of a peasant or common laborer. In fact, there is not one trace of dialect or description of the storytellers and their background in Gonzenbach's collection because she translated the tales directly into German and only inserted sparse footnotes. The language she uses is literary German. As she recorded the tales on paper and sought the "appropriate" German words and expressions, she probably thought about what an educated German might expect. She had to find the forms and words that this implied German reader would approve and probably also censored herself, unless the peasant women already censored themselves by omitting curse words, sexual inferences, and other speech that had no place in the literature of this era's polite classes. Nevertheless, Gonzenbach had a great affinity with the peasant storytellers, recording the violent conflicts of class and gender more or less as the women experienced them. Gonzenbach's translation of the Sicilian tales is perhaps more "authentic" than the tales of the Brothers Grimm, and certainly more important because of her careful transformation and attentive reception of tales told by women.

Anyone familiar with many of the extant Sicilian dialect versions of the tales Gonzenbach recorded, such as those collected by Giuseppe Pitrè, whom I shall discuss in the next chapter, knows how different they are from those produced in her high German renderings. At the same time, it is striking to see how close Gonzenbach remained to the plots and the terse, abrupt manner in which the tales were obviously told. The dialect tales give a good indication of the tone and color of the tales, and fortunately, Gonzenbach's German "equivalents" do not embellish or improve the tales with smooth transitions and clearer motivation. Gonzenbach respected the "authorial" and ideological perspective of the narrators. Of course, there is no clear uniform ideology in the tales, but Gonzenbach's translation keeps alive the anger, disappointment, hope, and hardiness of the storytellers, who view life from the bottom and do not mask their sentiments. Her work stands in contrast to that of the Brothers Grimm, who more or less "bourgeoisified" their tales for a middle-class audience and added a male perspective. Their tales have served as the model or typical fairy tale of the nineteenth century and thus have obfuscated crucial perspectives that Gonzenbach brings to light.

As I have argued in *Why Fairy Tales Stick: The Evolution and Relevance of a Genre*, it is foolish to generalize about the meaning of translations or appropriate way to translate because each text brings its own demands and difficulties.[14] For an educated woman such as Gonzenbach, to translate tales told by lower-class informants, mainly women, into an upper-class foreign language was not only a particular process of retention but also meant to confront how discontented people thought, spoke, and contended, or wished to contend, with oppression. Despite the different languages, Sicilian and high German, Gonzenbach managed to convey the spirit of insurrection and provocation with which the tellers imbued their tales. My English

translation, completed at the beginning of the twenty-first century in contemporary American vernacular, is another transformation of the oral tales
that has multiple purposes.

The first overall purpose is to recover some of the important work by late
nineteenth-century female collectors and folklorists whose perspective on
collecting, translating, and tradition may differ significantly from those of
the male folklorists, thereby altering our concept of what constituted an oral
wonder tale and literary fairy tale in the nineteenth century. In his classic
work *The British Folklorists*, Richard Dorson deals briefly with the work of
Busk, Mary Frere, Alice Bertha Gomme, and Charlotte Burne. But there were
other important storytellers in France like Lévesque, whose collection of tales
I described above, and in Italy like Carolina Coronedi-Berti, who published
Novelle popolari bolognesi in 1874, among others who deserve investigation.
Thus far, few scholars have explored their works, or studied how gender may
play a role in recording, translating, editing, and publishing oral wonder
tales. As I have already remarked, the gender bias of the Grimms' tales can be
clearly demonstrated when their edited versions are compared with those of
Gonzenbach.

This leads me to my second purpose. Our notions of fairy tales that encompass oral folk tales have been greatly determined by the collections of
Perrault, the Brothers Grimm, and Andersen—not to mention Disney. Yet
there were competing collections in the nineteenth century that shed greater
light on differences in the modes of telling, collecting, and editing tales.
Though nineteenth-century British and American folklorists endeavored to
bring out the differences with their translations and collections, there are still
many key works that need translating and close study to spell out the cultural
and gender differences. The Grimms' tales may forever remain the "classical" collection of the nineteenth century, but this distinction should not go
unchallenged, and through further examination of the other collections we
might reach a better understanding of why the Grimms' tales became established as the paradigm of classical folk and fairy tale. The renowned German
scholar Heinz Rölleke, a superb philologist, has been at the forefront of those
critics who have shown that although the Grimms' tales stem from an oral
tradition, they are more literary products than authentic folk tales. But such
revelations do not entirely enable us to appreciate the complexity of collecting, editing, and translating oral tales. There is nothing "immoral" in what
the Grimms did, as John Ellis would have us believe, and nothing immoral in
editing and appropriation.[15] Yet it is crucial for the understanding of folklore,
fairy tales, and cultural history that the complexity of the process of their collection be open to study and evaluated and compared with other collections

This is the third purpose of my translation of Gonzenbach's tales. My
process began with a candid realization that I would not be able to produce
authentic Sicilian tales and was translating a translation of dialect tales that

might have been altered by Gonzenbach or even her sister, Magdalena. Such a realization made me even more eager and curious to undertake the translation because my work might allow me to learn about different perspectives on Sicilian folklore and fairy tales in general that were embedded in Gonzenbach's collection: the views of predominantly peasant and lower-class women, Gonzenbach and Magdalena, the buried motifs from Greek, Roman, Arabic, French, and Spanish sources, the social class struggles in the nineteenth century, and the differences between the Sicilian tales and those in the Mediterranean region and on the Continent. Even within the collection itself, I saw the possibility to illuminate different gender attitudes in the same region of Sicily, and in closing this chapter, I want to comment on two Sicilian versions of the same tale type, "The Courageous Maiden," which was translated by Gonzenbach into high German, and "The Story of the Three Sisters," collected in Sicilian dialect by D. Salvatore Morganti and published in dialect by Hartwig, who was in charge of the final manuscript. The tale appeared as a kind of addendum to Gonzenbach's collection, and I translated it into English from Sicilian.

The plot of the two short tales—both five manuscript pages—is similar. Three sisters, who are poor and without parents, make their living by spinning. They sell their flax in town, and one day the oldest decides to buy food and wine there. On her way home, a dog robs her. The same thing happens to the second sister. The youngest sister, however, races after the dog, discovering a palace with splendid beds, food, and treasures. She returns to her sisters and convinces them that they should move to this castle, which they do. During the night, however, the two older sisters are scared out of their wits by a weird voice. Once again, it is the youngest who discovers that the voice belongs to the ghost of a dead lady, formerly a duchess, who cannot rest until she gains revenge on her lover, who unjustly murdered her. The duchess promises the sister that she may inherit the palace if she tricks her former lover, a nobleman, to come into the house, where she is then supposed to kill him. Out of sympathy with the duchess, the lovely maiden fulfills the request and murders the nobleman. With the help of her sisters, they drag him out of the palace, bury him, and inherit the palace.

Though there are clear stylistic differences between the high German and Sicilian dialect, it is surprising to read how Gonzenbach's terse German text captures the colloquial style of her informant in much the same manner that Morganti did. Both tales reflect the desperate situation of the sisters and sympathize with them. Nevertheless, there are contrasting perspectives with regard to gender. In Morganti's tale, when the older sister is robbed by the dog and tells her sisters what happened, the middle sister calls her a fool. In Gonzenbach's version, the sisters are polite and say nothing. Morganti's sisters are competitive and hostile toward one another. Gonzenbach's sisters are more gentle and kind to each other. Throughout Gonzenbach's narrative, they support each other while Morganti shows how they mock each other.

The most important difference between the two texts concerns the ending of the tales. Morganti's story reads:

> "I remember everything," he [the nobleman] responded, "and I fall to your feet and ask your pardon for all the suffering that I've caused you. I've changed, and I'll now be your loyal and tender lover until death. Pardon me, my love."
>
> They made peace and went to sit down at the table to eat, but as he approached her to throw himself into the arms of his lover, the maiden quickly took out a dagger and stabbed him in his heart.
>
> "I'm dying," he said as he fell, "by treacherous hands."
>
> The maiden grabbed him by his hair and dragged him down to the foot of the stairs, and she buried him where he had buried his lover. The three sisters became owners of this rich palace, but they were not happy because the price of blood is always bitter.[16]

Gonzenbach's story reads:

> "Can I also have the honor of dining with you tonight?" she said, and the nobleman stayed there. During the meal, however, she handed him the bottle with the sleeping potion. As soon as he had drunken a little of it, he sank into a deep sleep. Then she took a little knife and slit his throat so that he died for his sins without confession or absolution. Soon after the maiden called her sisters, and all three dragged him to a deep well and threw him into it. At midnight the door opened once again, and the dark figure entered and said to the youngest sister, "You have saved me through your courage, and now all these treasures belong to you. Live well. Tonight I have come for the last time because now I have found peace."
>
> Upon saying this, she disappeared and never returned. Meanwhile, the three sisters remained in the magnificent castle, and each one of them married a fine gentleman. Indeed, they remained happy and content, and we were left without a cent.[17]

Morganti plainly does not approve of the actions of the three sisters, while in Gonzenbach's narrative they are amply rewarded for their behavior. It seems as though Gonzenbach's female peasant informants favored a tale of revenge and articulated their feelings in this version. We know that their lives were hard, and their husbands and lords often beat them. Nor did the informants ever become rich. "The Courageous Maiden" was doubtless some kind of wish fulfillment on their part. Morganti represents the sisters in a more critical vein, and their revenge spoils their rewards. Apparently, he or his informant did not think that the sister should have murdered the nobleman. It would seem that the male perspective incorporated into this dialect tale reflects the attitudes of men who find murder permissible by a man but not by a woman.

My conclusions, however, cannot be fully documented. We do not know exactly who Gonzenbach's informant was, nor whether she altered the tale and presented a more harmonious picture of the sisters than what was in the original tale. We do not know Morganti's informant, or if he edited his tale. What we do know is that both tales focus on gender conflict and reveal the brutal nature of relations during this period. In addition, we know that such conflicts have not disappeared, neither in Sicily or the rest of the world. As we have seen in the tales of Lévesque collected by Smith, the Roman tales collected by Busk, and the Czech and Slovakian tales written by Němcová, all from the same period, persecution of innocent heroines was a major theme that they all sought to communicate through written transcriptions, transformations, and translations. Most important is that they endeavored in some manner or another to represent a feminine perspective and keep it alive, even though there may be problematic features to the way "original" voices and perspectives are disseminated through print.

To translate the conflicts from oral and literary tales as well as transform them into discourses that have contemporary relevance and need further investigation is, I believe, a major task of scholars who work in the field of folklore and fairy-tale studies. Perhaps it is impossible to authenticate words that were once told and are buried with their tellers, but it is possible to approximate, transform, and appropriate their printed equivalents by paying respect to obfuscated voices and neglected words of the past.

6

Giuseppe Pitrè and the Great Collectors of Folk Tales in the Nineteenth Century

Despite the comprehensive histories of European and American folklore, such as Giuseppe Cocchiara's *The History of Folklore in Europe* (1952), Dorson's *The British Folklorists* (1968), Simon Bronner's *American Folklore Studies: An Intellectual History* (1986), and Rosemary Zumwalt's *American Folklore Scholarship* (1988), there are still numerous folklorists and their collections of tales that need more discussion, elaboration, translation, and analysis. The great progress that had been made in folklore studies and ethnography in the twentieth century has reached a standstill in the twenty-first century, even as important projects in the study of folk tales such as the *Enzyklopädie des Märchens* in Göttingen and the Gutenberg Internet site are ongoing. Folk and fairy tales are still read and taught in universities and the public sphere, but there are few places where serious historical, anthropological, and ethnological work is being maintained as well as supported, and the mass media have basically continued to spread ignorant notions about fairy tales. Universities in Europe and North America are not supporting the humanities as strongly as they used to do, and the significance of folklore as a cultural field has diminished, leading to the reduction and elimination of programs and departments. Yet stories, old and new, continue to breathe, and need to be given space and places to breathe so that unknown voices can be heard and included in history.

Initially, the collecting and study of folk tales was undertaken in the nineteenth century by professionals outside the university until their work was recognized as invaluable for gaining a full sense of history. The acknowledgment of folklore studies as a "legitimate" field of study was slow and difficult in coming. Its value was never firmly established at the university level, and now that the university has become more of a corporation than a place of learning, particularly in the United States and United Kingdom, folklore has moved even more to the margins than ever before. Unfortunately, in my opinion, the present marginalization of folklore studies and storytelling can only lead to promoting ignorance and devaluing history.

I have partially addressed this topic in the previous chapter by focusing on the neglected role of women in nineteenth-century folklore. But there are many more collectors and storytellers, men and women, whose works need to be recovered, if not discovered, for they brought about what I call the golden age of folklore toward the end of the nineteenth century and beginning of the twentieth century in Europe and North America. The reason why this epoch is and remains so important is because learned people finally began turning their attention to all aspects of folk life and the oral traditions of folk tales, recording, editing, and publishing them. This international "movement" also included the founding of museums, archives, and other institutions to "preserve" or safeguard the artifacts of cultural heritages. That is, learned people from different social classes began uncovering and examining the unstudied as well as unusual and usual practices and artworks of the common people. They also realized that they were a part of the folk, and that the folk mattered. Furthermore, they began drawing important connections to the rich literary tradition of fairy tales and their connection to oral traditions.

In his superb analysis of American folklore studies, which includes pertinent references to developments in Europe, Bronner remarks that folklore studies was

> an outgrowth of a subjective dialogue on social conditions between members of the professional middle class and their changing society. During the nineteenth century, many members of this class who called themselves folklorists or, more broadly, "scientific men and women" unearthed a usable past which had been hidden by the rapid material transformation of the present. For these Victorians, folklore was a body of material set squarely in the past, even if it could still be heard on the lips of the "backward portions of society." And the past was directed forward. In a period marked by often-paradoxical combinations of, on the one hand, spreading imperialism, industrialism, and militaristic masculinity and, on the other, utopianism, antimodernism, and feminism, *folklore* and *folklife* became keywords in a new scientific awareness of the past which would, in turn, furnish the emergent social order.[1]

In the particular case of oral folk tales, what the early folklorists realized was that the stories led them to uncover what Bronner labels a usable, hidden past. It is thus not by chance that the rise of folklore begins with struggles to form nation-states while transforming absolutism and constitutional monarchy. All the reform movements were first inspired by the democratic and revolutionary spirit of the late eighteenth century, and the new political sensibility and ideological thinking of the middle classes caused many intellectuals to turn their attention to those deep cultural values that were shared by the common people and learned classes.

To a great extent the Brothers Grimm, pioneers of folklore, were motivated to make the German past usable to foster a united nation, and as they started collecting all kinds of folk tales in the first decade of the nineteenth century, they were following other middle-class writers such as Johann Karl August Musäus (*Volksmärchen der Deutschen*, 1782–87), Benedikte Naubert (*Neue Deutsche Märchen*, 1789–93), and Johann Gustav Büsching (*Volkssagen, Märchen un Legenden*, 1812) who were already editing fairy-tale collections.[2] In addition, Albert Ludwig Grimm (*Kindermährchen*, 1809), Karoline Stahl (*Fabeln, Mährchen und Erzählungen für Kinder*, 1818), and anonymous authors published literary fairy tales for children based on oral tales. When the Grimms published the two volumes of the first edition of their *Kinder- und Hausmärchen* (*Children's and Household Tales*) in 1812 and 1815, intended primarily for learned adults, it set off (unintentionally) a chain reaction that had massive repercussions for the dissemination and study of folk tales in Europe and North America. Not only did the Grimms publish their tales with important notes. They also began writing a series of scholarly studies of medieval literature and put out a call in 1815 for other German scholars to join them in collecting tales. The opening of their circular letter reads as follows:

> A society has been founded that is intended to spread throughout all of Germany and has as its goal to save and collect all the existing songs and tales that can be found among the common German peasantry (*Landvolk*). Our fatherland is still filled with this wealth of material all over the country that our honest ancestors planted for us, and that, despite the mockery and derision heaped upon it, continues to live unaware of its own hidden beauty and carries within it its own unquenchable source. Our literature, history, and language cannot seriously be understood in their old and true origins without doing more exact research on this material.[3]

The results of this letter and the continual publication of the Grimms' *Children's and Household Tales*, which grew larger with each new edition up through 1857, and their numerous scholarly works on legends, myths, and sagas, can be seen in the manifold German and Austrian collections of the nineteenth century, such as Friedmund von Arnim's *Hundert neue Mährchen im Gebirge gesammelt* (1844), Johann Wilhelm Wolf's *Deutsche Märchen und Sagen* (1845), Kaspar Friedrich Gottschalck's *Deutsche Volksmärchen* (1846), Friedrich Panzer's *Bayerische Sagen und Bräuche* (1848), Franz Josef Vonbun's *Volkssagen aus Vorarlberg* (1850), Ignanz and Joseph Zingerle's, *Tirols Volksdichtungen und Volksbräuche* (1852), Heinrich Pröhle's *Kinder und Volksmärchen* (1853), Theodor Vernaleken's *Alpenmärchen* (1863), Christian Schneller's *Märchen und Sagen aus Wälschtirol* (1867), and Josef Haltrich's *Deutsche Volksmärchen aus dem Sachsenlande in Siebenbürgen* (1885). The Grimms had a direct and indirect influence on all these collections, and these works are only the tip of the iceberg in German-speaking lands.

The Brothers Grimm were also in contact with aspiring folklorists in other countries, and their influence was multifaceted. For instance, Wilhelm Grimm began writing to Thomas Crofton Croker in England, translating his *Fairy Legends and Traditions of the South of Ireland* (1825) in 1826 as *Elfenmärchen*, and Croker published an essay by the Grimms in a later edition of his collection. The Brothers Grimm were already exchanging ideas with Edgar Taylor, who published the first English translation of their tales as *German Popular Tales* in 1823.[4] This book, along with a second volume published in 1826, went through many different editions in Great Britain and the United States, and was the primary translation of the Grimms' tales until the 1880s. Yet Taylor's translation was more of a free adaptation that catered to young readers, and in many respects Taylor's successful Anglicization and infantilization of the tales set a "model" for literary fairy tales in England in the nineteenth century. As David Blamires points out,

> With all its faults, Taylor's translation has achieved a sort of classic status of its own. If modern readers were aware that it is a period piece, that would not much matter, but most do not realize how skewed a picture of the Grimms' collection they get through reading Taylor. Not that Taylor attempted to camouflage what he was doing in adapting, combining and expurgating his originals—on the contrary, he signalled his changes very frankly in the notes he appended to the tales. But what he presents is not what a modern reader would be entitled to expect.[5]

Another famous European writer of fairy tales, Andersen, also owed a debt to the Brothers Grimm, whom he once visited in Berlin. To a certain degree, the fusion of the oral and the literary into the "classic type" of fairy tale was due to the Grimms. That is, the Grimms modified the "raw" tales, told in diverse dialects, and their tales underwent dramatic changes in Taylor's hands. All this led to a strange case of misrepresentation of so-called genuine folk tales or tales suitable for children. But most important, despite heavy editing and translations into the language of the educated elite, was the immense production of folk-tale collections in different countries of Europe. Some of the more significant folk-tale books are: in Italy, Angelo De Gubernatis's *Le Novelline di Santo Stefano* (1869), Vittorio Imbriani's *La novellaja fiorentina* (1871), Coronedi-Berti's *Novelle popolari bolognesi* (1874), Domenico Comparetti's *Novelline Popolari Italiene* (1875); in Ireland, Samuel Lover's *Legends and Stories of Ireland* (1837), Patrick Kennedy's *The Fireside Stories of Ireland* (1870), and William Butler Yeats's *Fairy and Folk Tales of the Irish Peasantry* (1888); in England, Joseph Ritson's *Fairy Tales* (1831), Sabine Baring-Gould, *Notes on the Folklore of the Northern Countries of England and the Borders* (1866), and Joseph Jacobs's *English Fairy Tales* (1890); in France, Emmanuel Cosquin's *Contes populaires de Lorraine* (1860), Jean-François Bladé's *Contes et Proverbes recueillis en Armagnac* (1867), François

Luzel's *Contes et Récits populaires des Bretons armoricains* (1869), Charles Deulin's *Les Contes de ma Mère l'Oye avant Perrault* (1878), Paul Sébillot's *Contes populaires de la Haute-Bretagne* (1881), and Achille Millien's *Petits Contes du Nivernais* (1894); in Norway, Peter Christen Asbjørnsen and Jorgen Moe's *Norske folke-eventyr* (1852); in Denmark, Sven Grundtvig's *Gamle danske minder i folkemunde* (1854); in Portugal, Adolfo Cœlho's *Contos populares portugueses* (1879); in Czechoslovakia, Němcová's *Czech Folk Tales and Legends* (1845–48), and *Slovakian Fairy Tales and Legends* (1857–58); and in Russia, Afanasyev's *Narodnuiya Russkiya Skazki* (1860–63), Khudiakov's *Velikorusskiya Skazki* (1860–62), and E. A. Chudinsky's *Russkiya Narodnuiya Skazki* (1864).

Many more books could be added to this list, and many of the collectors produced additional collections of tales and also scholarly studies. In England, after the foundation of the British Folklore Society, a great effort was also made by British and American folklorists to translate folk tales from other countries, such as India, China, Japan, and Africa. Yet their full impact has never been appreciated because the majority of the European folk-tale collections have not been translated or studied in English-speaking countries. For instance, until recently, one of the most exceptional of the great nineteenth-century European and American folklorists, Pitrè, was ignored, and thus I want to turn to his life and works to demonstrate how he is an exemplary representative of those learned, dedicated folklorists who tried to make the past usable so that we might learn something about ourselves.

Giuseppe Pitrè

In an obituary published in the *Nation* soon after Pitrè's death in 1916, the extraordinary American scholar Thomas Frederick Crane, a gifted folklorist in his own right, made this comment in comparing Pitrè to the Grimms:

> Wide as the scope of their [the Grimms'] labors, it did not equal in extent the field cultivated by Pitrè, and after the *Kinder- und Hausmärchen* (*Children's and Household Tales*) and the *Deutsche Sagen* (*German Legends*) the interests of the brothers became almost exclusively linguistic and lexicographical. Pitrè, on the other hand, was all his life a practicing physician, and took a prominent part in the civic affairs of Palermo, being Syndic, or Mayor, for many years. The Grimms were chiefly concerned with the tales and legends of Germany and its medieval literature: Pitrè throughout his long life devoted himself to every branch of folk-lore—popular tales, legends, songs, children's games, proverbs, riddles, customs, etc.—and collected himself an astounding mass of material, only a part of which is represented in the twenty-five

volumes of the *Biblioteca delle tradizioni popolari siciliani* (*The Library of Sicilian Folklore*, Palermo, 1871–1914).[6]

Born in Borgo, a lower-class district in Palermo, on December 22, 1841, Pitrè came from a family with a strong maritime tradition. His father, Salvatore, was a sailor and worked on transatlantic ships, and his mother, Maria Stabile, was the daughter of a seafaring family. Unfortunately, Pitrè's father died in 1847 from yellow fever while he was in New Orleans, and Pitrè and his younger brother, Antonio, were compelled to move into their maternal grandfather's house in Borgo. This early death brought the young Pitrè closer to his grandfather, Giuseppe Stabile, and it also strengthened his mother's desire to further her son's education rather than encourage him to become a sailor. Thanks to the support of her tightly knit extended family and the help of a priest, she was able to provide educational opportunities and security for her two sons. These close, warm relations among his relatives and friends in the Borgo district stamped Pitrè's positive attitude toward the common people his entire life.

Already, as a young boy, he began collecting proverbs, maritime expressions, and songs, and it soon became clear that he had a literary bent, plus was especially curious about the history of the common customs and beliefs of Sicilians mainly from the lower classes. When he turned thirteen, he entered a Jesuit seminary, San Francisco di Paola, where he received a rigorous classical education. He was among the best students at this school, and had begun seriously to collect proverbs and study the history of Sicily. During this time, however, the Italian insurrection against the Austrians erupted, and Pitrè, who, like many of his schoolmates, was a dedicated patriot, was inspired by the idea of an independent united Italy, which also included a liberated Sicily. So he left school in 1860 to enlist in Giuseppe Garibaldi's navy, even though he disliked the sea and suffered from seasickness. During spring 1860 he traveled to different port cities such as Marseilles, Genoa, and Naples, the only time he ever left the island of Sicily, and fortunately was not involved in any battles.

When the uprising was quelled and the Italians defeated, he returned to Sicily to finish his studies and enrolled in 1861 as a student of medicine at the University of Palermo. His mother, her family, and a priest, Francesco Coniglio, continued to further his education, and Pitrè did not disappoint them. In fact, he surpassed their expectations. Not only did he excel in his study of medicine, but he also became an accomplished scholar of literature and history. During the five years of his studies, he began publishing articles on proverbs in the Sicilian journals *Borghini* and *Favilla* and taught Italian literature at the Conservatori di Musica. It was also during this time, in 1865 to be precise, that he made the acquaintance of Salvatore Salomone-Marino, also a young student of medicine, who became one of his most intimate friends and closest collaborator in folklore research until they had a falling out toward the end of the nineteenth century.

When Pitrè completed his studies in 1866, he began teaching Italian literature almost immediately at the Ginassio Vittorio Emanuele, a high school in Palermo, because he could not find work as a physician, and because he now wanted to help support his mother and her family in return for all their help. He soon lost this teaching position, however, because of a dispute with a vindictive official, who was later punished for indiscriminate behavior. As a result of this incident, Pitrè decided to begin practice as a private doctor just when a major cholera epidemic spread throughout Sicily between 1866 and 1867. He dedicated himself to aiding hundreds of people stricken with cholera and soon came to realize how important it was to continue practicing medicine while pursuing his interests as a folklorist.

Pitrè either walked or traveled by horse and buggy to his patients, and it was often through contact with them along with their relatives and friends that he collected and wrote down songs, proverbs, and tales. From this point on until his death, he became widely known in Palermo as the little doctor who took notes and even wrote entire books while riding in his horse and buggy. Nobody dared disturb him while he concentrated on his work. In a revealing reminiscence of a visit with Pitrè, the Swiss folklorist Walter Keller wrote:

And so we went down the stairs where his servant was already waiting for us in front of the house with an old-fashioned coach drawn by a single horse. "Please allow me to introduce my *traveling study*," Pitrè said to me and asked me to climb in.

"Padrone," the servant said to the doctor, "I've put the mail on the table in the coach for you."

Indeed he had! The inside of the coach had been transformed into a small study with a desk, and the walls contained all kinds of shafts, secret folders, and invisible pockets from which Pitrè took out manuscripts, books, magazines, and letters.

"You see," he explained to me, "for years I've taken care of almost all my correspondence in this traveling study."

"Aha!" I thought. "That's why the handwriting of his letters is so unclear and shaky."

"And it's inside here that I've written a good part of my books, always on the way from one sick person to the next. I can't conceive of how I could have otherwise completed my large collections and wrapped up everything during my lifetime. This coach bounces softly, as you can see, and Old Fritz, my faithful horse, doesn't trot very fast so that I can work here very nicely. You can get used to anything."[7]

And Pitrè always seemed to get used to everything. By 1868, he had gathered enough folk songs to publish his first major book, *Canti popolari siciliani* (*Sicilian Popular Songs*), based on a work that had influenced him as a young man, Giuseppe Giusti's *Raccolta di proverbi toscani* (*The Collection of Tuscan*

Proverbs, 1852). Pitrè's collection became the first in his twenty-five volume series, *Biblioteca delle tradizioni popolari siciliane* (1871–1913), supported by the Luigi Pedone Lauriel, one the first great publishers in Palermo, who was dedicated to Sicilian history and folklore. Their meeting was serendipitous, and their collaboration was exceptional. Pitrè never demanded money or royalty in these early years for his work, and Lauriel totally supported all his endeavors.

When Pitrè began his serious work in the field of folklore, he was not given much credit because folklore was not considered a respectable or significant field of research, even though numerous scholars in Sicily and Italy had started publishing important works. In fact, journalists and educators frequently ridiculed him. For instance, when the four volumes of *Fiabe, novelle e racconti popolari siciliani* (*Sicilian Fairy Tales, Folk Tales, and Stories*), which constituted volumes four through seven of the *Biblioteca*, appeared in 1875, they were dismissed as vulgar, indecent, and trivial by many journalists, critics, and academicians, especially since the tales and stories were published in Sicilian dialect. Yet it was precisely Pitrè's devotion to the neglected "authentic" traditions of the Sicilian people that made his work so valuable.

Unlike many of his predecessors in Europe, Pitrè endeavored to provide accurate renditions of the spoken word in dialect and also wrote historical studies about the customs and belief systems of the Sicilian people to supply a cultural and historical context for his work. Not only did Pitrè collect materials from his patients and friends, but he also recruited his own family to work with him—his mother, who had often sung sea ballads to him when he was a child, contributed to his collections—and he began corresponding with interested scholars on the island and the Continent. Many of them sent him tales or information, which he included in various collections. In 1877, he married Francesca Vitrano and had three children with her, Maria (b. 1878), Rosina (b. 1885), and Salvatore (b. 1887). Although all the children helped him with his research, it was mainly Maria who assisted him in all his work until she married an Italian diplomat in 1904 and then went to Brazil. To say the least, Pitrè was always in need of collaborators, for his historical research and collecting were phenomenal, and he was always grateful for the least bit of information that pertained to Sicilian folklore.

As early as 1869, he cofounded the literary journal *Nuove effemeridi siciliani* with Vincenzo Di Giovanni and Salomone-Marino, and this publication enabled him to share his work as well as develop a greater understanding of the latest folklore research on the Continent and in England. The journal lasted until 1882. The year before publication was stopped, Pitrè had been seriously ill, but during his convalescence, Lauriel persuaded him to start a new journal dealing mainly with folklore. So together with Salomone-Marino, he founded *Archivio per lo studio delle tradizioni popolari* in 1882, and this famous periodical, international in scope, lasted until 1907, and contained a wealth of folklore material. Moreover, as editor, he came into contact with many of the leading folklorists in Europe and the United States. Among his correspondents were Comparetti, Alessandro D'Ancona, Ernesto Monaci, Constantino Nigra, Gubernatis, Pio Rajna, Michele Barbi, Benedetto Croce, Ernesto Renan, Wilhelm Manhardt, Sébillot, Hugo Schuchardt, Menéndez y Pelayo, Gaston Paris, Karl Krohn, Francis James Child, Busk, Ralston, and Crane, to name but a few. This vast correspondence is significant, because the letters (over seven thousand) that he wrote and received reveal how erudite and knowledgeable Pitrè had become with regard to other folklore traditions, how astute he had become in interpreting the immense amount of materials and documents that he had gathered, and how helpful he was when other scholars turned to him for assistance. While he was editing the *Archivio*, he also developed another series, *Curiosità popolari tradizionali* (*Folklore Curiosities*, 1885–90), in sixteen volumes, containing songs, proverbs, customs, and tales.

Impressive as these accomplishments may be, they almost pale in comparison to the twenty-five volumes he published in his *Biblioteca* between 1871 and 1913. In a certain sense, all these books constitute a major collaborative effort between Pitrè and the people of Sicily, with the help of friends, scholars, and assistants. But the major responsibility for the conception of the *Biblioteca*—the notes, the editing of folklore, and all the songs, poetry, legends, folk tales, proverbs, ghost stories, anecdotes, idioms, customs, medicine, clothes, utensils, and regional history—lay with Pitrè.

At the same time that he carried out his extensive folklore research and worked as a medical doctor, he was gradually drawn into politics. While Pitrè never joined a party and disingenuously considered himself apolitical, the tenor of his work and social background show how disposed he was to support the common people's causes. And certainly they had great trust in Pitrè, who had always prided himself on being frank and honest in all his relations. So given his sincerity and popularity, he was "drafted" as a candidate and elected as an independent counselor (consigliere) of the Comune di Palermo, and was soon regarded as one of the most beloved representatives of the people in his district. (Eventually, in 1915, he became a senator.) But his major passion remained the study of folklore. In 1909 he established the first folklore museum, Il Museo Etnografico Siciliano, in a former convent on the outskirts of Palermo, and it housed all the tools, costumes, pottery, etchings, and other artifacts that Pitrè had personally collected over the years. Finally, thanks to Pitrè, the first chair in folklore, which he called Demopsicologia (psychology of the people), was founded in 1911 at the University of Palermo, and he taught an introductory course on the history of demopsicologia in 1911–12. His lectures were only recently published as *La Demopsicologia e la sua storia* (*The Psychology of the People and its History*) in 2001, ninety years after he had delivered them.

Yet despite all the honors Pitrè received at the beginning of the twentieth century, he was devastated by personal tragedies in his latter years. His daughter Rosina, who had married in 1906 and become pregnant the following year, perished in the Messina earthquake of 1908. His son, Salvatore, who had graduated from the University of Palermo in 1911 and become a medical doctor, died from food poisoning in 1912. His eldest daughter, Maria d'Alia Pitrè, who had assisted him in his research and left Sicily in 1904 to live in Brazil, was his only child to survive him when he died in 1916.

Pitrè's Concept of Folklore

Pitrè's attachment to the Sicilian people was profound and boundless, and because of this, he has often been criticized for romanticizing the Sicilian folk and its traditions. Some scholars have charged him with creating an image of common Sicilians as pure, innocent, and noble "primitives," downplaying many crude and deplorable aspects of the Sicilian folk and even the role of the Mafia as a criminal organization. Others have complained that he edited and censored some texts that he gathered with the purpose of establishing respect and honor for the Sicilian folk. In other words, his view as a folklorist was allegedly skewed, and one critic has argued that his representation of the evolution of Sicilian culture resulted from many fixed binary divisions such as rural/urban and nonliterate/educated that he conceived to uncover what he saw as the authentic Sicilian spirit.

Some of these allegations may, indeed, be true, but they are also simplistic, for it was precisely this passionate love for the common people, almost an obsession, that drove him to become more and more scientific in his research. He aspired to grasp not only the "Sicilian" qualities in the habits, customs, rituals, and mentality of the folk but also the similar modes of oral narrative representation and thinking that the Sicilians shared with other European peoples. Paradoxically, Pitrè's romanticism led him to become more international, rational, and comprehensive in his research, and resulted in his producing a huge treasure of materials that do not romanticize the Sicilian people or lead to their "romanticization."

If anything, his collections, historical commentary, and anthropological research reveal checkered and diverse traditions that demand a nuanced and careful analysis, even though it may be true that Pitrè, like all folklorists of his time, sought to fulfill his own personal mission to preserve the essence of the Sicilian folk and open other people's eyes, especially those of the educated classes in Sicily, to what he thought they were missing. At one point in the preface to *Fiabe, novelle e racconti*, he observed that when common people in villages and cities were asked to explain the history of certain names, locations, or events, they always knew a great deal, but the educated people were at a loss because they never bothered to become intimately acquainted with this history. Pitrè wanted to compensate (perhaps overcompensate) for this neglect and sought to celebrate the accomplishments of common Sicilians.

Certainly there was and still is a social class "split vision" in the way history is recorded and remembered in all cultures. In Pitrè's day, he saw himself as an educated scholar who wanted to turn over the smallest stone to see what was beneath it, for he believed that the hidden history of the Sicilian folk constituted the hidden treasure of Sicilian culture. He came to believe, moreover, that this culture had unusual links to other so-called primitive cultures that revealed how the common people throughout the world thought, preserved customs and habits, and disseminated them through their stories.

As a young man Pitrè began his work not from a concept but rather from intuition, great curiosity, and a deep attraction to Sicilian songs and sayings that grew from his experiences in the Borgo district of Palermo. As he began to write down Sicilian songs and proverbs in dialect and study them, he also started to take a great interest in contemporary writers and Sicilian history. His early publications *Profili* (*Profiles*, 1864), *Nuovi Profili* (*New Profiles*, 1868), and *Saggi di critica letteraria* (*Essays of Literary Criticism*, 1871) reveal how broad his interests were, but there was a common thread in all these writings as well as his reviews and articles in journals: he wanted to restore the significance of oral literature and live expressions in Sicilian history; more precisely, he sought to document the authentic art and history of the common people. This is clear in three of his other early books, *Sopra i proverbi* (*On Proverbs*, 1863), *Saggio di un vocabolaroio di marina* (*Essay on a Maritime Vocabulary*, 1863), and *Lo Studio critico sui canti siciliani* (*A Critical Study of Sicilian Songs*, 1868).

Perhaps the greatest influence on his work at this time was, as I have already mentioned, Giusti's *Raccolta di proverbi toscani*, which laid the basis for his comparative method and philosophy of collecting. But Giusti was not the only important scholar who marked Pitrè's development as a folklorist. In one of the most comprehensive and insightful essays on Pitrè's work, Alberto Mario Cirese has emphasizes that although self-educated and driven by his passionate dedication to the Sicilian folk, Pitrè's phenomenal personal development and work as a folklorist did not come out of nowhere. The period between 1850 and 1875 in which Pitrè began taking an interest in folklore—a revolutionary and nationalistic period—was also the formative phase of this field on the Continent and in England, and once Pitrè decided to embark on a career as folklorist, he read widely and voraciously. By the early 1870s, when he was still a young man, he had already learned German, French, and English, and his knowledge of international folklore and scholarship was extraordinary—literally breathtaking. He was familiar with all the most recent debates, discoveries, and publications in several different languages. As Cirese notes, the foremost Italian scholars and folklorists such as Nigra, D'Ancona, Comparetti, and Imbriani had already begun publishing significant collections and essays.

But there were also contributions closer to home in Sicily that were not lacking. We should not omit the possibility that Pitrè might have known or eventually discovered much earlier precedents (the Catania collection of Giuseppe Leopardi Cilia that appeared in manuscript form approximately 1817 but was not published until recently; the notes furnished by Giuseppe La Farina in 1834 to Niccolò Tommaso's *Gita nel Pistoiese*; the few songs published by V. Navarro and G. R. Abati in 1843–1845); between 1857 and 1870 Sicilian culture manifested a lively interest in popular poetry and literature, and Pitrè was certainly influenced by this development. Lionardo Vigo's *Canti popolari siciliani* appeared in 1857, and between 1870 and 1874 he transformed them in *Raccolta amplissima*; from 1865 to 1867 Letterio Lizio Bruno published texts and tales that prefigured his *Canti popolari delle isole Eolie* in 1871; in 1867 Salvatore Salomone-Marino (who had just turned twenty-one and was six years younger than Pitrè) notably expanded the horizon of the publications and the other works that were then common in Sicily with his book, *Canti popolari siciliani in aggiunta a quelli del Virgo*; in 1868 a Sicilian journal published Niccolò Tommaso's letter, *Sui canti popolari*; in the same year Salomone-Marino showed how dedicated he was as an accurate researcher to the dates, facts and documents as he began to study the history of the popular Sicilian songs.[8]

But the Italians and Sicilians were not the only important collectors and scholars for Pitrè. He also knew of Gonzenbach, whom I discussed in the previous chapter. Though the daughter of a Swiss merchant living in Messina, she had published the first and highly significant collection of Sicilian tales, *Sicilianische Märchen* (*Sicilian Fairy Tales*) in German. Her work was introduced by the German historian Hartwig and edited by the meticulous scholar Reinhold Köhler, whose approach to the categorization of the tale types may have influenced Pitrè. Other German and Austrian scholars had already translated and edited noteworthy collections of Italian tales, and Pitrè was acquainted with these books as well. For instance, Georg Widter and Adam Wolf published *Volksmärchen aus Venetien* (*Folktales from Venetia*, 1866), edited once again by the enterprising Köhler in the *Jahrbuch für romantische und englische Literatur* (*Yearbook for Romance and English Literature*); Hermann Knust compiled his translation, *Italienische Märchen* (*Italian Fairy Tales*, 1866), also in the *Jahrbuch für romantische und englische Literatur*, and Schneller produced *Märchen und Sagen aus Wälschtirol* (*Fairy Tales and Legends from Welsh Tyrol*).

Before Pitrè turned his full attention to folk tales, however, he focused more on folk songs and published a revision of his *Lo studio critico sui canti siciliani* (*The Critical Study of Sicilian Songs*, 1870), the first edition of *Canti popolari siciliani* (1871) in two volumes, and *Studi di poesia popolare* (*Studies of Popular Poetry*, 1872), a collection of his essays and reviews. These three books constituted the first three volumes of his immense series *Biblioteca delle tradizione popolari siciliani*, and he had clearly determined that his life's work would be dedicated to recording every possible aspect of the art, customs, and history of the Sicilian folk. This "patriotic" commitment was, of course, reinforced by the political climate of the times. Pitrè had supported Garibaldi's efforts to unify Italy in the early 1860s, and was gratified by the final triumph of Garibaldi's army over the Austrian forces in 1870 that eventually brought about Italian unification. For Pitrè, this unification also allowed the Sicilian people to gain a sense of national pride, for the island would no longer be occupied and controlled by foreigners, and his so-called *popolarismo romantico* was an expression of this pride.

At the same time that Pitrè sought to extol the "genius" of the Sicilian folk and its culture, he was moving beyond this romantic glorification of the common Sicilian people, and began grounding his folk-tale collecting on a more concrete scientific and anthropological approach to understanding the history, evolution, and significance of all types of folk tales. General theories about the origins and spread of the folk tales leading to the formation of the literary tales were first conceived only at the beginning of the nineteenth century. The Brothers Grimm, key figures in this development, believed that fairy tales were derived from myths that had been religious at one time, but storytellers had gradually discarded their religious connotations, and the tales eventually became more secular, containing remnants of religious rites and customs often referred to as buried motifs. Their views were expanded by Theodor Benfey (1809–81), a Sanskrit scholar, who argued in his introduction to the Indic *Pantschatantra* (1859) that the fairy-tale genre originated in ancient India as an oral wonder tale, spreading first to Persia and then the entire Arabic-speaking world. Eventually, these tales were transmitted to Europe via Spain, Greece, and Sicily through trade, migration, and the Crusades. The Grimms and Benfey believed that there was one point of origin, or one place of birth (monogenesis), that led to the formation of different kinds of folk tales.

In contrast, Joseph Bédier (1864–1938), a French folklorist, eventually opposed their views and developed his notion of polygenesis in *Les Fabliaux* (1893); he maintained that the tales originated in different places and were cultivated by gifted storytellers. The notion of polygenesis had already been at the basis of the works of British anthropological scholars Tylor, Lang, and Frazer, who held that since the human species was similar throughout the world, humans responded to their environment in similar ways, thereby giving rise to identical tales that varied only according to the customs that the different cultures developed.[9] They preceded and differed from Bédier in that they believed that the common people as well as gifted storytellers cultivated the tales in their rituals and customs. The oral wonder tale was one among different genres or types of tales that were cultivated throughout the world, often with similar plots and themes. In particular, Tylor's two early works,

Researches into the Early History of Mankind (1865) and *Primitive Culture: Researches into the Development of Mythology, Philosophy, Religion, Language, Art, and Custom* (1871), left a deep impression on Pitrè, and he frequently referred to Tylor's notions in his writings on folklore.

In Aurelio Rigoli's significant study of Tylor's influence on Pitrè, *Il Concetto di sopravvenza nell'opera di Pitrè e altri studi di folklore* (*The Concept of Survival in the Work of Pitrè and Other Studies of Folklore*), he points out that Pitrè agreed with the basic tenet of Tylor's notion that folklore was a conglomeration of relics that originated among primitive peoples; they were kept alive and survived through the comportment, belief systems, and customs of the common people. As Rigoli notes, Pitrè was more cautious about attributing everything in folklore to relics of survival. Yet Tylor's ideas form the underlying concepts in Pitrè work, and by the time Pitrè concluded the last volume of his *Bibiloteca* in 1913, he noted:

> Anthropology and psychology have replaced history in many points, and with a precise and refined examination, these fields of study want now to explain the deformed residues of myths, superstitions, and symbols from ancient times. That which has existed in the human psyche for many years—that which has not been fully recovered according to the intelligent ethnological theory of Tylor—constitutes part of our own unconscious, transparent in our mental attitudes, in our poetical metaphors as well as in our philosophical concepts. It is the basis or substratum that explains the survival of tendencies, of particular ways of feeling and thinking in contention with all the other psychological manifestations.[10]

What is crucial to bear in mind is that Pitrè's reading of Tylor and other scholars reveals that even by the early 1870s, though Pitrè left the island of Sicily only once as a young man, and though it is uncertain how and when he developed the capacity to read English, French, German, and Spanish, not to mention many different Sicilian dialects, he had become an accomplished *international* folklorist with a comprehensive theoretical knowledge of developments largely in Europe—and later in North America through his correspondence with Crane. He was familiar with the most important folklore collections and scholars of folklore, and his early small publications such as *Saggio di fiabe e novella popolari siciliane* (*A Sample of Sicilian Fairy and Folk Tales*, 1873), *Nuovo Saggio di fiabe e novelle popolari siciliane* (*A New Sample of Sicilian Fairy and Folk Tales*, 1873), *Otto fiabe e novelle siciliane* (*Eight Sicilian Fairy and Folk Tales*, 1873), and *Novelline popolari siciliane* (*Sicilian Folk Tales*, 1873) indicate his wide-ranging interest in drawing parallels between Sicilian tales and those published and disseminated on the Continent. By the time he published the four volumes of *Fiabe, novelle e racconti popolari siciliani* in 1875, he had come to realize that the Sicilian tales were not only representative of Sicilian culture, and could be connected to the deeply entrenched customs, beliefs, superstitions, behaviors, and history of the Sicilian people, but they were also linked to the tales of other cultures that were engendered and evoked by comparatively similar natural phenomena and experiences.

If there were similarities in the Sicilian tales that could be traced to other European and Oriental collections, Pitrè attributed them to the fact that humans express themselves more or less in the same way when the environmental and psychological conditions are comparable. Here he was very much in accord with Tylor's *Primitive Culture* and other British anthropologists who proposed that humans have the same instincts and thus tend to produce similar rituals and tales. Although Pitrè did not discount communication, commerce, war, travel, theater, professional storytellers, and religious ceremonies that can account for the spread of particular tale types, he fundamentally believed that it was human nature and the human response to the environment that led to the same tale types. What was significant as well as exciting for Pitrè was the manner in which people from different regions of Sicily— and for that matter, the world—changed and varied the motifs of well-known tales, or created tales based on their peculiar and particular experiences to contribute to a so-called minor history. For Pitrè the minor was major. As he wrote: "History should not be a list of men, in which their outstanding acts are registered, but the revelation of ideas, passions, customs and civil interests, in short, of the life of a people, of a nation." Moreover, he took a political stance: "The history of the people is confused with that of its dominators. . . . [T]heir story has been taken and made into the same history of its governments without taking into consideration that they, the people, have a memory that is very different from that which is often attributed to them, whether it be from the side of the institutions or from the predominant powers."[11] Collecting was for Pitrè a "subversive" act, and his diverse collections, taken as a whole, were intended to offer an alternative to Sicily's official history.

Collecting relics of the past that had survived into the present was therefore an ethical act, and his definition of demopsicologia in his inaugural address held at the University of Palermo on January 12, 1911, makes this clear:

> For us demopsychology studies the moral and material life of civil people and non-civil people. The less civil they are, the more important the material is. This life is documented by diverse genres of the oral and objective traditions. Fairy tales and fables, stories and legends, proverbs and maxims, songs and melodies, puzzles and riddles, games and amusements, toys and playthings, performances and festivals, habits and customs, rituals and ceremonies, practices, beliefs, superstitions, fads, the world of manifestations and the occult, the real and imaginative world. This world moves, agitates, smiles, and moans at whoever knows how to draw near to it and to understand it. Its smiles, moans, and voices, insignificant for most people, are revelations for the man of

science who senses the long echo of open-hearted and fading genera-
tions of past centuries.

Pitrè was not simply interested in resuscitating the past; he wanted to endow
it with meaning in the present: "The demopsychologist, after having examined the current tradition, confronts it with the primitive traditions that are
still alive and establishes the entity, and in this way he finds the solution to
some obscure problem of the moral story of humankind: two processes, one
of psychic paleontology and the other critical anthropology."[12] In addition,
Pitrè sought to compare and contrast all the relics of the past with those from
other cultures. If certain customs and belief systems remained alive in the
diverse regions of Sicily, they had particular reasons that needed historical
explanation and could be best understood when comparing them with similar traditions in other cultures. This is one of the reasons he became so international in his research while remaining so dedicated to the Sicilian people.

Pitrè's Methods and the Historical Significance of His Collection

When Pitrè began to collect songs, proverbs, and tales professionally, he was
a young man in his twenties, and as I have emphasized, he did not have a
clearly defined method or concept of folklore. (Incidentally, this is true of
most European and American folklorists of the late nineteenth century.) His
approach to collecting oral tales, proverbs, riddles, and songs evolved as he
realized that the preservation of oral storytelling entailed a combination of
meticulous research and a deep theoretical understanding of the problems
involved in the transformation of the oral to the literary. It was obvious from
the beginning, however, that Pitrè wanted to give voice to humble and neglected narrators, who were the curators of Sicilian history, so to speak, and
this is why he kept the tales in their respective dialects.

Although there is not a great deal of documentation with regard to the exact methods Pitrè used in recording and editing all the tales, there is enough
information to provide a reliable account of his work. As is well known, Pitrè
did a great deal of collecting himself, especially in the district of Borgo, where
he was well acquainted with two of his best informants, Agatuzza Messia,
whom he knew as a child, and who told him forty tales, and Rosa Brusca,
who worked as a weaver and eventually became blind. He had apparently also
met another important narrator, Elisabetta Sanfrantello, who worked as a servant in Vallelunga. Women narrated about 60 percent of the tales that Pitrè
collected. In this regard, his collection is more balanced than Gonzenbach's
Sicilianische Märchen, which consisted of tales almost entirely told by women
and represented a particular feminine view of Sicilian culture. The tales told
by men tended to be different in style and content, and thus Pitrè's collection
allows readers to compare and contrast the manner in which women and

men narrated their versions of well-known tales, legends, anecdotes, and the proverbs that they include.

Pitrè generally took notes when he heard a tale told in dialect, and based on a hearing and possibly two or three, he reconstructed the tale using a mixed method that enabled him to keep the phonetic sounds while also retaining the dialect to make it as accessible as possible to a reading audience. In other words, Pitrè favored the Palermo Sicilian dialect as his standard in terms of spelling and grammar. Colleagues, friends, and relatives brought or sent him tales in different Sicilian dialects from all parts of the island, however, and he tried to remain as faithful to other unusual dialects and would explain the differences in his footnotes, which often included several variants. Pitrè tried scrupulously to provide variants in his notes because he regarded the tales as ethnological, historical, and social documents. His erudition was so great by the time he put together the four volumes of his collection that he could refer to variants in all parts of Europe and the Middle East and could trace the history of certain tales to the Greco-Roman period, frequently working like a detective to explain the derivation and deviation of a particular tale.

It is not clear to what extent Pitrè "censored" the tales or selected only those tales that reflected positively on Sicilian culture. Those critics who have asserted that Pitrè eliminated scatological references, brutality, and sexual innuendos from the tales have apparently not read the entire collection. Not only did Pitrè allow for "vulgar" language and stories with risqué and comical scenes—for instance, one in which a woman is made out of shit—but he also explained the metaphoric references to sex in his notes. If the majority of the tales are not as erotic, bawdy, and scatological as they might have been, it may be due to the fact that many of the tales were told by women with a different mind-set than men. Yet even the women did not shy away from sexual innuendos.

Pitrè divided the four volumes of *Fiabe, novelle e racconti popolari siciliani* into five sections: *fiabe populari comuni*, or common popular fairy tales, which constitute the bulk of the collection and include numerous fairy tales well known in Europe and the Middle East; *scherzi e anedotti*, or tall tales and anecdotes; *tradizioni storiche e fantastiche di luoghi e di persone*, or legends that deal with places and people; *proverbi e modelli di dire proverbiali spiegati con aneddoti e storielle*, or proverbial tales with anecdotes; and *favolette e apologhi*, or brief tales, fables, and animal tales. Altogether there are approximately four hundred tales—three hundred in the main body of texts, and a hundred variants in the notes that immediately followed each tale. There is also an appendix with seven Sicilian tales in Albanian dialect that was not included in the English translation. In addition, Pitrè wrote a preface to the four volumes, and included two long essays about this history of popular tales and the grammar of Sicilian dialect, which was later published separately as a small book.

If one considers that after the publication of *Fiabe, novelle e racconti popolari siciliani* in 1875, Pitrè published other significant collections of tales such as *Novelle popolari toscane* (1885), *Fiabe e Legende popolari siciliani* (1888), and *La Rondinella nelle tradizioni popolari* (*The Swallow in Folklore*, 1903), not to mention numerous tales that he printed in the *Archivio* and other journals, his collections constitute one of the richest sources of European folk tales in the nineteenth century, if not the richest ever. Pitrè was fully aware of just how fertile the tales were for understanding how European tales originated and were cross-fertilized, so to speak. After all, Sicily had been a country that had been constantly attacked, invaded, and occupied by the Greeks, Romans, Arabs, Turks, French, and Spanish for long as well as short periods of times. All of these occupations left their imprint on Sicilian culture, and many of the tales can be traced to storytelling traditions of these other cultures.

In her introduction to the late twentieth-century republication of *Fiabe, novelle e racconti popoplari siciliani*, Aurora Milillo maintains that the core of Pitrè's folklore program, and I would add, methods, can be ascertained in the first two tales in the collection, "The Tale Told Time and Again," told by the eight-year-old Mara Curatolo in Erice, and "The Parrot with Three Tales to Tell," told by Pitrè's most gifted informant, Messia, in Palermo. Milillo notes that in the first tale, Pitrè commented that nothing is arbitrary in a folk tale, which does not mean that everything is fixed. Significantly, this tale reveals that even the "infraction," the breaking of formulaic rules, belongs to the structure and function of the folk tale.

In "The Tale Told Time and Again," the little girl Elisabetta wins the wager with the merchant and takes over his shop by *not* beginning her tale with the formula "this tale has been told time and again." By breaking with the rules, she shows that storytelling includes infraction, and that breaking the rules may be necessary to gain what one wants. The story's young protagonist is opportunistic and clever, and uses an original way of starting her tale to enrich and empower herself. There are other aspects of this tale that neither Pitrè nor Milillo address that make it even more important as the collection's initial tale. The narrator is not only a female but also only eight years old, and tells her tale in an abrupt, somewhat-enigmatic manner that, for Pitrè, represented the "pure" and "authentic" style of the folk. It is also a tale of assertion, a takeover, by a young peasant girl, who stakes out a claim to her heritage using a promissory note that entitles her to the property that the merchant occupies. As an announcement, Pitrè's first tale can be regarded in some ways as his staking out a claim for the Sicilian folk to regain what belongs to them.

The second tale, again told by a woman, but a woman in her seventies, who lives in the city of Palermo and not in the country, is a much different statement about storytelling and folklore. "The Parrot with Three Tales to Tell" ultimately derives from the fifteenth-century Sanskrit collection *Shuka Saptatit: Seventy Tales of the Parrot*, and it is unclear how many intermediary stages and versions that it went through in the oral tradition before it entered Messia's repertory. What is apparent, though, is that Pitrè recognized its significance as a frame tale that similar to many collections like *Thousand and One Nights*, included several other tales that were connected to the meaning of the frame narrative. Just as the first tale reflects some of the brutal struggles over property and ownership along with the necessity to tell one's own story, so, too, the second tale is a frank commentary on the amorality of courting, desire, and seduction. Here the devious notary transformed into a parrot uses the storytelling to gain a woman that does *not* belong to him. Still, there is a certain ambiguity in his tale-telling, because in his three tales the notary depicts a courageous princess, who accomplishes amazing feats while searching for her lost doll. In the end she reclaims her doll and claims a husband at the same time. The princess has a "moral" right to her doll and proves her prowess by doing good deeds. On the other hand, the parrot or notary, who has sold his soul to the devil, connives and kills to obtain what he desires. While there is a simple and clear justice in the actions of the princess in the three internal tales, the conclusion of the frame tale leaves us with a more complex sense of what is just. The notary winds up with the woman who he has protected from another seducer, and only because of his brilliant ability to entertain through storytelling, he has won us over to some extent. We cannot be too upset by the death of the overly possessive husband or the defeat of the other seducer. The art of telling stories, as Pitrè's entire collection reveals, is more about learning how to survive under harsh conditions of life than learning how to lead a moral life.

Nineteenth-century Sicilian storytellers, no matter how much magic, fantasy, transformation, and humor were contained in their tales, always brought their listeners back to reality in the end. The endings or codas reveal how the storytellers were well aware of their own condition as well as the impossibility of realizing their fantasies. The verses vary, but the messages are similar.

> And so they lived on as husband and wife,
> While we toil away without a life.

> Now they are happy and content,
> While we sit here without a cent.

> My tale's been written, my tale's been told,
> Now you tell yours, because mine is old.

> They remained happy and content,
> While we still can't pay the rent.

Happiness was a fiction. Happiness was a wish bound to be unfulfilled in the lives of most of the storytellers and their listeners. But the stories were in and of themselves a fulfillment. The art of storytelling and listening enabled both tellers and listeners to extract meaning, "revenge," joy, and important knowledge from the narratives, just as storytelling continues to allow people today to confront their everyday vicissitudes. Though Pitrè may have edited many of the tales in his collection, he did not negate their essence: the mode of thinking of common Sicilians about work, sex, religion, law, other ethnic groups, money, and power.

One only has to read several of the Sicilian versions of "classical fairy tales" such as "Cinderella," "Donkey-Skin," "Rapunzel," "Beauty and the Beast," and "Puss in Boots" to grasp how Pitrè respected the narrators' voices along with their styles, and how he endeavored to record them as authentically as possible. Since women told most of these tales, they tend to be candid and stark depictions of extraordinary young women who cleverly shape their own destinies, in contrast to the male literary versions of Straparola, Basile, Perrault, and the Brothers Grimm. In "Date, Oh Beautiful Date," for instance, the sprightly Ninetta (Cinderella) toys with a prince in his garden until he falls desperately in love with her. She constantly evades him, even at three different balls, until he is at his wits' end. The prince's father must intervene to save his son's life, and he actually proposes to Ninetta for his son. In "Pilusedda," a version of "Donkey-Skin," related to the Cinderella-type tales, a clever young woman escapes her father's lecherous desires and uses three gifts from the fairies to entice a prince to marry her. In "The Old Woman of the Garden" ("Rapunzel"), after the young girl is abandoned by her mother, she is brutally treated by an ogress. Yet instead of running away from a tower with a prince, she shoves the ogress into an oven and makes peace with her mother. Here is the tale in its entirety:

The Old Woman of the Garden

Once upon a time there was a cabbage garden. The crops each year were becoming more and more scarce, and when two women began talking, one of them said:

"My friend, let's go and pick some cabbages."

"How are we to know whether anyone's there?" said the other.

"All right. I'll go and see if someone's keeping guard," the neighbor said. She went and looked.

"There's no one. Let's go!"

They entered the garden, gathered two good batches of cabbage, and left. Then they cheerfully ate the cabbages. The next morning they returned, but one of the women was afraid that the gardener would be there. However, since they didn't see anybody, they entered. Once again they gathered two good batches of cabbage and ate them all.

Now let's leave them eating the cabbages and turn to the old woman who owned the garden. When she went to her garden, she cried out: "Jesus! Some one's eaten my cabbages. Well, I'm going to take care of this. . . . I'll get a dog and tie him to the gate at the entrance. When the thieves come, the dog will know what to do."

All right, let's leave the old woman who fetched a dog to guard the garden and return to the two women. One of them said to the other:

"Let's go and pick some cabbages."

"No, my friend, there's a dog now."

"Not a problem! We'll buy some dry bread with our money and feed it to the dog. Then we can do whatever we want."

So they bought some bread, and before the dog could bark, they threw it some pieces. As soon as the dog became silent, they gathered the cabbages and left. Later on, the old woman arrived, and when she saw the damage, she cried out, "Ahh! So, you let them gather the cabbages! You're really not a good guard dog. Out you go!"

And so the old woman now took a cat to guard the garden and hid in the house, and as soon as the cat screeched *meow! meow!* she would grab the thieves by their throats.

The next day one of the women said, "Friend, let's go and pick some cabbages."

"No. There's a guard, and this means trouble for us."

"I don't think so. Let's go."

When they saw the cat, they bought some fish, and before the cat could *meow*, they threw it some fish, and the cat didn't utter a sound. The women gathered some cabbage and left. When the cat finished eating the fish, it went *meow, meow!* The old woman came running but didn't see anyone. So she picked up the cat and cut off its head. Then she said, "Now I'm going to have the cock keep guard, and when it crows, I'll come running and kill those thieves."

The next day the two women began talking with one another.

"Let's go and pick some cabbage."

"No, my friend, there's the cock."

"Doesn't matter," her friend said. "We'll take some grain with us and throw it to the cock so it won't cry out."

And this is what they did. While the cock ate the grain, they picked the cabbages and left. When the cock finished eating the grain, it crowed: "*Cock-a-doodle-do!*" So the old woman came running and saw that more cabbages had been stolen. So she picked up the cock, wrung its neck, and ate it. Then she called a peasant and said, "I want you to dig a hole just my size."

Afterward she hid herself in the long hole, but one of her ears stuck outside. The next morning the women came to the garden and didn't see a soul. The old woman had asked the peasant to dig the hole along the path that the women would have to pass, and when they came by, they didn't notice a thing. They passed the hole and collected some cabbages, and on their return, the woman who was pregnant, looked at the ground and saw a mushroom which was actually the old woman's ear.

"Friend, look at this beautiful mushroom!"

She knelt down and tugged at it. She pulled and pulled, and finally, she yanked out the old woman with all her might.

"Ahh!" the old woman said, "you're the ones who've been picking my cabbage! Just wait and see what I'm going to do to you!"

She grabbed hold of the pregnant woman, while the other scampered away as fast as her legs could carry her.

"Now I'm going to eat you alive!" the old woman said to the pregnant woman whom she had in her clutches.

"No! Listen to me! When I give birth, and my child is sixteen years old, I promise that, whether boy or girl, I'll send the child to you, and I'll keep my promise."

"All right," the old woman said. "Pick all the cabbages you want, and then leave. But remember the promise you've made."

The poor woman was more dead than alive when she returned home.

"Ah, friend," she said to her neighbor. "You managed to escape, and I'm still in trouble. I promised the old woman that I'd give her my firstborn when the child turns sixteen."

"And what do you want me to do?"

After two months, the Lord blessed the pregnant woman with a baby girl.

"Ahh, my daughter!" she said to the baby. "I'll raise you, give you my breast, but then someone is going eat you!"

And the poor mother wept. When the girl turned sixteen, she went out to buy some oil for her mother. The old woman saw her and said, "Whose daughter are you, my girl?"

"My mother's name is Sabedda," she replied.[13]

"Well, tell your mother to remember her promise. You've become a beautiful maiden. You're nice and tasty," she said as she caressed her. "Here, take some of these figs and bring them to your mother."

The maiden went to her mother and told her what had happened.

"The old woman told me to remind you of your promise."

"Why did I promise her?!" the mother began to cry.

"Why are you crying, mama?"

But her mother said nothing. After weeping for some time, she said to her daughter, "If you meet the old woman, you're to say: 'She's still too young . . .'"

The next evening the maiden went again to get some oil and met the old woman, who did the same thing as she had done the day before.

Meanwhile her mother thought, "It's now or in the course of two years that I'll have to separate from my daughter." So she said to her daughter, "If you meet the old woman, tell her, 'When you see her, take her, and the promise is kept.'"

Then the old woman soon appeared and asked, "What did your mother say?"

"When you see her, take her."

"Well then, come with your grandma, for I'm going to give you many things."

She took the maiden with her, and when they arrived at the old woman's house, she locked the maiden in a closet and said, "Eat whatever's there."

After a fair amount of time had passed, the old woman said, "I want to see if you've gotten fatter."

There was a little hole in the door.

"Show me, little one. Stick out your finger."

The maiden was clever. A mouse had come by, and she had cut off its tail and showed it to the old woman.

"Ahh! How thin you are, my daughter. You've got to eat for your grandma. You're so thin, and you've got to eat."

Some more time passed.

"Come out, my daughter, so I can see you."

The maiden came out.

"Ahh! You've become nice and fat. Let's go and knead some bread."

"Yes, grandma. I know how to do it."

When they finished kneading the bread, the old woman had her heat up the oven.

"Light it for your grandma."

The maiden began to clear it out to heat the oven.

"Come on. Do it for grandma," the old woman said. "Let's put the bread in the oven."

"But, grandma, I don't know how to put the bread into the oven. I know how to do everything else, but I don't know how to put the bread into the oven."

"Well then," said the old woman, "I'll put the bread into the oven. You just have to pass it to me."

The maiden took the bread and gave it to the old woman, who said, "Pick up the iron slab that closes the oven."

"But grandma, I don't have the strength to pick up the slab."

"Well then, I'll pick it up."

When the old woman kneeled down, the maiden grabbed her from behind and shoved her into the oven. Then she picked up the slab and used it to close the oven.

"Now there's nothing more to do here. So I'll find out where my mother is."

As she went outside, a neighbor saw her.

"Well, you're alive?!"

"Why, should I be dead? Now, listen to what I'm going to tell you. I want you to look for my mother. I want to see her."

The neighbor went and called her mother, who went to the old woman's house. When her daughter told her everything that had happened, she became very happy, and they took charge of everything in the house.

They remained happy and content,
While we still don't have a cent.

Told by Elisabetta (Sabedda) Sanfratello in Vallelunga[14]

There are several beast bridegroom tales such as "Marvizia," "The King of Love," "King Dead Horse," and "The Serpent," and in each story a young woman is put to severe tests to rescue an enchanted prince or tame a beast. In rare instances, as in the traditional tale of "Beauty and the Beast" by Madame Leprince de Beaumont, she does this as a sacrifice to save her father, but more often she does it to prove that she is valiant, smart, and competent.

In classic fairy tales that feature men such as "Count Joseph Pear," a comical version of "Puss in Boots," the episodes often involve ruthless struggles. In this tale a female fox, not a cat, helps a peasant. And the fox helps the peasant to pretend to be a count, and thus fool a king and his daughter. But the peasant is ungrateful, and in the end he smashes her head so that the fox will not be able reveal to the princess that he is really from the lower classes. This brutal ending is not untypical in the Sicilian folk-tale tradition. Other tales that have been widely diffused and become popular in Western culture such as "The Beauty of the Seven Mountains of Gold," "The Magic Purse, Cloak, and Horn," "The Fig-and-Raisin-Fool," "Water and Salt," and "Master Joseph" do not mince words about the violent struggles experienced by protagonists who set out into the world to improve their station in life. Life was hard and cruel for most people from the lower classes, and the relics of the past that surface transparently in all the tales reveal the hopes and wishes for wealth, food, revenge, and power.

But there is also a lot of humor in the different types of tales collected by Pitrè. Many of the comical stories about Saint Peter reveal an irreverent attitude toward this particular saint, who is often pompous and pretentious. In the tales about Saint Joseph and Saint Michael, the saint is depicted more like a fairy, a fata, than a biblical saint. The humor can also be satirical. One of the harshest tales in the collection is "The Shoemaker and the Monks," in which Peppi, a poor shoemaker, literally destroys a monastery and all the monks because they are so corrupt. In fact, there is a strong anticlerical strain that runs through many of the tales such as "The Monk and the Brother," "The Priest and His Shepherd Friends," "The Bourgeois Gentleman and the Preacher," and "The Sexton's Nose." Though Sicilians tended to be religious and revered God, they did not revere the local priests and sextons all that much. They were also critical of each other and outsiders—that is, people from other cities, towns, and regions. Some of the more comical tales like "The Simpleton from Calabria" and "The Petralian" deal with the gullibility of country bumpkins. Other stories such as "The Thief of Sicily and the Thief of Naples" and "The Neapolitan and the Sicilian" extol the cleverness of Sicilians, who always prove themselves smarter than the Neapolitans, just as some tales reveal how city people from Palermo become lost souls in the country.

Although there are some delightful nonsense tales such as "King Ridiculous" and "The Four Numskulls," the most biting and humorous tales by far concern two "folk heroes," Firrazzanu and Giufà. Despite some similarities between the two protagonists, they stem from two different traditions, and

Pitrè pays homage to their roguish behavior that undermines the norms of decency by including fifteen tales about Firrazzanu and fifteen about Giufà. There may be some connection to the tales about the wise fool Hodja Nasreddin that began circulating in the Mediterranean and Slavic countries during the sixteenth century. Firrazzanu is also similar to the sly character Bertoldo Bertoldino, who was a popular figure in many regions of Italy. He is always conscious of what he is doing and generally profits from the pranks he plays. On the other hand, Giufà springs from tales told about a noble protagonist in the Arabic folk tradition of the medieval period, and gradually took on a much more complex character. Unlike Firrazzanu, Giufà is not conscious or aware of the consequences of his actions. He understands the world in a literal sense that leads him to do brutal things. Frequently his mother must rectify his actions, which cause the deaths of other people including his own sister. Giufà is clearly a fool, but he is not a wise fool. He is laughable because he always brings out the superstitions, amorality, and injustice in Sicilian society.

Pitrè did not shy away from documenting the contradictions of the Sicilian people. The latter part of his collection is filled with legends, stories based on proverbs, and animal tales that tend to be more realistic and historical than the fairy tales in the first two volumes. The legends read like landmarks of Sicily, telling a history of occupation and survival. The proverbs—and Pitrè assiduously collected hundreds in other books—ground the sayings in the customs formed by Sicilians over centuries. Many are similar to parables, as are the animal tales that owe a debt to Aesop. The tales such as "Brancaliuni" and "Friend Wolf and Friend Fox," however, usually end on a tragic note or with hard justice.

In my estimation, the four volumes that constitute *Fiabe, novelle e racconti popolari siciliani* are more important than the Grimms' tales because Pitrè was from the lower classes, was raised speaking a Sicilian dialect, and understood the people from whom he collected his tales in dialect. He was also fastidious in his recordings and provided variants and histories of the tales in his notes. There are over four hundred texts, originally in Sicilian dialect, that cover a wide range of tale types often told in a rough and disjointed style. As a result, some of the tales are jarring because they lack description and are crude. For the most part, though, they have a charming earthy quality, reflecting the customs, beliefs, and superstitions of the common people in Sicily more clearly than most European collections of the nineteenth century portray the experiences of common people in their respective countries. As a side effect, they expose just how *literary* the Grimms' tales are as well as other collections of tales written down by educated European collectors in the nineteenth and early part of the twentieth century.

Pitrè admired the simplicity, honesty, and candor of the common people, and he was intent on preserving their stories as they told them because they were filled with unvarnished "truths" that still spoke to the conditions in his day and age. Because they are tales of survival that have been transmitted over centuries, they have a unique quality, for they depict the world as it is without questioning the magic and impossibility of the events. Pitrè felt great empathy with the people who recounted these tales. He kept their simple, frank words in Sicilian dialect and ironically felt compelled to instruct the educated on how to grasp what the *popolo* said and did. Though much is lost in an English translation, which I recently published with Joseph Russo, it can still offer insights into the power of the spoken word and to a certain degree preserve a great heritage that deserves to be known in other languages. Pitrè's greatest contribution to folklore was his effort to allow Sicilian stories from the peasantry and urban lower classes to breathe, and this effort led to the establishment of folklore as a recognized discipline in Sicily. In his time he accomplished this task more than he realized, and in 2012, his complete collection of Sicilian dialect tales will finally be translated into standard Italian. Folklore research may be suffering from neglect, but there are numerous folklorists and scholars of fairy lore who are still trying to make the past usable for the present.

7

Fairy-Tale Collisions, or the Explosion of a Genre

According to [Theodor] Adorno, "culture" represents the interests and demands of the particular as against the homogenizing pressures of the "general"—and takes on an uncompromisingly critical stance towards the existing state of affairs, and its institutions. . . . The conflict is especially glaring, the clashes particularly bitter and relations singularly fraught with catastrophic consequences in the case of the fine arts—the foremost area of culture and the powerhouse of its dynamics. The fine arts are the most hyped up area of culture; for that reason they cannot resist making ever new forays into fresh territory and waging guerilla warfare in order to forge, pave and plot ever new pathways to be followed by the rest of human culture ("art is not a better, but an alternative existence," noted Joseph Brodsky, "it is not an attempt to escape from reality, but the opposite; an attempt to animate it"). Creators of art are by their very nature adversaries or competitors in activities which managers would, after all, prefer to make into their own prerogatives.

Zygmunt Bauman, *Culture in a Liquid Modern World* (2011)

Though it may seem somewhat strange to skip from the nineteenth century to the end of the twentieth and beginning of the twenty-first century to discuss the irresistibility and inexplicability of the fairy tale as a genre, I believe this chapter is appropriate because it will demonstrate just how expansive the fairy tale has become and also how unheard voices speak through the visual arts. Moreover, it also connects some of the subversive and moral aspects of the whalelike fairy tale in unimaginable ways that have paradoxically been imagined. It is difficult for us to resist the imaginable of fairy tales that take us seriously and realize the unimaginable.

One could possibly argue in fact that nothing is unimaginable these days. Everything has become so relative and liquid that the boundaries between reason and fantasy have collapsed. Consequently, it has become impossible for serious artists to accept the traditional structures and "goodness" of fairy tales in a globalized world that appears to have gone haywire. And yet there are profound meanings in the classical fairy tales that stem from human conflicts of the past and still speak to us. As I have tried to show, fairy tales embody worlds of naive morality that can still resonate with us if their underlying dramas are re-created and re-designed to counter as well as collide with our complex social realities. Collisions do not have to end in destruction. They are necessary to disrupt and confront clichés and bad habits. They are necessary to shake up the world and sharpen our gaze. In this regard, contemporary fairy-tale artworks, though often dystopian, still pulsate with utopian fervor.

From the nineteenth century up through the 1960s, visual artists generally celebrated the opulent and extraordinary optimism of the fairy tale in diverse works—paintings, sculptures, illustrations, photographs, cartoons, and films.[1] Their felicitous visions have dramatically shifted in the last fifty years, however. No longer do they interpret and portray fairy-tale texts, or conceive images of fairy-tale realms, as enchanting dreamworlds that lure the eye to bask in an idyllic setting or divert the viewer from the ugliness of the everyday world. On the contrary, contemporary artists have approached fairy-tale topics from a critical and skeptical perspective, intent on disturbing viewers and reminding them that the world is out of joint and fairy tales offer no alternative to drab reality. Their subversive views of the fairy tale collide with traditional norms and conventional expectations of fairy-tale representations as well as the false, rosy images that the Disney Corporation and other popularizing artists and publishers have disseminated for close to one hundred years. Indeed, they *defy* pulp-produced and sanitized images that publishers and media moguls have spread.

Paradoxically, to save the essence of hope in the fairy tale, contemporary visual artists have divested it of beautiful heroes and princesses along with cheerful scenes that delude viewers about the meaning of happiness, and at the same time they have endowed the fairy tale with a more profound meaning through the creation of dystopian, grotesque, macabre, and comic configurations. Their works collide with past fairy-tale conventions by engendering extraordinary, imaginative narratives through images that compel viewers to question whether it is possible to lead a so-called fairy-tale life in a rapidly changing world that appears to champion brutality and greed over beauty and kindness.

Fairy-tale collisions stem, in my opinion, from the conflicts of the 1960s, when the civil rights and antiwar movements, followed by a resurgence of feminism and educational and political reforms, led many young people to believe in the power of the imagination, revolutionary transformation, political justice, and utopian hope. Yet virtually none of the wishes and dreams of the 1960s' generation have been fulfilled. Instead, we wallow in a world filled with conflict, false promises, corruption, and material greed. As a consequence of the deterioration of social, political, and cultural conditions, numerous artists have employed the fairy tale, not to encourage utopian urges, but rather to pierce artificial illusions that make it difficult for people to comprehend what is happening to them. They ironically imply that viewers can come to terms with reality through their fairy-tale images that are intended to disturb or provoke anyone who encounters them. The encounter is clearly meant to be a collision—a fortuitous one—that will make viewers stop and think about the meaning of fairy tales and happiness. It is also an act of re-creation, for viewers are obliged to imagine their own reality and narratives while gazing at the image.

There are two major tendencies in fairy-tale re-creations and collisions that have struck my eye in the past decades—and there may be more, depending on how one views the different techniques and styles of the artists. The first tendency, what I call remaking and re-creating classic tales, which I discussed somewhat in chapter 3, concerns explicit references to well-known, if not canonical, fairy tales such as "Cinderella," "Bluebeard," "Little Red Riding Hood," "Snow White," "Beauty and the Beast," and "Hansel and Grethel" in the representation. Given the sexist disposition of most of these popular tales, the artists who use them explicitly as their subject matter tend to embody a startling critique of the stories in images that urge, if not drive, viewers to rethink what they know about the tales. The second tendency, what I label conflicted mosaics, consists of paintings, sculptures, and photographs that draw on an assortment of fairy-tale fragments to evoke a sense of wonder, if not bafflement. The images are otherworldly, bizarre, and lush. They are not associated with any one particular fairy tale but instead are fairy tales unto themselves. Most do not evoke utopia or promise happiness. They are simply otherness or realms of estrangement.

Both these tendencies are widespread in Europe and North America, and it is impossible to summarize the fascinating visual fairy-tale works that have been produced from 1970 to 2012 because hundreds, if not thousands, of images have been produced through painting, illustration, graphics, animation, design, digital images, photography, and so on. Therefore, I shall explore the significance of the two tendencies in fairy-tale collisions with a focus on the recent 2012 exhibit Fairy Tales, Monsters, and the Genetic Imagination, held at the Frist Center for the Visual Arts in Nashville, Tennessee, and I shall also comment on the works of many other talented artists who have been experimenting with the fairy tale along the same lines.[2] Here it is important to bear in mind the words of John McEwen, who notes that 70 percent of the artists in England who have become professional since the mid-1980s are women: "Art lies beyond age, race, or sex but is nonetheless affected by them all. The worldwide rise of women artists is the greatest artistic revolution of this age."[3]

In fact, in the particular case of fairy tales and other popular stories, the views of women artists and writers have clashed, and they continue to clash vividly with the mainstream production of these narratives: fairy tales are no longer what they seem to be and are no longer once upon a time. As collisions, they are part of our time.

Re-creating Classical Fairy Tales

In my opinion, the two most extraordinary contemporary artists who have totally revamped the manner in which viewers are to regard and interpret classical fairy tales and other popular stories are Paula Rego and Kiki Smith. Both dismantle literary and painterly norms and expectations with feminist humor and rage and cause spectators to rethink what they believe fairy tales mean and how they might re-create narratives in their own minds, just like Rego and Smith do. Or not! For there is a dark side to the visions of Rego and Smith.

In 1985 Rego stated:

> My favourite themes are power games and hierarchies. I always want to turn things on their heads, to upset the established order, to change heroines and idiots. If the story is "given," I take liberties with it to make it conform to my own experiences, and to be outrageous. At the same time as loving the stories I want to undermine them, like wanting to harm the person you love. Above all, though, I want to work with stories which emerge as I go along. It is something I have done in the past, and now I wish to do exactly that.[4]

Rego is indeed the storyteller/painter as subversive artist par excellence. Whether she depicts scenes based on Portuguese folk tales, nursery rhymes, classical fairy tales, or stories from her own experiences and dreams, she delves into their grotesque and surreal aspects to grasp as well as exorcise oppressive and troubling elements related to experiences that most people do not want revealed or discussed. Deep-seated wounds are reopened, many of which are buried in tales that are generally meant to soothe the anxious mind. They are colorfully resurrected and plastered in her works.

In 1989 she created the *Nursery Rhymes* series, published as a book with thirty-five images in etchings and aquatint, turning classical delightful verses for children into haunting scenes of cruelty, abuse, horror and comedy. Although Rego had already revealed in her early surrealistic paintings how she would challenge the fluid, realistic, and traditional forms of narrative, these engravings were among the first she created to serve as counterpoints to known texts and were her first experimental etchings. As Marina Warner remarks in her splendid introduction to *Nursery Rhymes*, Rego's tales "constantly surprise the viewer with unexpected reversals. Her sympathy with *naïveté*, her love of its double character, its weakness and its force, led her to nursery rhymes as a new source for her imagery."[5]

In *Little Miss Muffett, Three Blind Mice*, and *Who Killed Cock Robin?* the funny nonsense of the rhymed verses are offset by Kafkaesque images of insects and animals that are filled with dread. There is little to laugh about when the tentacles of a gigantic half-human beetle that threatens Little Miss Muffett. The farmer's wife seems more vicious and sadistic than the large blind mice. They are *not* a sight to see as they helplessly dance before a woman with a raised knife. The beetle, the fly, and various birds who seek to bury cock robin are more menacing and absurd than caring, and the sparrow appears to be proud of having killed the robin. The image in *Baa, Baa Black Sheep* is one of Rego's most provocative illustrations: instead of a boy asking, "Baa, baa, black sheep, have you any wool?" she portrays a young girl entranced by a gigantic ram, sitting on a stool and embracing her. Next to them are three bags of wool on a wooden shelf. The girl, whose face is averted from viewers, has one of her hands raised with three fingers showing, as if she is asking for the three bags of wool and making a bargain with the ram, who towers over her, holds her in a sexually fraught embrace, and gazes down at her with self-assurance. Has she made a sexual bargain for the wool? The girl is already enclosed and rubbing up against his genitals. In the background, as if a joke, a little boy who lives down the lane is watching the sensual engagement.

Rego's "grotesquely perverse" images of children's nursery rhymes hark back to the first great picture book of the nineteenth century, *Struwwelpeter* (1845), known in English as *Slovenly Peter*, by Heinrich Hoffmann, who drew sadistic cartoonlike illustrations of children being burned up by fire, blown away by a wind, or having their fingers cut off by a bogeyman. Hoffmann wanted to warn children about the consequences of disobedience through his illustrations. According to him, parents could do no wrong and had to be obeyed. Rego's images, in contrast, suggest that the world is discombobulated, and that childhood is a period of abuse and danger for children, for adults take a sadistic sexual pleasure in administering punishment. This is most clear in *The Old Woman Who Lived in a Shoe*. In this etching, a strong old woman whipping a bare-assed young boy who is stooped over takes center stage at the bottom of an open shoe that resembles a theater, with tiers of people either watching the whipping or involved in conversations. These people, adults and children, are clearly well-dressed, middle-class onlookers, who react differently to the beating—some with glee, some entranced, and some indifferent. Nobody is prompted to intercede. The brutal sadistic punishment is apparently pro forma, and even the boy appears to accept it. Rego makes the hideous nature of such abuse more shocking by revealing the callousness of the viewers.

Rego is a partisan artist. She takes sides—particularly for children and women—as she seeks to uncover the darkness of stories that we read and tell ourselves. But she does not depict people as helpless victims. Rather, they are enmeshed in distorted social relations. In 1992, she followed *Nursery Rhymes* with a probing exploration of J. M. Barrie's *Peter Pan* that turns the sentimental fairy-tale play into a fierce survival-of-the-fittest drama. Rego produced approximately twenty-five etchings and aquatints, from which fifteen were chosen for the publication of the Folio Society's book *Peter Pan, or the Boy Who Would Not Grow Up*, introduced by Andrew Birkin. Whereas Barrie made it clear in his play that the adventures in Neverland were all make-believe, Rego's illustrations suggest otherwise. They are filled with brutal images of a mermaid drowning Wendy, Tiger Lily mercilessly tied to a rock, Captain Hooks's menacing face peering into the underground home of the lost boys, cannibalistic pirates carrying off the naked lost boys, and Hook dueling a strange-looking Peter, who appears as a diminutive older man in typical dueling outfit while the lost boys are anxiously bound together in front of an alligator swallowing a dog.

Rego's largest major image in the collection, *Neverland*, depicts a small shadow cutout of Peter in the upper left and a full-grown Wendy in a night-gown descending in the air on to the island. It seems that they are landing in death's realm, for Captain Hook, whose face is the skull of death, is being drawn in a cart by peasant-looking pirates. Wendy is landing in the water next to the skull of an ox. Other animals, including the alligator and a hippopotamus, are swimming in the water alongside naked lost boys and Indians in canoes. All the play's characters are in this landscape that does not portend well for Wendy, despite the smile on her face. Clearly, Rego's idea of life in Neverland collides with Barrie's concept. Perhaps one could say that she exposes everything Barrie was afraid to write, for her images are brooding scenes from the play that evoke sadistic pleasure and disturbing urges. Most of the characters, never portrayed in an identical manner, are trapped, fighting, or mocked. Rego's re-creation of *Peter Pan* is a profound questioning of Barrie's own creation and an appropriation that calls for a new retelling.

This call for retelling is the salient feature of two of Rego's superb re-creations of "Snow White" and "Little Red Riding Hood." In 1995, she totally rendered the Disney image of Snow White banal with several lurid pastel images of a domesticated Snow White, who is brawny, solemn, and mute. Though Rego used different models to portray Snow White, they all tend to be homely middle-aged women, whose condition depends on the context in which they find themselves—humiliated as a stepmother puts panties on her; arrogant and vain as she holds one of her father's trophies, with the stepmother kneeling and grimacing in the background. In *Snow White Swallows the Poisoned Apple*, Rego depicts the violent death as a Snow White in the traditional Disney garb. But this Snow White appears to have been violated on a disheveled couch. She clutches her skirts as if she has lost not only her life but also her virginity. This is a Snow White who has not survived the ordeals she has been made to suffer, whether it be the jealousy of her stepmother or her own desire to be the fairest of them all.

Figure 3.
Paula Rego, *Snow White Swallows the Poisoned Apple*, 1995.
Pastel on paper, mounted on aluminum. Courtesy of Paula Rego
and the Marlborough Fine Art, London, Ltd. © Paula Rego.

In contrast to the Snow White series, Rego's Little Red Riding Hood series of 2003 represents an optimistic view of a mother and grandmother protecting a girl from male predators. In a series of six colored pastels, she comically illustrates how a mother dressed in red arrives to cut open, using a pitchfolk, the belly of a middle-aged man. Indeed, she is elegantly dressed, and in the final image, the mother sits in an office chair splendidly dressed with a wolf fur wrapped around her neck. As we shall see, numerous women artists have been drawn to "Little Red Riding Hood" because of the gender conflict, and because the Perrault and Grimm versions tend to make little girls responsible for their own rape and/or demise. Rego re-creates a version in which women are capable of saving themselves.

All her remakes of classical fairy tales—similar to Breillat's remake of "Bluebeard" in chapter 3—question how women and children are raised and treated and project borderline images of loving care and brutality, joy in life and sadistic punishment. The complex sensual ambiguity of human behavior is at the heart of other fairy-tale re-creations such as *The Little Mermaid* (2003), a pastel on paper that depicts a grown woman in a bathing suit as refuse on a beach, or the three Pinocchio pastels on paper, which blur the affection of the Blue Fairy and Gepetto for a lifelike boy, or *Prince Pig's Courtship* (2006), a colored lithograph based on Straparola's "The Pig Prince," marking the oppression of a disheartened woman. Rego bores into the troubled psyches of the characters of her tales and is not afraid to spill blood and guts in her re-creations.

This is also true of Smith as subversive artist and storyteller, who has often used fairy-tale motifs in her works. When I think of her artistic re-creations, I think of blood, the body, rupture, and movement. Nothing ever stays still or fits exactly into our frame of reference in her artworks. Whatever medium she uses, and wherever she travels literally and figuratively, she scatters parts of bodies, objects, and stories all over studios, museums, galleries, books, and other places. The British term for gypsy in English is traveler, and of course, gypsies are wonderful storytellers, subversive and provocative. In many ways, Smith is the consummate traveler as artist. She is elusive and keeps all her tales open ended.

Smith tells all sorts of stories through her art, and they keep changing as the modalities of her art change. In the case of the fairy tale, her work is in keeping with the second phase of feminist and postmodern writers and illustrators of fairy tales that became productive in the 1980s, especially Angela Carter, Tanith Lee, and Robert Coover, whose works are disconcerting, and unsettle our views and understanding of traditional tales. Like these writers, Smith focuses on bodies and blood, fluidity and flexibility, surprising formations through rearrangement of object relations, and the provocation of new associations within spectators who are challenged and might be stimulated to form their own stories. Take the tale of "Little Red Riding Hood." How is a viewer to read "Little Red Riding Hood" after viewing Smith's installation *Telling Tales* (2001) or the exhibit Prints, Books, and Things (2003)? Are the sculptures, color photographs, paintings, drawings, stop animation, and lithographs related? That is, do they tell a single, carefully conceived, neatly structured story? I would argue no, with one proviso. Since the same artist, who has been fascinated by the "Little Red Riding Hood" story and other fairy tales such as "Sleeping Beauty" and "Rumpelstiltskin" for the past twenty-five years, has created these works, there are bound to be connections between them. But I would argue that each artwork tells a different story, and they all tell the story of Little Red Riding Hood anew, each time we gaze at the images.

It is well known that Little Red Riding Hood in the two classical versions by Perrault and the Grimms is not a heroine. She is more of a wimp. Either she stupidly agrees to an assignation with the hungry wolf and thus is complicit in her own rape/violation and death (Perrault), or she needs the help of a hunter to free her from the wolf's belly (Grimm). This is not Smith's Red Riding at all, and like Carter and the best fairy-tale writers, she provides us with multiple versions of Red Riding Hood not simply as heroic but also fleshed out in different contexts, suggesting a variant to the traditional girl.

In her stunning four-feet-high sculpture *Daughter* (1999), cocreated with Margaret De Wys and made out of nepal paper, bubble wrap, methyl cellulose, hair, fabric, and glass, we are presented with a young girl wearing a red wool cape and hood that contrast with her white dress. Wild strands of hair cover her face and head—perhaps the wolf's fur. Her mouth is slightly open, and her hazel eyes glance upward as if she were somewhat desolate, perhaps lost. She is transfixed, not moving. Who is she? A mutant? The daughter of Little Red Riding Hood and the wolf? Was Little Red Riding Hood not harmed?

The wolves are rarely vicious or dangerous in Smith's images. In the glass paintings of *Gang of Girls and Pack of Wolves* (1999), the bronze sculpture *Wolf* (2000), and the lithographs *Companions* (2001), the wolves are noble, sturdy, and larger than life, but more friendly and protective than threatening. They remind me of the wolf in Carter's "The Company of Wolves," which ends with the female protagonist holding the wolf in her arms after having apparently tamed him. In her work, Smith is asking, What is the relationship of the wolves to young women? Are wolves, wolves, not predatory men? Why have we defamed wolves? Perhaps the wolves as wolves protect young women? Perhaps women and young women were born with blood-red hoods and capes from wolves, as is suggested in the lithograph *Born* (2002)? The wolf's hair appears to stream into the hairy capes and hoods of mother and daughter like blood or red flames. Smith relates several of her pieces such as *Rapture* (2002) to the life of Saint Genevieve, the patron saint of Paris, said to have been born from a wolf's womb.[6] If women are born of wolves, they may inherit their intrepid character. They are certainly not fearful, and neither is Smith in the enigmatic photos of herself as a witch dressed in black in *Sleeping Witch* (2000), nor are the nude women in the *Spinster Series I and II* (2002) the typical miller's daughters. Though they appear to be tied to their spinning wheels, they have a quiet confidence about them.

Smith's transformation of the female protagonists of fairy tales into confident and self-possessed women is brought about by a transformation of their bodies, dress, function, and format along with their relationship to their environments. In her *Blue Print Series* (1999), consisting of fifteen etchings and aquatints, she portrayed a disturbed Dorothy from *The Wizard of Oz*, reflecting not only the dilemmas of the young girl swept off to a strange land but also the struggles of Judy Garland, for Dorothy is Judy and Judy is Dorothy, US fairy-tale icons of the twentieth century. In two other etchings based on

Figure 4.
Kiki Smith, *Born*, 2002. Lithograph, 68 x 56 in. Photo courtesy
Universal Limited Art Editions, Inc. © Kiki Smith and Universal
Limited Art Editions, Inc.

Lewis Carroll's *Alice's Adventures Under Ground*, created in 2000 and 2002,
Alice appears in two contexts: in the first engraving she appears in a pool of
her own tears, anxiously fleeing some danger that obviously has frightened
a strange group of fowls and animals; in the second she sits on a hill and
watches a flock of geese fly away from her. It is not clear why, but this Alice
seems self-composed.

In each instance, in the etchings of Dorothy and Alice, Smith wants us to wonder what is bothering the girls, and whether they will resolve an apparent dilemma. The re-creations of Dorothy and Alice invite us to rethink the stories that we have been told about each girl. The tales we conceive may not be happy, but like the texts of many feminist writers and critics, they will likely subvert what we have generally been conditioned to believe as universal stories that are good for our children and own souls—stories that many believe should not be touched. Feminist artists (no matter how political they may or may not be) are always touching things and messing them up. Smith has a magic touch that disturbs and enchants. She continually changes the female figures of fairy tales, myths, and religious legends, keeps them moving, to reveal their multidimensionality, and does not leave out the blood and gore. Like Rego, she is attracted to the dark and mysterious side of fairy tales and feels compelled to retell them with a feminist critique.

This critique is evident in numerous re-creations of fairy tales. For example, although Claire Prussian's fairy-tale paintings, which consist of two-part digital pieces, iris prints hung on top of and next to ornate wallpaper with patterns similar to the focus of the print, are not optimistic, they are shockingly enlightening insofar as they compel the viewer to reflect on the glib happiness in fairy tales and nursery rhymes. Prussian has written on her Web site: "I am also concerned with the imagery in patterns and what it tells us historically. Recently I completed a series based on the dark side of nursery rhymes and fairy tales. It is interesting that people protect their children from what they perceive to be unpleasant, yet the subject of these poems and stories is anything but unpleasant."[7]

On a bright sunny day, Jack is threatened by a gigantic hand, which will rip him out of a flowery setting and perhaps demolish him as his mother looks on. Hansel ends up locked in a cage, and Grethel stands by helplessly. A forlorn Cinderella leans against a garden wall with a broom and without a prince as she watches her stepsisters about to have their eyes pecked out. A young woman, who does not look like a princess, looks askance at a gigantic phallic frog that palms a golden ball as he emerges from a covered well. She is dressed in modern apparel and does not appear to be a princess, even though there is a castle in the background. Little Red Riding Hood emerges from the bloody belly of the wolf on a linoleum black-and-white checkered floor, saved by a massive hand holding a bloody knife. Perhaps, after this bloody deed, she may not really be saved. Prussian's images question whether happiness is possible in a savage world that appears covered up by the banality of homey wallpaper. In many respects, she deflowers tales meant to deceive us by their innocent appearance.

In 2004, the New Zealand painter Sharon Singer also produced an extraordinary body of oil paintings that retell many well-known fairy tales, offering brilliant and often disturbing insights into how they relate to the momentous changes in our contemporary chaotic world, marked by globalized violence,

Figure 5.
Claire Prussian, *Cinderella*, 1998. The caption reads,
"A two-part digital iris print." Courtesy of Claire Prussian.

rapid movement, and the breakdown of community and identity. Singer's images, or better yet, her imaginings of fairy tales and children's dolls, are exotic projections that refuse to yield to the destructive tendencies of our times. They resonate in splendid color, abnormal shapes, and distorted forms that express startling associations with past and present stories, and thus generate new stories that necessitate transformation.

Little Dread Riding Hood, for instance, recalls the familiar tale of a naive girl gobbled up by a wolf, but this alarming image gives the story a radically different slant. Singer's "Dread" Riding Hood is here a feisty young woman with dreadlocks seemingly riding on a wolf, tamed and muzzled. It is unclear whether she is actually riding him because she is wearing skates, and the wolf appears to be more like a hobbyhorse than anything else, just as her basket appears to carry trinkets instead of food to nourish her granny. Different hues of "redlike blood" fuse to add luster to a forceful young woman who is to be reckoned with, perhaps "dreaded," because of her courage. On the other hand, Singer's images of "Bluebeard" or "Jack and the Beanstalk" tend to minimize dread. The blue feathers of Bluebeard's beard along with his pierced ears, white hair, and narrow features make him seem more like a homeless, lonely man than a serial killer. Jack's small head atop a giant's torso implies that the relationship between big and small, power and powerlessness, is symbiotic. Jack seems out of place and yet attached. The vast pale blue gray violet background suggests a realm of unlimited space in which one could easily lose oneself. Singer's surrealist paintings are often haunting images of well-known fairy-tale characters and creatures lost in a maze. The tales she retells through her paintings are baffling and enigmatic, prodding our curiosity, and questioning our "normal" views of art and storytelling.

It is interesting to note that almost all the contemporary feminist artists who have been concerned with fairy tales have focused on revising "Little Red Riding Hood" because it is the most popular memetic tale that enunciates the gender conflict and alludes to the problem of rape.[8] An entire book, *Aftérouge* (2006), has been devoted to the collective memory of artists and writers who have been affected by "Little Red Riding Hood."[9]

Aside from this collective endeavor, individual artists such as Vanessa Jane Phaff produced thirty-six silk screens on canvas in 2002 that retell the story of "Little Red Riding Hood" in an unusual graphic style recalling a children's picture book, except here the girl is courageous and smart, and eventually appears to tame the wolf and sleep with him in bed. A vibrant feisty Little Red Riding Hood can be found on the Deviant Art Web site, where there are four images of "Little Red Riding Hood," by three male conceptual artists, Shane Madden (Canada), Jerry Cai (Canada), and Ivik Nier (Russia).[10] Donna Leishman, a Scottish graphic and digital artist, has produced two dissonant and subversive digital revisions of "Little Red Riding Hood" and "Bluebeard," challenging the way we view, read, and hear classical fairy tales while permitting us to intervene in the narrative.[11] Emma SanCartier, a Canadian artist,

Figure 6.
Sharon Singer, *Little Dread Riding Hood*, 2005.
Oil on canvas, 59 1/10 x 52 in.
Courtesy of Sharon K. Singer.

provided a Red Riding Hood illustration for the cover of *PRISM international*, which recalls Singer's tantalizing oil painting. In SanCartier's piece, a young woman is dressed in a red duffle coat and is walking a submissive wolf—a sign of changing times?[12] Also in 2010, Sarah McRae Morton produced a unique oil painting, *Red Riding and Goldie Locks Encounter Each Other and Scandinavian Animals*, for her exhibition the Marrow of Tradition.[13] Here, too, the wolf appears harmless as Red Riding Hood meets Goldie Locks in a surreal room filled with a deer and other animals.

The Snow White images are, of course, different but just as subversive. Elena Sisto's portrait *Snow White* (1998), in oil on canvas, depicts a fair-faced head on a pillow looking more like a comatose zombie than a beautiful princess. Dina Goldstein, a Canadian photographer, produced a fascinating photo series, *Fallen Princesses*, in 2009 that comments critically on the Disney world and raises many questions about the lives women are expected to lead versus their actual lives.[14] In her macabre portrayal of Snow White, she depicts the gruesome fate of the young woman, who is the spitting image of Disney's Barbie heroine. She stands in the middle of a suburban living room holding two of her children in diapers, one crying, and the other sucking her thumb. Another daughter is pulling on Snow White's skirt, while a fourth is crawling in a corner of the room. A tiny bulldog is sniffing the ground. Snow White stares solemnly into the camera while her princelike husband sits on an easy chair and watches a sporting event on television. He is holding a can of beer and is totally detached from his family. Goldstein's provocative photos are only the tip of the iceberg with regard to fairy-tale experimentation by photographers.

For instance, Cindy Sherman has produced two series of photographs, *Fairy Tales* (1985) and *Disasters* (1986–89), to bring out the dark, macabre side of fairy tales.[15] Sherman uses dummies and protheses in grotesque positions, emphasizing the sexual disintegration and perverse aspects of fairy tales, viewed as ugly and grim. She does not allude to particular fairy tales. Rather, synthetic bodies are mashed into the ground in scenes that recall battlefields. Sherman's perspective on fairy tales is nightmarish.

In some respects, though, the images of Miwa Yanagi's *Fairy Tale* series (2004–6) are more disturbing.[16] Yanagi uses young mixed-race girls as her models in posed black-and-white photos—scenes taken largely from the Grimms' tales, but given a Gothic, chilling interpretation. She focuses on "Hansel and Grethel," "Snow White," "Cinderella," and "Sleeping Beauty" and emphasizes the struggle between young and old. Some of the girls use Playtex masks and wigs that make them appear to be hideous old figures, confronting beautiful innocent girls in bitter combat. Yanagi claims that there is beauty in cruelty, and the desperate scenes she photographs bring out the misogyny in our culture and subvert stereotypes.

Polixeni Papapetrou also employs young children in her posed color photographs.[17] Yet unlike Yanagi, she is more optimistic and seeks to display

Figure 7.
Dina Goldstein, *Snowy*, 2009. Photo.
Part of the *Fallen Princesses* series.
Courtesy of Dina Goldstein.

the innocence of childhood. In a series of fairy-tale photos, in which she often uses her own daughter Olimpia, she depicts sweet, innocent children in front of painted backdrops to contrast the naturalness of the young protagonists with the artificiality of the fairy tale. The opposition is striking in *The Witch's House* (2003), *The Girl Who Trod on a Loaf as Not to Spoil Her Shoes* (2005), and *The Little Match Girl* (2005). Papapetrou has also created an intriguing series of photos, *Wonderland* (2003–4), stressing the playful nature of Olimpia, dressed as Alice in Victorian garb. Olimpia confronts the characters of Carroll's fairy-tale novel painted on backdrops and interrogates their foibles.

Of course, other talented artists have concentrated on repicturing classical fairy tales. Judith Schaechter, a brilliant stained-glass artist, has created all sorts of fascinating fairy-tale images. One of them, *The Fisherman's Wife*, is a fabulous retelling of the Grimms' tale. Carrie Ann Baade, an American painter of surrealist phantasmagorias, has created a tearful princess holding hands with an old-fashioned prince whose head is topped by a bulging frog. Rima Staines, a talented British artist, has experimented with portraying different images of Baba Yaga, Red Riding Hood's grandmother, and the witch in

"Hansel and Grethel." To her mind, they are all related and part of one deity. The old woman

> appears as an incarnation of the crone or winter aspect of the female deities of old. She is the carrier of wisdom, the guardian of the life and death gates, the overseer of the cold months, and the stewardess of story. We talk nowadays of long, old, particularly northern, tales as Sagas. But in some quarters it is believed that this word saga was once the feminine of the word sage and that the written sagas of Scandinavia were originally sacred histories kept by female sagas or "sayers." Thus storytelling and wisdom-keeping were entwined in one person: "She who Speaks"—the Oracular Priestess. Her appearance in orally passed down fairy tales seems to stress the importance of story for gaining and nurturing wisdom.[18]

Her image of Baba Yaga appears at the beginning of chapter 4.

Aside from old witches and wise women, the young fairy-tale figure of Alice haunts the imagination of many artists. I briefly mentioned Smith's and Papapetrou's work with Alice. The experimental photographer Anna Gaskell also created two series of provocative images based on *Alice in Wonderland*: *Wonder* (1996–97) and *Override* (1997). Her staged scenes of preadolescent girls captured in strange contexts reveal the disturbed condition of the perplexed Alice. It appears as if Alice will never overcome the trauma of falling down the rabbit hole. Another image, *Hide* (1998), is based on Perrault's tale of incest, "The Donkey-Skin," and is often mistakenly referred to as a Grimms' tale, "The Magic Donkey," which does not exist. What does exist are the ominous depictions of parts of adolescent girls' bodies that suggest abuse and manipulation. In most fairy tales about incest the father is generally forgiven, but there is no forgiveness in these photos, just uncertainty about the identity of the young girls, and why they are posed in strange positions that provoke viewers to reflect on manipulation.

Conflicted Mosaics

Whereas the re-created fairy-tale artworks always cite well-known narratives, the fairy-tale mosaics generally project other worlds filled with fantastic motifs that generally suggest happiness in classical tales. Yet happiness appears to be evasive in these mosaics. The diverse images created by Meghan Boody, Frank Moore, Saya Woolfalk, Walter Martin and Paloma Muñoz, Marcel Dzama, Tracey Moffat, and Trenton Doyle Hancock are experimental compositions that collide with traditional images of fairy-tale settings while offering variations on the theme of fairy-tale otherness.

Boody has produced several series of extraordinary photos in which strange characters are placed in worlds in which they do not fit. For instance, in the bizarre pictures of *Incident at the Reformatory* (1995), human beings and animals assume erotic or everyday poses in baroque palatial settings made to appear ridiculous, for the animals are unsuitable in these fancy human constructions, and the humans pose in outrageous positions. In the series *My Doll* (1996), Boody shifts the setting for her provocative arrangements to the icy-white and frigid Arctic region and satirically alludes to several of Andersen's fairy tales, especially "The Snow Queen." In the six staged photos, prepubescent girls are pictured in snowscapes playing strange games or mingling with gigantic animals—a walrus and a prehistoric elephant as well as a mermaid. The young people are somber and seem to be indifferent to the icy waters and climate. They are out of place in an inclement world.

In a statement about another series, *Henry's Wives* (1997), Boody remarks: "Like a sorcerer selecting the perfect blend of sacrificial ingredients for his brother, Henry succeeds in sampling six distant varieties of womanhood. He seems to have hit upon a winning combination. The archetypes typically ascribed to each (i.e. the Betrayed Wife, the Temptress, the Saint, the Sister, the Bad Girl and the Mother) have served to lodge their images firmly in the collective psyche, casting a divine aura upon six women unhappy in love."[19] She likens Henry VIII to a "bellicose Bluebeard," and the six photos of the queens tend to be satirical portraits of the women who succumbed to a decadent king, just the opposite of many queens and princesses in classical fairy tales. In the final image of the series, *In the Garden So Green*, Boody appears to delight sadistically in the fate of the princesses and King Henry. It seems as though Henry as the frog king has drowned or is dying from swallowing too many golden balls (oranges). The garden is somewhat dilapidated. The five queens along with a nude girl on top of a fountain have different reactions to the frog's condition, from indifference or surprise to concern. Clearly, Boody's title plays ironically with the notion of some kind of verdant fairy-tale garden that she pictures more like a backyard disrepair populated by bizarre women caught up in comic antics.

While Boody tends to favor placing girls and women in unusual contexts that reveal oppressive conditions, Moore's work, especially his environmental oil paintings, vacillate between hopeful futurist scenes and dystopian images that reveal how destructive humans can be to the environment. *Oz* (1999–2000), a large oil painting, is a counterpoint to the optimism of L. Frank Baum's *The Wonderful Wizard of Oz*. Not only does Moore depict how humans are ruining the earth, but he also does not shy away from portraying animal abuse. His Oz is totally dystopian and clashes with Baum's hopeful vision of another world that would be more humane and egalitarian. In contrast Woolfalk projects a flourishing, flowery, utopian world in her pulsating video *Ethnography of No Place* (2007–8), created with the anthropologist Rachel Lears. The lushly colored images that keep changing are naive imaginings of the future. One of her major influences is Carroll's *Alice in Wonderland*, and in her multimedia work she combines painting, sculpture, live performance, and toys to offer a softer and more hopeful world than the one encountered by Alice.

But there is little utopianism in the island panoramas and traveler's snow globe series created by Martin and Muñoz; their winter fairylike images are deceptively beautiful because the eerie tiny figurines perform odd acts and are trapped or else traveling to nowhere. There is no sense of community in the globalized scenes, just stark alienation. In an interview about their snow globes that appeared in the *Penleaf* in 2008, Martin and Muñoz stated,

> I think we saw in the format of these commonplace kitsch objects a latent potential to express and explore aspects of the human condition that we were, and are still trying to come to terms with. The globe is an encapsulator. When all is said and done, it is essentially a novel framing device particularly well suited for the kinds of scenes we imagined. The sense of isolation and helplessness that permeates our narrative scenes is partly due to the intrinsic power of the snow globe format to encapsulate, miniaturize, and distort its subject matter.[20]

Generally speaking, the snow globes contain serene scenes and characters and are associated with joyful childhood. Shake a globe, and the snowflakes fall gently. The world remains at peace with itself. This is not the case in the Martin and Muñoz snow globes. In some of the globes, Humpty Dumpty (the egg) is all alone and perched dangerously, about to fall into the snow; a tiny traveler approaches two enormous white rabbits, which seem to be more like predators on a snow-covered cliff that features a barren tree; on a snow-covered island with factory-like smokestacks, a black sheep races away from a herd of white sheep that are being transported to the mainland to be slaughtered; a miniature man appears to force a woman on to a glazier. These are all puzzling images. In the humorous c-print on Plexiglas, *The Mail Boat* (2007), some strange pack animals are carrying the mail to a church while off to the side a man dressed in white speaks to a half man/half horse. There is an icy rock formation to the right, a man in red is jumping off the peak of a rock, and two businessmen in shirt and tie carry briefcases and appear to be discussing something on flat rock. Beneath them, two men with horse heads are also in conversation. And so it goes. Parody and pain form the contours of the snow globes and other artworks of Martin and Muñoz. Their fairy-tale collisions are weird realms that do not augur harmony and happiness.

And certainly, Dzama's wood-glazed ceramic sculptures do not promise much happiness either. In the ironic, *Welcome to the Land of the Bat* (2008), the cute but poaching white bats hover over a dying bear in a black background. There is something terrifyingly ominous about this scene. Are the bats descending like vultures to eat the helpless dark-blue animal? Who are these "angelic" bats that thrive on a wounded creature? The original title for this diorama was *Infidels*, designating an explicit political turn in Dzama's works. As Joseph Wolin observes,

> We might unpack allusions to current events from many of Dzama's new works, from the white bloodsuckers denoted as unbelievers (*Welcome to the Land of the Bat*) to a showcase of boyishly unabashed dissemblers (*La Verdad Está Muerta*) to the confluence of figures that can only be read as terrorists with some sort of sexualized power dynamic (*The Underground*). Dzama appears to have left behind the whimsy of his earlier, hermetic creations for a darker mode that acknowledges the darker world outside.[21]

Even the cute Pinocchio, for example, assumes a more sinister shape in *Room Full of Liars* (2008), a direct reference to the Bush government, in which the eight puppets exhibit growing noses, indicating the continual production of lies and corruption that extends into the present. Most disturbing is the ceramic diorama, *First Born* (2008), in which a gigantic bear tightly embraces a woman in a white dress yet grasps a baseball bat in his hand, while a dapper man dressed in a suit holds the bear's arm high. The bear appears to have knocked off the male heads like baseball balls, and a demure woman dressed in red looks on without an expression. Is the big gray-black bear a symbol of Barack Obama, who has arrived on the scene to knock off heads and mop up the Pinocchios of the past? Being born new in the United States might, it seems to Dzama, mean that there will be a clash with the old world, and his art appears to be on a collision course with the reality that he critiques and apparently wants to change.

Other contemporary artists such as Moffat and Hancock have also reformed fairy-tale worlds in compositions bound on a collision with traditional aesthetics and a status quo sensibility. In three of the images of her 2000 photo silk screen series, *Invocations*, Moffat depicts anxious trees that appear to guard the entrance to a dimly lit dense forest where a witch may be lurking to devour a young girl—a strong hint of "Hansel and Grethel." And yet in the twelfth invocation, a young girl dressed in a white nightgown enters the forest and seems to be frightening the gnarled trees. Perhaps the girl will change the traditional narrative of "Hansel and Grethel" and transform the forest by herself? Perhaps she will learn to appreciate the forest? Moffat opens the forest to a psychodramatic exploration.

Hancock, influenced strongly by expressionism, surrealism, the Bible, and comic books, has developed another fairy-tale narrative in his artworks, which include drawings, collages, oil paintings, and installations. Since the beginning of the twenty-first century, he has continuously worked on a fantasy that he calls *The Story of the Mounds*. Using different modalities of art, Hancock depicts the battle between half-human, half-plant mutants called Mounds and the Vegans, evil creatures, who want to destroy all the Mounds. It is unclear who will triumph at the end of Hancock's narrative, but his paintings such as

Meddler (2008), a mixed media on paper, reveal that the world is never safe from intruders, who haunt his visions and narratives of other worlds.

Whether contemporary artists re-create traditional fairy tales or shape their own fairy-tale mosaics, their works unquestionably represent a discontent with the way their actual realities are configured and how social arrangements have been deformed. In fact, dissonance is the key to understanding all their works, especially those with fairy-tale motifs. This is why the recent fairy-tale artworks are so startling. Fairy tales originated and derived from wish fulfillment coupled with a desire for other moral worlds. They had always been told, serving to compensate for the impoverished lives and desperate struggles of many people. Whatever the outcome of a fairy tale, there was some sort of hope for a miraculous change. There still may be hope in the fairy-tale collisions of contemporary artists, but it is tempered by the piercing truths of their imaginative visions that compel us to re-create traditional narratives and rethink the course our lives have taken.

Appendix A

Sensationalist Scholarship:
A "New" History of Fairy Tales

In early modern Europe, then, what was a mixed-media environment characterized by talking and manuscripts became even more mixed by the addition of mass print. Again, we need to stress that mass print did not replace talking or manuscripts. Major media generally accumulate; they do not supplant one another. We also should emphasize that mass print did not at any point or in any place become the predominant mode of communications. For several centuries after the introduction of mass print, literacy rates remained low. People who can't read—and that was the majority of the European population until the late nineteenth century—do not read manuscripts or printed texts. They talk. Orality, though not primary orality, survived well into the modern era even where print and literacy spread fastest and penetrated most deeply. And even among people who were literate, talking and manuscripts hardly disappeared once printing and printed matter became widely available. For many—and perhaps even most—purposes it remained easier to talk to someone than to write a note to them, and easier to write a note to them than to print one.

—Marshall Poe, *A History of Communications* (2011)

The Historical Background to the Publication
of *A New History of Fairy Tales*

On July 30, 2005, Ruth Bottigheimer upset many of the folklorists attending the Fourteenth Congress of the International Society for Folk Narrative Theory in Tartu, Estonia, by delivering a paper titled "Fairy Tale Origins, Fairy Tale Dissemination, and Folk Narrative Theory," which dismissed the oral tradition as providing the source of literary fairy tales and proclaimed that Straparola was the inventor of the fairy-tale genre.* Her paper was largely based on her book *Fairy Godfather: Straparola, Venice, and the Fairy Tale* (2002). Until Bottigheimer had promoted Straparola to the position of "god" of the fairy tales, few scholars had paid much attention to the anonymous Italian author, whose collection of stories, *Le piacevoli notti* (*The Pleasant Nights*), published in two volumes, contain about fourteen eclectic fairy tales and fifty-nine stories with riddles.[1] A "best seller" in its time, its allure can be attributed to several factors, as I pointed out in *Fairy Tales and the Art of Subversion*:

> His use of erotic and obscene riddles, his mastery of polite Italian used by narrators in the frame narrative, his introduction of plain earthly language into the stories, the critical view of the power struggles in Italian society and lack of moralistic preaching, his introduction of fourteen unusual fairy tales into the collection, and his interest in magic, unpredictable events, duplicity, and the supernatural. Similar to Boccaccio, Straparola exhibited an irreverence for authorities, and the frame narrative reveals a political tension and somewhat ironic if not pessimistic outlook on the possibilities of living a harmonious happy ever after life.[2]

It must be said, however, that Straparola was not a great stylist; he plagiarized many Latin tales, translating them into the vernacular Italian, and imitated contemporary writers. The foremost Straparola scholar in Italy, Donato Pirovano, who edited the definitive contemporary edition of *Le piacevoli notti*, remarks about Straparola's linguistics:

> In this general average tone, where there are no centrifugal impulses and extremes (it has already been pointed out how Straparola tended to tone down the lexical expressionism of Morlini), the dialect expression and the Latin cast, together with the phonetic variants and frequent hyper-corrections, reveal the strong linguistic accomplishment of the author in the direction of the models of the novella tradition and are the tell-tale of a more general narrative project directed at bringing about a literary consecration of the fairy tale of the oral tradition.[3]

Therefore, Bottigheimer's claims in her paper delivered in Tartu to folklorists, who generally subscribe to a theory of orality as the source of the literary fairy tale, were bound to be provocative.

----

*I am including two book reviews, of works by Ruth Bottigheimer and Willem de Blécourt, as appendixes so as not to distract readers from exploring my chapters on how difficult it is to explain the irresistible and inexplicable fairy tale. I did not want to weigh down my chapters by long critiques of these books. Yet I feel compelled to deal with the books here at some length because they reflect what I see as worrisome tendencies in fairy-tale scholarship. In particular, I am concerned that young students might be misled by what I'll argue are reductionist theses. Sometimes readers gloss over appendixes. I hope that in this case, they will not do so, and that they will also forgive me if I am a bit harsh in my critique.

Ben-Amos, one of the foremost folklorists in the world, decided to give her paper and book, *Fairy Godfather*, another hearing and organized a roundtable, the European Fairy Tale Tradition: Between Orality and Literacy, for the 2006 fall meeting of the American Folklore Society in Milwaukee. He invited Jan Ziolkowski, a renowned medievalist, and Francisco Vaz da Silva, a noted European anthropologist, to comment on Bottigheimer's book, which Ben-Amos also critically reviewed during the roundtable. Bottigheimer was allowed time to respond to their papers. All the papers from this session were revised and expanded into articles, published by the *Journal of American Folklore* in summer 2010.[4] The major points of contention were Bottigheimer's claims that Straparola was the founder of the fairy-tale narrative, described as a "rise tale," reflecting the rise of the mercantile and bourgeois classes; Straparola's tales set a model for other writers, especially the French; it was through print literature that tales were disseminated and reached the peasantry, who had not been intelligent enough to create their own wonder tales; and Straparola lived and worked in Venice, catering to a wide circle of artisans, who were literate. Though nothing is known about Straparola, such as where he was born, where he lived, or what his profession was, Bottigheimer made it seem that she knew everything about him and defended her biography, which the roundtable participants seriously questioned.

Responses to *Fairy Godfather*

As Ziolkowski, Vaz da Silva, and Ben-Amos demonstrate in their lengthy essays, Bottigheimer's *Fairy Godfather: Straparola, Venice, and the Fairy Tale* is one of the most narrow, positivist studies of folklore and fairy tales ever produced. Ziolkowski begins his essay by stating, "The book will not become a landmark in folkloristics in general, and only time will tell if it has a lasting impact even within fairy-tale studies."[5]

Ziolkowski, author of the comprehensive study *Fairy Tales from before Fairy Tales: The Medieval Latin Past of Wonderful Lies* (2007), chastises Bottigheimer for ignoring numerous Latin texts that have their origins in an oral tradition and were fairy tales before tales were given labels. According to him, Bottigheimer ignored evidence that the Greeks and Romans as well as other European, Asian, and African people were telling tales during the pre-Christian era and early antiquity, laying the foundation for a literary genre that gradually flowered in Paris, *not in Italy*, during the 1690s, when the sociocultural conditions were more favorable than in Italy for designating certain tale types as belonging to the fairy-tale genre. The narrative sequence of Bottigheimer's rise tales, which she attributes to Straparola, can be read differently and expanded to comprehend many other tale types and narrative patterns. But by limiting just fourteen of Straparola's tales to a tight definition, what Ziolkowski calls a "perverse agenda," Bottigheimer overlooks the wide range of different kinds of oral wonder tales that Straparola drew on to write his tales.[6] Aside from his own significant work, Ziolkowski cites other studies, such as *Formes médiévales du conte merveilleux* (1989), edited by Jacques Berlioz, Claude Brémond, and Catherine Velay-Vallantin, and *Märchen und mittelalterliche Literaturtradition* (1995) by Clausen-Stolzenberg, to show that oral tales existed and at times informed numerous literary romances, lais, poems, and exemplas. Yet as Ziolkowski notes,

> Tradition of the oral sort turns out to be a phenomenon Bottigheimer presents as being hopelessly elusive before the introduction of phonographic recording in the 1870s. A slogan, probably around fifty years old and quaint in ways that would have disconcerted its original exponents, advocates that we "Question Authority," but Bottigheimer follows a simpler (and possibly simplistic) principle of "Question Orality." In her view, not only is it pointless to conjecture about oral traditional literature before unambiguous records of it survive, but in addition it is wrongheaded to suppose that oral tale-telling ever made a creative contribution to the fairy-tale tradition as she defines it in the subtitle of her book.[7]

In general, Ziolkowski does not argue for privileging the oral over literature but rather against positivist approaches such as that used by Bottigheimer, who relies on strict divisions and absolutes along with a speculative history. Moreover, he contends that

> we have an obligation to approach each and every story with an open eye to possible orality lurking behind literature as well as to possible literature behind orality. Old dichotomies have broken down over the past decades in the understanding of medieval literature: it has been recognized that Latin texts from the Middle Ages could have features indebted to orality, popular culture, and secular tastes, while the literary products of medieval vernaculars could be literate, learned, and Christian.[8]

Complementing Ziolkowski's essay, which focuses on Bottigheimer's rejection of oral wonder tales that stem from antiquity, the Middle Ages, and Eastern traditions, Vaz da Silva questions the accuracy and authenticity of Bottigheimer's biographical depiction of Straparola, showing how she created a fictitious biography depicting the unknown Italian author as a fairy-tale hero inventing fairy tales. Moreover, he demonstrates that she invented her own history of storytelling that excludes 95 percent of the European population from creating and disseminating tales in an oral tradition. As Pirovano explains:

> The biography of Giovan Francesco Straparola still remains an unfathomable mystery. The almost absolute absence—at least in the present state of research—of documents that concern him is aggravated by the

impossibility of extracting definite facts about his life from his works. There are only vague hints that give access to conjectural hypotheses in which various scholars of the past centuries have exerted themselves, certainly in a noble but fruitless way. Frequently they managed to reconstruct Straparola's life, but these reconstructions were rarely persuasive if not groundless.[9]

Vaz da Silva also points out the contradictions in Bottigheimer's claim that Straparola's tales appealed to an urban and artisan readership, but ultimately nourished Europe's hungry folk imagination even though his stories were filled with reference to upper social classes in the sixteenth and seventeenth centuries. He asks:

> If there is a congruence between plot success and the preoccupations of the audience, then why would tales crafted for the specific situation of an urban Venetian readership become the characteristic lore of illiterate rustics across Europe and beyond? And why would tales offering imaginary escape from all-too-real poverty register success among the upper classes? Clearly, the principle of reference to social reality, which Bottigheimer uses to explain why a rise plot should have been successful in sixteenth-century Venice, fails to explain the reception of urban rags-to-riches plots among illiterate rustics as well as among aristocrats. In other words, the principle that is used to account for the invention of the genre fails to account for its diffusion.[10]

Vaz da Silva also offers numerous examples of how folk and literary tales meshed. Moreover, he proves conclusively that Straparola was not the primary influence on French writers of the 1690s, as Bottigheimer claims, but rather that numerous *French* oral tales and literary romances then in circulation influenced writers such as d'Aulnoy, Lhéritier, and Perrault.

Vaz da Silva's critique is reinforced by Ben-Amos's essay, in which he demonstrates that Straparola's plagiarizing and patchwork style followed the fashion of his age and also the tradition of oral storytelling:

> In borrowing tales and passing them on to new audiences, Straparola acted as an oral storyteller in the garb of a writer. Using the relatively new media of print, he continued a behavior common and appropriate to oral culture. Within this new era, his work became a reservoir of tales culled from diverse sources, a reservoir that, as John Colin Dunlop long ago pointed out, was very popular in France. *Le piacevoli notti* thus became a source for literary fairy-tale writers who did not have direct access to oral tradition.[11]

But it is not only the clear references to orality within Straparola's two-volume collection that concerns Ben-Amos. Like Ziolkowski, he provides evidence that there were numerous oral tales in ancient Egypt and Asia that became well known in Europe long before Straparola put pen to paper. And Europeans, despite the rise of Christianity and the witch hunts, continued to spread tales that involved pagan beliefs and rituals. As Ben-Amos observes, "Tales about supernatural miracles, holy men, fairies, and animals that enriched mortals were told in legends and fairy tales both before and after the fourteenth and fifteenth centuries, the time when Richard Whittington lived and then became the subject of a legend about a cat-less land, and both before and after the sixteenth century when Straparola incorporated into his anthology a version of 'Puss in Boots.'"[12]

One of Bottigheimer's major arguments throughout her essays and books is that the absence of documentation of fairy tales (as she narrowly defines them) is proof of the absence of fairy tales in the lives of the peasantry until Straparola and others began writing and publishing their tales. As Ziolkowski, Vaz da Silva, and Ben-Amos reveal, however, there is more than sufficient documentation about storytelling and texts that indicates a long tradition of oral wonder tales incorporating fairy-tale motifs, topoi, characters, and patterns. In premodern Europe before and after Christianity took hold, people, learned and nonliterate, believed strongly in witches, fairies, life after death, walking ghosts, vampires, devils, miraculous intervention, and so on. During the European witch hunts, which took many different forms from approximately 1480 to 1700, the testimonies of suspected witches, declared witches, witnesses, and prosecutors read like bizarre fairy tales, and certainly were part of the stuff that storytellers used to entertain or inform their audiences. The festivities and evening gatherings, in which all kinds of tales were told but never recorded, must have been filled with tales of fairies, witches, mermaids, dwarfs, ogres, dragons, devils, angels, saints, magical objects, potions, herbs, kings, queens, peasants, flying and talking horses, talking cats, dogs, and foxes, and so forth.

These tales were never recorded because the few learned people who could write had no interest in collecting and writing them down, and if they did, they stylized them for a different audience. Besides, these tales were always told in dialect, and there were no orthographic standards or grammars that facilitated the recording of tales told by peasants, laborers, and artisans. Almost every person in premodern Europe breathed the stuff of wonder tales and other types of tales that contained a mixture of pagan beliefs and early Christian religious stories. In his thought-provoking book *Strange Histories*, Darren Oldridge remarks:

> In the period covered by this book—from the late Middle Ages to the beginnings of modern science at the end of the seventeenth century—the prevailing system of belief permitted many ideas that now seem unfamiliar or ridiculous. Can the dead walk? Most people in medieval Europe believed they could, and orthodox Christians assumed this would happen en masse at the time of the Last Judgment. Can witches

fly? Even the most trenchant opponents of the persecution of witchcraft in sixteenth-century Europe believed this was possible. Just like us, the people who accepted these things relied on a body of knowledge to help them evaluate the facts of the world, and just like us, they inherited this knowledge from the culture in which they were born.[13]

A belief in fairies, witches, devils, and ogres became dangerous in European societies that punished people for heretical expression and behavior, and the peasantry, always suspicious of their learned superiors, were not about to tell them tales that were part of their intimate culture. Certainly, women were most hesitant to tell their tales to male interlocutors of the educated class. As Ben-Amos maintains:

> The slim documentary evidence of fairies in the belief systems of medieval European societies is not a testimony for their absence, and ignoring their documented presence creates a blind spot in the practice of literary empiricism. After all, ephemeral beliefs and communication occur regardless of their documentation. The meager references to fairies in contemporaneous writings are a function of the nature of medieval documents and of the attitude toward the fairies rather than a testimony to their true prevalence in belief systems. With no church and no cult to support them, the fairies were relegated to the cultural periphery. Consequently, the evidence of their significance can be inferred most readily from the testimony about their vanishing: comments about their disappearance attest to their earlier presence. In the words of Chaucer's "Wife of Bath":
>
> > In the Old days of King Arthur, today
> > Still praised by Britons in a special way,
> > This land was filled with fairies all about.[14]

Indeed, the belief in fairies has never vanished, and fairy tales as part of oral and literary culture can be considered a minor subversive genre that infiltrates major dominant culture whenever it can. When Barrie had Peter Pan cry out to the largely adult audience of his 1904 play in London and ask them whether they all believed in fairies, the answer was a resounding "yes!" And whenever and wherever the play is produced in the twenty-first century, the answer remains the same.

Bottigheimer's Rebuttal

Bottigheimer's *Fairy Tales: A New History*, to which I shall now turn, is a response to her critics. In her book, she essentially rehashes her nomination of Straparola as the inventor of literary fairy tales and adds Basile as his coinventor, while also setting herself up as the main authority in terms of defining fairy tales. She rewrites the history of the fairy tale by focusing on book commerce and contends that only the publication of books enables us to understand how writers created their fairy tales as well as how the tales were transmitted and received. Bottigheimer treats common people with disdain, making no effort to understand how language and communication evolved, nor how tales were disseminated orally before printing machines were invented. She concentrates on the publication records of three countries—Italy, France, and Germany—and excludes the rest of the world from her analysis, as though only Europe gave birth to fairy tales. And she establishes generic fairy-tale categories, which serve to hinder an understanding of why writers composed their fairy tales and how they created them.

In chapter 1, "Why a New History of Fairy Tales?" Bottigheimer sets the tone of her book by declaring: "It has been said so often that the folk invented and disseminated fairy tales that this assumption has become an unquestioned proposition. It may therefore surprise readers that folk invention and transmission of fairy tales has no basis in verifiable fact. Literary analysis undermines it, literary history rejects it, social history repudiates it, and publishing history (whether of manuscripts or of books) contradicts it."[15] Here and elsewhere in her book, Bottigheimer rarely cites sources or offers references. Who has said so often that the folk invented and disseminated fairy tales, and is she speaking about oral or literary fairy tales? Who are the historians who have claimed that only the folk invented fairy tales? She does not mention that in the last forty or fifty years, folklorists, literary critics, historians, and scholars of folklore and fairy tales from many different countries have been more interested in the intersections between the oral and literary traditions than trying to privilege one over the other. Bottigheimer wants to establish a paper tiger: the dichotomy between oral and literary traditions, and the privileging of oral tales. What does she mean by the abstract conglomerations of literary analysis, literary history, social history, and publishing history that refute the oral transmission of tales? Which groups of people, institutions, or methods prove that only Bottigheimer knows who the true inventors of the fairy tale are?

Indeed, this is what her opening chapter sets out to do. Bottigheimer begins with one of the most misleading, if not most simplistic, definitions of folk tales I have ever read: "Folk tales differ from fairy tales in their structure, their cast of characters, their plot trajectories, and their age. Brief, and with linear plots, folk tales reflect the world and the belief systems of their audiences. . . . Folk tales are easy to follow and easy to remember, in part because they deal with familiar aspects of the human condition like the propensity to build castles in the air."[16] In fact, folk tales, especially oral wonder tales, are much more diverse than Bottigheimer suggests and have many remarkable similarities with literary fairy tales and other genres, such as myths, legends, and anecdotes, making it difficult to define a typical "authentic" fairy tale, as I have tried to demonstrate throughout this book. Nevertheless, Bottigheimer provides us with strict demarcations that, in her view, will for once and for all enable us to know what a fairy tale really is.

Actually, according to Bottigheimer, there are *two* types of fairy tales, both invented by Straparola: restoration fairy tales and rise fairy tales. "Restoration fairy tales are firmly based in the world of human beings," Bottigheimer states. But she then goes on to outline a plot in which a member of the nobility (a king or queen) is banished or driven from his realm, and regains it through enduring tests and trials. "Rise fairy tales begin with a dirt poor girl or boy who suffers the effects of grinding poverty and whose story continues with tests, tasks, and trials until magic brings about a marriage to royalty and a happy accession to great wealth."[17] These definitions are so vague and formulaic that they could fit thousands, if not hundreds of thousands, of narrative types and schemes. Furthermore, Bottigheimer does not consider many other theories developed by Propp, Claude Lévi-Strauss, Brémond, Louis Marin, or Steven Swann Jones, to name just a few scholars who have endeavored to explicate the patterns in folk and fairy tales in great detail.[18] She does, however, discuss why tales about fairyland are different from fairy tales, asserting that "the distinguishing characteristics of tales about fairyland—two parallel universes and sometimes unhappy endings—make their differences from fairy tales obvious. Despite these fundamental differences in location and outcome, tales about fairyland are often, and confusingly, lumped together with human-centered and real-world-based fairy tales."[19] Yet Bottigheimer does not attempt to understand the social history of fairies that can be traced to Greek and Roman antiquity and the worship of certain goddesses.[20] Nor does she consider that fairies (and related creatures such as nixies, sirens, mermaids, and sylphs) were part of the real human world and belief systems. What concerns her most is to establish her own categorical definition of two types of literary fairy tales and demonstrate that the "unfettered country folk" could never have told tales that engendered what Straparola and Basile supposedly engendered—the genre of the fairy tale.

In her next chapter, "Two Accounts of the Grimms' Tales: The Folk as Creator, the Book as Source," she again rehashes what folklorists and literary critics have known and been discussing for the past forty years. She also attacks the Brothers Grimm and accuses them of falsifying the genuine folk quality of their tales, or should I say, Wilhelm, for he was the brother most responsible for editing the Grimms' *Children's and Household Tales* from 1819 onward. Bottigheimer stresses that many of the Grimms' informants were from the middle class or could read, and that the brothers idealized the German folk—a view that was carried on and maintained by German folklorists in the twentieth century and scholars from other countries. But she forgets to note that most, if not all, of the Grimms' tales have oral sources, and most can be traced to other countries and collections of folklorists in other countries. Whether the Grimms' conception of the folk was right or wrong, they were responsible for the significant collecting of oral tales in Europe throughout the nineteenth century, and Bottigheimer does not credit them for endeavoring to encourage learned people to pay more attention to nonliterate people along with their beliefs, rituals, and customs. Instead, she alleges that

> the Grimms themselves were poor judges of the folk that they claimed to be the pure creators of and the uncontaminated disseminators of oral narrative. In the years of their collecting for the first volume of the First Edition, Wilhelm and Jacob must have been remarkably ignorant about Germany's folk. Despite the personal poverty of their adolescent years in Cassel, they had passed their childhood among Hesse-Cassel's privileged and had spent their early manhood in libraries and archives, and, when ill health forced it, in spas. Unworldly, inexperienced, and like the tales they recorded, generally innocent of sexual knowledge, they were personally naive about the peasantry's earthly world. Thus it is not surprising that they projected the simplicity with which they were personally familiar onto the tales they were collecting, and beyond them, to the folk they believed in.[21]

Perhaps, though, she should have read the letters that the brothers exchanged between themselves and the recent biography by Stefan Martus to obtain a better understanding of the Grimms.[22] The brothers were not the total bookworms and naive dreamers that she makes them out to be. They were not interested in mixing with and catering to the upper classes and always had contact with people from both the lower and upper classes. It is true that they were diligent students, but they also were down-to-earth and knew that they had to work hard to support their family after their father's early death. Only one brother, Wilhelm, went to a health spa in Halle, not a luxurious spa attended by both brothers, as Bottigheimer suggests. Jacob traveled to Vienna and then to Paris and saw the ravages of war and its effect on the common people, and then wrote about them. The brothers knew more about sex and bawdy jokes than Bottigheimer pretends, and the tales they collected—among them, many tales about soldiers—do in part reflect the "earthly world."

Throughout her book Bottigheimer works with assumptions, declarations, and questionable evidence as if only she knew the truth about history. Yet she is an unreliable historian. In chapter 3, "The Late Seventeenth- and Eighteenth-Century Layers," she wants to prove that the talented French writers of the 1690s all knew Straparola's and Basile's works, and could not have been influenced by a French oral tradition that, according to Bottigheimer, did not even exist. Many of the women writers, however, such as d'Aulnoy, Lhéritier, de la Force, and Murat, and even Perrault, make references to nannies and servants who told them tales. Some of the best scholars in France have documented the influence of French folklore and orality in the writing of the tales.[23] Often the women writers performed their tales orally in salons. With the exception of Murat, none of the writers ever mentioned Straparola in their letters or memoirs. As for Basile, none of the French writers could read Italian much less the Neapolitan dialect in which Basile wrote his tales. Still, Bottigheimer states: "I've examined Lhéritier's and Perrault's tales of the good and bad sisters and their respective magical rewards and curses. I've compared them with each other and with the two Basile tales that preceded them. And I've concluded that Perrault may well have had his niece's tales as well as Basile's two tales in front of him when he composed 'The Fairies.'"[24]

Once again, Bottigheimer gets carried away by her imagination. We have no knowledge whatsoever about Perrault's practice of writing. We do not know whether he copied or worked with Basile's and Lhéritier's texts. It is most unlikely that he could decipher Basile's unusual Neapolitan dialect and baroque stories. But there is more likelihood that Perrault may have known some oral tale related to the cycle of "the good and bad girls" that circulated not only in France but also in Germany, the Slavic countries, Greece, and Italy. This is not to say that we must privilege the oral over print, but as various French scholars have endeavored to explain, we should be aware of oral influences in printed tales that can be traced linguistically, philologically, stylistically, and historically to all kinds of oral tales.

The oral components in Straparola's and Basile's tales are striking, but in chapter 4, "The Two Inventors of Fairy Tale Tradition; Giambattista Basile (1634–1636) and Giovan Francesco Straparola (1551, 1553)," Bottigheimer uses her definitions of the fairy tale as restoration and rise tale to eliminate any possibility that either Basile or Straparola may have based their tales on oral sources, or tried to imitate oral performances that may have influenced their writing.[25] Once again, Bottigheimer makes all sorts of allusions to Straparola's and Basile's lives that make it seem as if their tales were formed either by their own imaginations or through reading books. It is crucial, however, to stress again that we know absolutely nothing about Straparola, and that he may not have even lived in Venice or addressed his tales to the urban artisans who supposedly devoured his books. The truth is that we must rely on slight textual evidence in the case of Straparola, and historical records and texts in the case of Basile—two very different writers.

Since I have already dealt with Straparola earlier, I just want to add that the author himself reveals his debt to the oral storytelling tradition in the book, frame narrative, and some of the tales. Straparola admits that the tales are not his; his narrative is based on a gathering of upper-class people, who tell tales that they have heard before, and a couple of them are in dialect. All of them bear witness to an oral influence, including the telling of riddles. In the case of Basile, who chose to invent ten bizarre peasant women to tell the tales in his collection *The Tale of Tales* (*Lo Cunto del li cunti*), it is clear from the dialect, the hybrid plots, and his known performances in courts that he was thoroughly conversant with a lower-class tradition of storytelling.

Naples, the south of Italy, and Sicily were treasure chests of oral storytelling, and Basile, who was not from the aristocracy and traveled throughout Italy, was clearly familiar with oral tales and literary works. His brilliance—the use of folk dialect to mock baroque mannerist conventions—seems to have eluded Bottigheimer.

In her final chapter, "A New History," she again indicates a disdain for common people and oral traditions: "If we look forward from Straparola toward the fairy tale future, we see a publishing phenomenon with printed texts carrying fairy tales from one place to another. The ubiquitous and mysterious folk and nursemaids remain, but as consumers of fairy tales rather than as producers."[26] Given the fact that anywhere from 70 to 90 percent of the population in Europe was nonliterate; Latin dominated the books published in the sixteenth and seventeenth centuries; books were often purchased by collectors, placed in libraries, and not read; there are few records of people reading print fairy tales; people from all classes read aloud in an oral tradition; books were expensive; and most people spoke and communicated in some kind of dialect, we must ask what the common people were doing to amuse themselves in the medieval and Renaissance periods. We must ask why the learned people ignored writing down the tales of the common people. We know, though, that once learned people actually started to investigate in the nineteenth century what tales common people were telling, they found hundreds, if not thousands, that were not influenced by books, and many were oral wonder tales.

Bottigheimer forgets to add that books circulated mainly among the aristocracy and upper-middle classes, and many of the French and German writers of the eighteenth and nineteenth centuries wrote extraordinary literary fairy tales that show no connection to restoration and rise tales. As to her remarks about common people, who she turns into passive consumers unable to create their own wonder or magic tales, they are lamentable. Perhaps if she studied how peasants and laborers developed certain rituals, how tales and songs were performed in their homes and at work, how they confessed their beliefs about elves, fairies, and witches in fabricated stories to their persecutors, and how town criers circulated tales, she might have granted them some intelligence and creativity. But Bottigheimer goes even further than denying the majority of European people any power of original storytelling; she appears to diminish the tales of all other peoples in the world: "In a large sense the international spread of fairy tales can be explained within a history of a predominantly Italian creation, French editing, and German re-editing that took place in a context of commercial mechanisms within book distribution networks."[27] This statement—unless you subscribe to Bottigheimer's prescriptive definition of a fairy tale—explains nothing and indeed is untrue. Fairy tales, even the kind Bottigheimer celebrates, were told, copied, and disseminated by word of mouth and manuscript in many other parts of the world long before Straparola was born.

Ideological Simplifications and Implications

What is perhaps most disturbing about Bottigheimer's *Fairy Tales: A New History* is her seemingly objective use of terms and methods to conceal a "perverse ideological agenda" as Ziolkowski notes in his essay. Perhaps she is unaware of her own ideological prejudices, and the negative effects they may have for students and scholars of folklore and fairy tales, but they clearly color her views.

In her talk "Authorizing Fairy-Tale History? Disciplinary Debates and the Politics of Inequality" at the 2010 meeting of the American Folklore Association, Cristina Bacchilega comments:

> When Bottigheimer writes, "Rise fairy tales are a product of that quintessential engine of modernity, the printing press," this seemingly matter-of-fact statement, which is more a declaration than a historical truth, participates in a larger and powerful discourse that has represented modernity as strictly literate as well as simply European, and has configured the difference between oral and print traditions into a strategy of control and domination. Why does this matter? Whether the fairy-tale genre is considered exclusively within European and literary history, or as a genre whose ties to expressive cultures and comparative literatures are inflected by global dynamics, has significant implications for ascribing a place for lay and subaltern knowledges in history.[28]

If Bottigheimer had been serious about writing a new, more balanced, interdisciplinary history of the fairy tale, she might have begun with a discussion about the evolution of human communication throughout the world, and how humans exchanged information and developed narratives based on daily experience, work, rituals, and beliefs. Though there is no exact date as to when human language and cognition developed, most historians agree that it was at least three hundred thousand years ago, long before alphabets, script, and printing presses. That is, all people on earth lived and communicated by gestures and word of mouth thousands of years before such a thing as a fairy tale as we know it today came into being. Yet tales of various kinds were invented and cultivated, and as Tomasello points out in *The Origins of Communication,*

> Natural languages also contain cognitive resources for construing whole events or situations in terms of one another, that is, for creating the various kinds of analogies and metaphors that are so important in adult cognition—such as seeing the atom as a solar system, love as a journey, or anger as heat. Also, children's growing skills of linguistic communication enable them to participate in complex discourse interactions in which the explicitly symbolized perspectives of interactions clash and so must be negotiated and resolved. These kinds of

interactions may lead children to begin to construct something like a theory of mind of their communicative partners, and, in some special cases of pedagogical discourse, to internalize adult instructions and so begin to self-regulate and to reflect on their own thinking—perhaps leading to some types of metacognition and representational redescription. The internalization of discourse interactions containing multiple, conflicting perspectives may even be identified with certain types of uniquely human, dialogical thinking processes.[29]

The primary learning processes of language and cultural communication were—and still are—based on imitation, instruction, and communication. What is important for the study of fairy tales and any other narrative form is a comprehension of its evolutionary tendencies. Tomasello writes:

> Cumulative cultural evolution depends on imitative learning, and perhaps active instruction on the part of adults and cannot be brought about by means of "weaker" forms of social learning such as local enhancement, emulation learning, ontogenetic ritualization, or any form of individual learning. The argument is that cumulative cultural evolution depends on two processes, innovation and imitation (possibly supplemented by instruction), that must take place in a dialectical process over time such that one step in the process enables the next.[30]

As metaphoric tales were told and circulated thousands of years before print, they served social functions, were retained through memory, and were passed on from generation to generation. It is difficult to say when oral wonder tales originated, but there are traces, signs, patterns, and plots in early ancient manuscripts that reveal how all people came to know the world through metaphor, ritual, custom, and transformation. Tales were not named or categorized according to genre, yet it is clear that most of the fairy-tale motifs, topoi, characters, plots, and conventions existed in oral traditions (and some continue to do so) long before learned people learned how to write and categorize narratives.

An interesting case in point is *Thousand and One Nights* (*Alf Laila wa Laila*), which is omitted from discussion in Bottigheimer's essays and books. The tales in this collection were originally Persian, and stemmed from oral storytelling traditions of the eighth and ninth centuries. As Paul McMichael Nurse highlights in *Eastern Dreams: How the Arabian Nights Came to the World*,

> Travel and trade mean exchanges not only of goods but also of ideas and information. Although their exact provenance is unknown, based on such internal evidence as cultural references and terminology it is believed that many of the stories in the *Nights* originated with Indian, Arab, Persian, Greek, Roman and possibly Chinese travellers, merchants, and soldiers plying travel routes from the Balkans to the

China Sea. Rest stops were spent around campfires or in the occasional caravanserai—walled hostels catering to travellers—dotting the roads. At these times, it was customary to swap stories to while away the restful hours before setting out again. The more popular tales were thus transferred from place to place while being continually modified according to regional customs and circumstances, much as a joke will assume local colour and familiar allusions for better comprehension.[31]

The development of the *Nights* from the Oriental oral and literary traditions of the Middle Ages into a classical work for Western readers is a fascinating one. The tales in the collection can be traced to three ancient oral cultures—Indian, Persian, and Arab—and they probably circulated in the vernacular hundreds of years before they were written down some time between the ninth and fourteenth centuries. The apparent model for the literary versions of the tales was a Persian book titled *Hezâr afsân* (*A Thousand Stories*), translated into Arabic in the ninth century as *Alf laylah wa-laylah* (*Thousand and One Nights*), for it provided the framework story of a caliph who kills his wife because she betrays him. Then for the next three years, he takes a new wife every day and slays her each night after taking her maidenhead to avenge himself on women. A vizier's daughter, assisted by her slave girl, finally diverts him from this cruel custom. During the next seven centuries, various storytellers, scribes, and scholars began to record the tales from this collection and others, and shape them either independently or within the framework of the Sheherezade/Shahriyâr narrative. The tellers and authors of the tales were anonymous, and their styles and language differed greatly; the only common distinguishing feature was the fact that they were written in a colloquial language called Middle Arabic, which had its own peculiar grammar and syntax. By the fifteenth century, there were three distinct layers that could be detected in the collection of those tales, forming the nucleus of what became known as *Thousand and One Nights*: Persian tales that had some Indian elements and had been adapted into Arabic by the tenth century; tales recorded in Baghdad between the tenth and twelfth centuries; and stories written down in Egypt between the eleventh and fourteenth centuries.

Nurse emphasizes the important role played by the *rawi*, professional storytellers or reciting storytellers, in the dissemination of the tales that were addressed mainly to people of the lower classes, disdained by the educated classes. The rawi still exercise their profession in Morocco today. Nurse also notes that many of the tales come from written compilations and literary antecedents, and were constantly being changed when told and written down. In the process they became truly international, and Nurse explains,

It is known that stories from the *Nights* were circulating in "westernized" versions in Europe many centuries before their printed appearance, cropping up in oral form in Germany, France, Italy and Spain, although it is unclear whether manuscript versions of sundry *Nights* tales were in circulation. All the same, it is likely some *Nights* stories were present in Europe from around the twelfth century, arriving through Arabized Sicily or Moorish Spain to be absorbed into the European folklore tradition.[32]

Among the hundreds of tales that were recorded by scribes were stories that followed Bottigheimer's plots of restoration and rise tales, such as "The Fisherman and the Genie," "The Tale of the Three Apples," "Aladdin and the Magic Lamp," and "The Ebony Horse." In addition, there were fairy tales of initiation and marriage rituals; tales with fairies, flying horses, and wizards; and tales dealing with incest, child abuse and abandonment, rape, slavery, exploitation, deceit, miraculous intervention, and so on. Were these tales told in Venice during Straparola's time? We don't know for certain, but we do know something that Bottigheimer never discusses: Venice was the most important trade center with the Byzantine Empire and the Muslim world, and it is quite possible that not only goods but also tales were exchanged in this port city, which was known for the performing arts and book publishing. Though there was a higher rate of literacy in Venice than in most Italian cities, more than 70 percent of the people in the city could not read adequately, and even those who could read did not necessarily understand what they read. As Brian Richardson points out in *Printing, Writers, and Readers in Renaissance Italy*, "What is striking from a modern point of view is that children could learn to read without necessarily understanding fully what they read: because of the force of tradition and the lack of prestige of the vernacular as a written language among teachers, reading in one's native language did not play a part in the traditional curriculum."[33] Girls were rarely taught to read. Many people could only write their names and yet were considered literate.

In *Literacy in Early Modern Europe: Culture and Education, 1500–1800,* R. A. Houston states,

> The imperfect nature of early modern sources generally makes it necessary to categorise people as literate or illiterate. However these are at best seen not as discrete categories, but as steps in a hierarchy of skills. At the same time, seeing and listening could bridge the gap between literate and illiterate. What is more, literacy can be used for different purposes: to serve some practical or *functional* end such as economic need among tradesmen, in which case reading and writing would be advantageous; or to fulfil a religious need, where reading alone is all that is commonly required.[34]

Literacy was also used by the church and governments constituted by the upper classes to subject the lower classes to authoritative regulations, social codes, laws, and manners. Few books in the sixteenth century were secular and fiction. Even when they were read, they were frequently read aloud and in groups. For the most part and in most of Europe, orality of different kinds was the dominant mode of cultural communication among all social classes. Cultural conditions and languages were diverse throughout Europe, and the stories and social practices of the lower classes were not considered worthy of attention. Tales were rarely recorded, just as Bottigheimer never bothers to explore oral mediation in all the classes and the possible connections between the classes in regard to storytelling. If she had done so, we might find a different picture of Straparola and Basile in her book. We certainly would have a different view of the *Le piacevoli notti* and *Lo Cunto de li cunti* along with the significant roles they played in mediating oral and literary stories that helped foster the genre of the literary fairy tale. As it stands, Bottigheimer's "new" history of the fairy tale can only be considered sensationalist "scholarship."

Appendix B

Reductionist Scholarship: A "New" Definition of the Fairy Tale

Poetry is that which comes purely from the soul transformed into word and thus springs continually from a natural drive and innate ability to grasp the soul—folk poetry arises out of the soul of the collective whole (*Ganze*); in my opinion, artistic poetry stems from the individual. This is why the new poetry names its poets, while the old does not know any to name. It's not at all made by one person or two or three, rather it is the sum of the collective whole. It remains inexplicable how this collective whole was put together and got going. As I have already said, however, it is not any more mysterious than water that gathers (from different sources) in a river to flow together. I find it unthinkable that there ever was a Homer or author of the *Nibelungen*.

—Jacob Grimm, letter to Achim von Arnim, May 20, 1811

In his new book, *Tales of Magic, Tales in Print: On the Genealogy of Fairy Tales and the Brothers Grimm*, Willem de Blécourt seeks to "jolt" folklorists and fairy-tale specialists throughout the world so that they realize that only he (not Bottigheimer) knows when fairy tales truly began to exist, and only he can determine the empirical "truth" of their history based on his knowledge of print literature.[1] To be fair to de Blécourt, his scholarship is admirable, and his evidence and arguments, though flawed, are to be taken seriously. The difficulty with his book concerns his sweeping, often-misleading generalizations, an attitude comprised of what Germans call *Besserwisserei* ("know-it-all"), and particular ideological theories regarding folk culture. But I am getting ahead of myself. I would like first to summarize the contents of de Blécourt's book before offering a critique of what I consider to be its shortcomings. I also want to emphasize that despite my disagreements with de Blécourt, his book may help some scholars look more closely at print literature and its interaction with folk tales, fairy tales, and folklore in general.

In addition to a prologue and epilogue, de Blécourt's book is divided into seven chapters: "The Devil in the Detail," "A Quest for Rejuvenation," "The Girl in the Garden," "Magic and Metamorphosis," "The Substitute Storyteller," "Journeys to the Other World," and "The Vanishing Godmother." In the prologue, "The Magic of the Printed Word," de Blécourt outlines his thesis and intentions. He maintains that

> fairy tales are not more than a few centuries old and that they did not constitute a continuous oral tradition. . . . If some fairy tales, such as the Dragon Slayer, the Magician and His Pupil, the Magical Flight, the Girl Without Hands or the Water of Life, appear to have a history reaching back into the sixteenth century or into medieval times, the question is whether these predecessors can reasonably be called "fairy tales," without granting them characteristics and meanings they did not previously possess.

Indeed, de Blécourt asserts that folklorists, beginning with the Grimms, turned history on its head with the assumption that there was a pagan or ancient oral tale to which every particular tale type of fairy tale could be traced. Since it is impossible to uncover this history, according to de Blécourt, most folklorists created "myths" about peasants and oral traditions. He maintains that the only way to establish a "true" history of fairy tales is by comparing printed versions of a basic tale type and starting with the first print appearance of a tale. Time and again, he contends that "European fairy-tale communication took place in a printed environment." Lower-class people did not recount fairy tales, and when they finally did, it was because of print literature. The dissemination of fairy tales

> took place primarily among members of the nobility and the bourgeoisie. Only during the nineteenth century did fairy stories percolate down to the lower classes, as a form of *"gesunkenes Kulturgut"*—and even then it may only have been because a collector asked for it and his informant dimly remembered having heard it at school or having read it at some point. The situation where one finds an experienced storyteller in command of a well-rehearsed repertoire of *fairy tales*, such as for instance in mid twentieth-century Hungary, is the result of a fairly recent development, considerably aided by the teller's knowledge of printed stories.[2]

In determining the definition of a fairy tale, de Blécourt relies strangely on the bible of folklorists, so to speak: the recently revised *The Types of International Folktales: A Classification and Bibliography*.[3] I say "strangely" because de Blécourt spends a good deal of time throughout his book criticizing the historical-geographic school that gave birth to this reference work. Moreover,

The Types of International Folktales notes every instance in which literary versions are known for each tale type, and the number of times this occurs is scant. Most of the tales listed, in short have no known literary analogues. Be that as it may, de Blécourt focuses on the classified tales within the ATU 300–749 range, or the so-called wonder tales. Yet he constantly excludes what he views as tales that are not "real" tales of magic, without defining what he means by magic. For example, he declares that stories with devils and death are religious tales, not fairy tales. He also claims that stories about fairies, witches, and werewolves from the early modern period cannot be considered fairy tales but instead are simply tales about fairies, witches, and werewolves, even if they include magical transformation. They could only appear in "genuine" fairy tales in the nineteenth-century printed tales when people stopped believing in them (if they really did). Therefore, these staple characters, if they existed before the nineteenth century, cannot be considered part of the oral fairy-tale arsenal or repertoire.

The reason he deals largely with the Brothers Grimm and their collections of tales in the nineteenth century is that their stories are mainly based on traceable literary tales, and they had a profound influence on story collecting in Europe. Moreover, the Grimms narrowed the definition of a fairy tale and transformed the tales into stories to educate children. This pedagogical intention led them to edit and refine their tales so that they could be effectively told. The historical lineage of fairy tales thus is literary, in de Blécourt's opinion, and the common people played little or no role in the origination and dissemination of fairy tales until the nineteenth century, when more of them began to read. (It should be noted, however, that only 30 percent or less of the German-speaking people could read then.)[4]

Given de Blécourt's ideological premise and/or bias, he selects seven major tale types in the Grimms' *Children's and Household Tales* (*Kinder-und Hausmärchen*) and uses tales in the Grimms' collection in each chapter to show how they are more literary than oral and can be connected to a long history of similar printed tales. In chapter 1, he discusses "The Devil with the Three Golden Hairs" to argue that this tale was a nineteenth-century invention, and folklorists are engaging in speculation when they trace it to the Middle Ages. There is no concrete evidence. In the process he attacks the scholarship of prominent folklorists Lutz Röhrich, Propp, Thompson, and Bengt Holbek by showing that the Grimms and their young informants, Marie and Amalie Hassenpflug along with Dorothea Viehmann, borrowed motifs from a French literary tradition to tell this tale.

In chapter 2 he studies "The Golden Bird," using an old essay by Austrian literary critic Albert Wesselski, whose early twentieth-century theories are generally considered outdated.[5] Nevertheless, he resurrects Wesselski's ideas to try to prove Haney and Propp wrong when they insist that this tale is related to the Russian "Firebird" story and dismisses the notion that there was an indigenous development of fairy tales in Russia, without doing much research on this topic.[6] According to de Blécourt, the Grimms' version of "The Golden Bird" stemmed from a conglomeration of literary and religious texts and could not have existed until the Grimms shaped it in the nineteenth century.

In chapter 3, de Blécourt begins by stating that an "underlying 'peasant culture' of the tales of magic in the KHM [*Children's and Household Tales*] is nowhere in sight. Instead the texts can be understood as a product of the interaction between the brothers and their young, female supporters." This is a productive remark, to which I shall return at the end of this appendix, but de Blécourt uses it primarily to show that all the tale types of the magic flight (ATU 313) such as "Hansel and Grethel," "The Foundling," and "The Water Nixie" have nothing to do with a continuous oral tradition, even though, he admits, there were numerous similar stories about magical flights, elements, and motifs in pre-Christian oral stories and literature. De Blécourt is mainly interested in revealing how young women played a key role in providing the Grimms with their tales based on literature. Provocatively he asks, "Why would the girls, each in their own way, also not have told what they had read? As is clear from the records, they not just reproduced stories but incorporated elements they had found elsewhere, heard from each other and from the brothers. The oral exchanges were cemented by printed texts."[7] He also argues that more attention should be paid to gender differences in the telling and recording of fairy tales.

Chapter 4 shifts the focus to the Grimms' tale "The Thief and His Master" (ATU 325, the magician and his pupil), and here de Blécourt disputes the ancient Indian origins of this tale type and maintains that, in fact, there was a possibility that European literary tales may have influenced Eastern tales due to colonialism. Whatever the case may be, de Blécourt reveals that the Grimms' informants were probably familiar with French Orientalized tales, which he contends are not really fairy tales because they are concerned with sexual deviance and the acquisition of magic for power.

De Blécourt turns to three tales in chapter 5—"The Learned Hunter," "The Carnation," and "The Iron Stove"—to show that the so-called peasant storyteller, Viehmann, from the town of Zwehrn, was neither a peasant nor a model common storyteller, as the Grimms and numerous other folklorists have described her, and that other people from Zwehrn may have been the real informants from this community. In addition, the Grimms' sources were probably broadsides, chapbooks, or books.

Chapter 6 is a critique of folklorists who believe that there are strong ties to shamanism in fairy tales. The shamanistic characteristics generally involve journeys to another world and resurrection. "To shamanistic theorists fairy tale texts are decontextualized; they do not represent a nineteenth- or twentieth-century story-telling reality. Instead, they are seen as timeless representatives of a prehistorical unwritten tradition."[8] Here he analyzes four tales—"The Princess on the Glass Mountain," "The Shepherd in the Service of a Witch," "The Ogre's Heart in the Egg," and "The Tree That Grows Up to the Sky"—in an effort to prove that shamanistic beliefs were not connected to the fictitious elements in fairy tales.

Finally, in chapter 7, de Blécourt selects the cycle of "The Kind and Unkind Girls" (ATU 480), best exemplified in the Grimms' collection by Mother Holle, to discuss how Warren Roberts's 1958 book on this topic is misleading because it "presumes a distribution through largely oral channels."[9] De Blécourt argues that the earliest manifestation of the subtype occurs in a mid-nineteenth-century chapbook that Roberts ignores. In de Blécourt's opinion, Roberts neglected all printed editions, despite the fact that Roberts relied heavily on *The Types of International Folktales*, which does indeed contain literary sources. The key story in the Grimms' collection is "Mother Holle," and de Blécourt denies that there is any connection to pagan deities (without studying the associations with Nordic and Slavic goddesses as well as early tales of Baba Yaga).[10] The tale of "Mother Holle" involves a fairy, and thus, since fairies stem primarily from a literary tradition of the twelfth and thirteenth centuries and had nothing to do with the everyday beliefs of the common people, it is evident, he maintains, that tales about kind and unkind girls along with fairies were inventions of aristocratic and bourgeois writers, who may have even had a great impact in India, because the didactic focus of the tales in the cycle is on cultivating young girls so that they exhibit proper behavior. De Blécourt concludes this chapter by stating,

> Rather than being the paragon of orality, the Kind and Unkind Girls positions fairy tales in at least one of their proper slots: education. Their dissemination by teachers, the inner missionaries of Western society and often belonging to the clergy themselves, has so far been underestimated in folklore research and deserves urgent attention. Tales of magic only became part of a feeble oral tradition at a very late stage in Europe's history; instead of traditional they formed part of the movement to combat genuine oral traditions as "superstitious."[11]

In his book's epilogue, de Blécourt reiterates his thesis that fairy tales were primarily dependent on literary sources, and makes some "wild," if not inflammatory, assertions:

> During the early and modern period, European society was not just attempting to come to terms with magic; it became saturated with literacy. If the latter was not actively promoted through compulsory education, it was dominantly present in religion, law, and commerce, even though there may have been subtle differences between Protestant and Catholic practices. Within this context the presumption of a separate lower-class "oral culture" is inconceivable, if not a major historical fallacy. Not everyone may have been able to read, but with an increasing frequency people became available who could and there was no ques-

tion about the lucrative market for cheap prints. . . . With this book, I hope to have enhanced the probability that many later orally recited and subsequently recorded fairy tales had their basis in printed form, from cheap booklets, broadsides to newspapers, rather than the other way around. Folklorists in search of an idealized orality, however, strove to conceal the connections as much as possible.[12]

Fallacies and Contradictions

Throughout de Blécourt's book he writes as if folklorists had conspired to invent "romantic" notions of the folk and folklore that silenced the "true" originators of the fairy tale along with Wesselski, Manfred Grätz, and Rudolf Schenda.[13] So let me state once again, there is much to be learned from his study about the relationship between literary and oral fairy tales. Ironically, however, his fastidious, selective research proves the opposite of his claim in that he provides interesting textual evidence of a strong oral/literary tradition of fairy-tale storytelling in Europe.

De Blécourt decries the distortion or lack of history in works by folklorists and fairy-tale specialists. Yet there is little comprehensive history in his own study except for a positivist linking of printed texts of tales and speculative assessments of how and why different informants of the Grimms were influenced by reading printed texts, as if they only read books and did not tell oral tales. His starting point is typical of conservative "historians," who recount history from the point of view of the ruling classes, for his perspective assumes that commoners throughout history (including slaves, peasants, workers, women, and children) did not have a culture and did not tell tales worth recording, while everything the upper classes did was significant to record. Although de Blécourt seems to recognize that tales evolved and continue to evolve, he ignores many different factors that play a role in the historical evolution of storytelling, not only in Europe, but also throughout the world. For instance, he makes the following comments:

> An historical development of fairy tales is not just restricted to their content when ogres can change into devils or cats into frogs. Tale types themselves are part of an evolution; when folklorists designated a type, they effectively froze it in time and when they ordered a type thematically, the genetic relations with other types became obscured. When they assigned fairy tales a history going back as far as prehistorical times, they placed them effectively outside time, ignoring their temporal embeddedness. . . . Since fairy tales were supposed to belong to an anonymous "people," researchers have hardly payed proper attention to the production of tales. Yet the texts themselves, when put into temporal sequence, show constant meddling. Fragments were forgotten, half

remembered, replaced, rewritten and improved. In the process whole new stories and story types came into being. . . . If classical motifs suddenly appear in nineteenth-century stories, it is more an indication that its author had a classical education than that these stories survived for centuries in oral tradition—provided they are genuine classical motifs and not a figure of later interpretation.[14]

While I, too, have difficulty with the classification categories of *The Types of International Folktales*, I would not say that folklorists have frozen them in time and obscured relations. Here it is important to note that, as de Blécourt certainly knows, not all folklorists are alike, and there have been major disputes among them as to what constitutes folklore, a wonder tale, or the different types of tales that have been told and collected.[15] *The Types of International Folktales*, which de Blécourt employs to serve his own purposes, can be useful within limits, and various folklorists and literary critics have elaborated the categories creatively and judiciously as well as criticized and expanded on them. Folklorists have also abused them and taken them at face value. In the past, numerous folklorists earnestly sought to explore the changing contents and structures of the fairy tales long before the classifications of *The Types of International Folktales* were proposed in the early twentieth century. The more that folk tales were collected throughout the world in the nineteenth century, due in part to the Brothers Grimm, the more learned professionals became aware what was missing in history and what striking similarities worldwide there were among the tales. De Blécourt omits any discussion of the nineteenth-century anthropological school of folklorists (Tylor, James George Frazer, Lang, Ralston, Edwin Sydney Hartland, Pitrè, and many others) who developed notions of the polygenesis of folk tales and studied both oral and literary sources to analyze various genres of tales. Thanks to this school of thought and later scholars who favored historical and anthropological structuralism, numerous twentieth-century studies have opened our eyes to the evolution of tales in close and remote places and enabled neglected voices to be heard and unusual customs to be studied.

If de Blécourt truly believed in the evolution of fairy tales, as he says he does, he might have begun his book with an evolutionary history about storytelling and language in Europe. By necessity, he would have had to start with oral storytelling traditions. Fairy tales were told in pagan and Greco-Roman periods before they were recognized as such in the seventeenth century. Scholars like Burkert, Anderson, Hansen, Carl Lindahl, Röhrich, and Ziolkowski, among many others, have demonstrated that there were myths, stories, anecdotes, fables, and fragments similar to fairy tales in pre-Christian times and early modern Europe. The most significant "fairy tale" of the second century, "Cupid and Psyche" in Apuleius's *The Golden Ass*, is generally recognized by reliable classical scholars as a product of an oral tradition or heavily influenced by oral storytelling.[16] Besides, Apuleius himself was considered to be a great rhetorician and may have disseminated his tales orally as well as in written form. De Blécourt never discusses the possible influence of *Thousand and One Nights*, which were in oral and print circulation from the ninth through the eighteenth century and may have entered European regions through commerce and cultural exchanges in Spain, Italy, Greece, Sicily, and other Mediterranean countries.[17] In addition, the Crusades in the twelfth and thirteenth centuries may have led to direct contact with Eastern stories. Tales of magic that involved miraculous transformation along with supernatural characters, creatures, and animals were spread throughout Europe before the definition of fairy tales commenced in the eighteenth century. All early religions including Judaism and Christianity are full of them. Some of the oral magic tales already exhibited features of the later fairy tales, but there was no concept of genre. Tales were hybrids and crossbreeds.

How is it possible, then, for de Blécourt to exclude a discussion of tales in pre-Christian or pagan times of history, when people of all ranks and classes told tales, developed rituals, created gods and fates, and worshipped imaginary deities? Isn't it important to consider, as numerous folklorists and anthropologists have tried to demonstrate, that there were links between cultural practices of pagan people and those of the Greeks and Romans, and that there are numerous pagan relics in early modern history?[18] Isn't it conceivable that there were different class cultures in the Greco-Roman and early modern European periods that produced different types of storytelling? They ranged from court poets, traveling troubadours and actors, street callers, female salonnières, soldiers, journeymen, and merchants to common people in public and private spheres.

Communication, moreover, was predicated on a vast number of dialects from the Greco-Roman period through the nineteenth century, and it did not interest rulers and educated elites to record the hundreds of thousands of different tales that people told. Besides, learned people did not always speak or comprehend the dialects. Most histories of literacy of European countries estimate that 90 percent or more of the people were illiterate up through the eighteenth century.[19] They could not and did not write down their tales, songs, memoirs, and so on. When de Blécourt asserts that literacy began saturating Europe after the invention of the printing press, he has not done his homework. When it comes to storytelling, orality reigned in all social classes and still does up through today. As Françoise Waquet remarks in her book *Parler comme un livre: L'oralité et le savoir (XVIe–XXe siècle)*: "In placing the intellectual world under the major sign of writing and print, and in reducing the works of the mind to texts to read, one has forgotten the manner in which knowledge also circulated and still circulates at its highest level: the word."[20] Of course, by this she means the spoken word.

Not only did most learned Europeans read aloud and in groups up through the seventeenth century but they also participated in courtly performances and theatrical events that were called féeries in the seventeenth century and led eventually to the development of fairy-tale operas and plays. Talk was the mode of communication that led to relevance in all walks of life. We still communicate stories and information daily mainly through talk, whether we are professional storytellers or ordinary people. Our social class and education also determine our language, enunciation, and access to mass media for dissemination. While de Blécourt regrets that not enough work has been done in studying gendered ways of producing tales, he does not consider social class in his history of the evolution of fairy tales. He has no sense of class struggle in the public sphere when it comes to the battles over owning and appropriating stories, even though he views himself as an expert on witch hunts and the Inquisition, when peasants and also upper-class people were compelled to tell conflicting, extraordinary stories about magical flights, dangerous journeys, witches, fairies, demons, and other invented creatures from the fifteenth through the seventeenth century.

De Blécourt's assertion that there was only a feeble oral storytelling tradition among peasants is speculation, especially if we include documented stories of confessions and accusations, folk gatherings, and folk customs and festivities. Instead, he should simply have said that we do not have enough information about storytelling and fairy tales before the nineteenth century, because those learned people who could write did not collect tales from the peasantry and workers and frowned on their stories. They wrote about their own concerns. They documented their own relevance. Jerry Toner, Peter Burke, Danièle Alexandre-Bidon, Didier Lett, Marie-Thérèse Lorcin, and many other scholars of the Greco-Roman, medieval, and baroque periods have indicated that there were particular and different cultural traditions of storytelling throughout Europe.[21] Some important studies of common people's belief systems have also demonstrated how widespread the belief in witches, fairies, demons, ogres, and werewolves was up through the nineteenth century. It was not until the twentieth century—and in fact, late into the twentieth century—that scholars began exploring the conflicting stories told during the witch hunt period, and thus realized why and how people told so many different stories about witches, and how they were deprived of speaking their minds. Yet de Blécourt does not mention these studies, nor does he acknowledge that common people may have always told stories that either contained staple characters and motifs of fairy tales, or even the type of story of magic that he authorizes as a genuine fairy tale.

When he talks about the crucial role that learned people played in writing down stories, romances, myths, and so forth, he makes a significant contribution to our understanding of how educated writers and readers functioned in the fairy tale's evolution. Without their works, we would not be able to understand how tales evolved. As he says, they "meddled" in the evolution of the tales in all sorts of ways, eliminating, adding, and changing plots, characters, and motifs. But this is what all good storytellers do in all walks of life, and since most of the learned people did this when orality reigned, it is clear that many changes are due to oral exchanges. And many changes are due to the exchanges that upper-class people had with lower-class people who could not read and write. Sometimes upper-class people even acknowledged the oral storytelling of common people in their literary works.

During Louis XIV's reign in France in the seventeenth and early part of the eighteenth century, the great proponent of modernism, Perrault, indicated that his tales were influenced by stories that he had heard from his nanny. Some critics have refused to believe him, but there were also other writers of fairy tales at the end of the seventeenth and beginning of the eighteenth century who claimed to have heard their stories from lower-class informants. There is no reason to disbelieve them or Perrault, especially when they themselves were fond of telling their written stories orally in salons or among themselves, or when Louis XIV himself expressed delight in fairy tales.

What is important about this particular period, approximately 1690–1710, is that all the conditions for the institutionalization of a literary genre called conte de fée or fairy tale had been met: composition through writing by gifted writers, mainly women; production, publication, and dissemination of the tales by publishing houses that had to meet the approval of the royal authorities; and an expected reception or audience of readers, who would circulate the tales and perhaps write tales themselves. Once the French authors—and French was the dominant language among the elites in Europe—set the standard for printed fairy tales, the literary genre began to flower throughout Europe. But this did not mean that the oral tradition of telling fairy tales and other kinds of tales abated. The impact of the French literary fairy tales led to a fruitful exchange between the literary and oral traditions of storytelling that continues up through today. De Blécourt's dismissal of orality blinds him to the fact that the social institutionalization of the literary genre by the French enhanced a productive process that can be traced back in time even before the French to the Italians Straparola and Basile, both evidently influenced by oral tales, and even to the Greco-Roman period, when writers told tales in public places. The reason why I place so much emphasis on the French role in establishing the literary fairy tale is that this period of rising industrialism and mercantilism enabled greater distribution of books in the vernacular along with greater contact among urban and agrarian communities. The new technologies enhanced the oral dissemination of stories; they did not eliminate them.

De Blécourt seems to think that it was only in the nineteenth century, when most social classes had become literate or were about to become literate, that tales of magic began to be spread throughout Germany—and his focus is narrowly on German-speaking regions, whereas many other regions in Europe were highly illiterate. This is why he goes to great lengths to show how numerous tales that the Grimms supposedly collected by word of mouth were actually told or sent to them by literate lower- and upper-class informants. Yet this is neither news nor new scholarship.

Rölleke, perhaps the foremost Grimm scholar in the world, has long since uncovered facts about the Grimms' informants. His voluminous work has led to different interpretations and assessments of the Grimms' tales as "pure" folk tales.[22] But he reaches different conclusions about the Brothers Grimm than de Blécourt does. In examining the role that the educated aristocratic informants from Haxthausen played in providing fairy tales for the Grimms, he demonstrates that "the Brothers Grimm were well aware of the interplay of the oral tradition and its temporary written recording through that what Wesselski had once called 'fairy-tale cultivation' and defined their own role from this position in the taking and giving [of tales]."[23] In many of his different essays, Rölleke brings out the mutuality of the oral and written processes and explains that even if an informant was educated, he or she might have been strongly influenced by an oral tradition. It is to Rölleke's credit that we understand more about the role that literature and educated informants played in stamping the "folk" tales of the nineteenth century, and vice versa, and he does not dismiss the oral storytelling tradition among peasants.

Certainly, as Jürgen Beyer in a recent *Folklore* article comments, there is still more that folklorists must undertake to understand what "folk" and "orality" mean. He states: "Folklorists studying narratives from the nineteenth century are also dealing with tales of the 'folk,' but only with a small part of them. Many nineteenth-century narratives are forever lost, but a very substantial body of material—written, urban, multi-cultural, Christian—is to be found in collections outside folklore archives. It is time to have an unprejudiced look at this source material."[24] Implicit in Beyer's "plea" for me is also a call for folklorists (and literary critics and historians) to endeavor to understand the interplay between the orality and literacy of all kinds of tales and documents in the formation of genres like the fairy tale, and if possible, reach back into pre-Christian periods. One need not only study collections of folk tales and literature to grasp how fairy tales were formed; church records and cultural artifacts that pertain to relations and practices among people are also good sources.

De Blécourt claims that the Grimms' collection was "contaminated" from the beginning because they concealed the literary sources of their tales and due to their romantic pedagogical zeal. He thus devalues their role as *cultivators* of fairy tales and other simple genres, such as legends, tall tales, fables, animal tales, and anecdotes. Furthermore, he misinterprets the purpose of the Grimms' collecting and editing of the tales. In an essay about the role that the eccentric Romantic writer Clemens Brentano played in the formation of the Grimms' collection—we must remember that the Brothers began gathering tales on his behalf during the first decade of the nineteenth century—Rölleke notes that the Grimms did not recall hearing fairy tales in their youth, and that Brentano's early work on folk songs and tales involved literary and oral tales, influencing the brothers. In many respects, he inspired the Grimms.

Brentano is responsible for and the cause of the Brothers Grimm interest in the phenomenon of the fairy tale. He decisively stamped their
ideal style by his references to the appropriate old sources and references to the oral tradition, above all by the high estimation of [Philipp
Otto] Runge's fairy-tale contributions [they were in dialect] as well
as his own tendencies to adapt tales through his own publications of
fairy tales such as "The Little Mouse," the story about "Little Chicken,"
"Bearskin," and so on. The Brothers Grimm subordinated themselves
at first to all of this without conditions. That is, they learned from and
through Brentano to develop their extremely successful method that
they practiced and that involved contaminating related textual versions, restoring corrupted passages, and especially the reconstructing
of what they held to be an original fairy-tale tone. Most of all, however,
in their search for fairy tales they followed the same path indicated by
Brentano from the very beginning: only texts and subjects that corre-
sponded to their ideal of a fairy tale came under their purview or found
favor before their eyes. The so-called real transmission of folk material,
which distinguished itself in the end by abstruse, fragmentary, obscene
or even rebellious elements, did not occur to them and does not occur
in their collection.[25]

Here it is important to clarify what "contamination" or "meddling" means.
From the beginning, the Grimms and other folklorists had an ideal notion
of what a true folk tale was, no matter what genre. They assumed that there
had been some kind of pure primeval tales (*Urmärchen*) that gave birth to
genuine tale types, which engendered versions created by all sorts of storytellers. The Grimms therefore considered any variant of an ideal tale type
that contained great stylistic or substantial changes as contaminated in some
way. That is, whatever "ruined" the putative genuine folk elements was regarded as artificial and detracted from the folk spirit of the tales. This notion
of contamination lasted among folklorists well into the 1960s. De Blécourt
has rightly criticized it, but contamination has its curious aspects when we
examine the Grimms' work on folk tales, for they meddled constantly with
the different versions of the tales they received from their informants, while
trying to shape what they believed to be the most genuine representation of
a folk tale. To their minds, their acts of contamination were actually acts of
purification.

In an incisive study of the poetics of *The Children's and Household Tales*,
gathered by the Brothers Grimm, Jens Sennewald develops Rölleke's notion
of the Grimms as modernist and romantic cultivators of folk tales, not just
fairy tales. His book is an antidote to de Blécourt's negative assessment of the
Grimms as "forgers" and misleading depiction of them as writers for children. In his debate with Arnim about natural and artistic poetry as well as the

meaning of fairy tales, Jacob Grimm makes clear what the brothers' intentions were:

> Here my old phrase that I have already used earlier to defend myself [is signficant]: One should write according to one's ability and internal drives and not orient oneself to outside forces and adjust comfortably to them. Thus, the fairy-tale book has not been written for children, but it is welcomed by them, and that makes me very happy. I would not have worked on the fairy tales with pleasure if I had not believed that the most serious and oldest people just as I myself would consider it as poetry, mythology, and history and regard it as important.[26]

It is to Sennewald's credit that he explores and explains the intentions and conceptions of the Grimms' as romantic writers and philologists, just as Jacob sought to clarify his and his brother's beliefs and methods to Arnim.[27] Sennewald emphasizes that there was not just one edition of their tales but rather seven, and that the narratives, consisting of fairy tales, animal tales, legends, religious stories, fables, and anecdotes, were edited and changed over the course of forty-seven years. According to Sennewald, the Grimms' other linguistic and philological works influenced the seven editions. Given the Grimms' great erudition and concerns, Sennewald maintains that the tales need to be considered as a collective whole, which, the Grimms believed, originated in antiquity and continued to be formed and reformed in a flowing process of remaking that sought to make words come alive, to resuscitate relics of the past and silenced words, so that they could speak for themselves in tone and structure. As part of the process, the Grimms saw themselves as excavators and cultivators who wanted to make the past livable for all people so that they could become at one with the tales' words. Such a task that the Grimms set for themselves demanded great artistry and philological knowledge. As Sennewald comments,

> The *poetry* of the *Children's and Household Tales* is the result of their authorship of a "romantic book." Their poetics is stamped by philological poetry: at each turn of speech the "prevailing mark" of the philologists is at work who produced highly poetical texts and permanently concealed this singular achievement. . . . The *Children's and Household Tales*, collected by the Brothers Grimm, became a "book that we are" through their poetics. The "we" of this book is one of brotherhood, of the "collaterals," as Jacob Grimm wrote. The figures of the *Children's and Household Tales*, the *female informant* and the *collector*, represent a "folk widely speaking," and it seems as if the closed collection, read as ethnographical record, reaches way beyond the borders of the book. Whoever turns to the tales of the "folk" after reading the *Children's and Household Tales* will find what let him turn to the tales: the structures and regularity of a "romantic book." A research of folk tales

that connects itself to the *Children's and Household Tales* and dedicates itself to finding "original" folk tales that correspond to the "instinctual doings of nature" follows the *prescribed* tracks of the *Children's and Household Tales.*[28]

Indeed, the Grimms paved the way for research—the collecting of tales and setting of "romantic" precepts of folklore in the nineteenth century. This is not to say that the Grimms were idealistic visionaries who misrepresented the folk and folk tales by claiming they all emanated from a pristine past or mysterious divinity. The German Romantics were often experimental, innovative, and highly educated. The Grimms intensely studied words, sayings, etymologies, themes, plots, and history, and pieced together hundreds of versions and variants of fairy tales to understand their core.

Sennewald laboriously analyzes how the Grimms framed their collections, and added the relevant portrait of Viehmann in the second 1819 edition as an imagined model storyteller of the folk and a figure in the tales. He examines the various introductions, systematic constructions of the tales, and intertextualities—all of which form a whole body or an embodied tradition. Sennewald contends that the Grimms shaped the body as space in which the fairy tales and other tales that stemmed from an oral tradition could breathe organically and naturally, and combined and cultivated them with printed versions so that readers of every class could figure within them. Sennewald states:

> The thesis that can be derived from the various constellations is: the knowledge that the *Children's and Household Tales* depict is the result of their poetics. The constellations can be read as *scientific* text only within the perimeter in which they are poetical text and vice versa. To perceive the folk tales of *Children's and Household Tales* as documents of a "live tradition" or a "natural" and universal *poetry* means to read them as a "romantic book." The more one emphasizes their *scientific truth* and follows up on it, the more one realizes the poetic features of the folk tales. The more one concentrates on their poetics . . . the more construction and constructiveness of that "truth" and its poetological value emerge.[29]

In contrast to Sennewald's meticulous exploration of romantic aesthetics and philology that formed the basis of the Grimms' conception and concretization of the tales, de Blécourt flattens their significance, especially the fairy tales. By squeezing the Grimms' fairy tales into a lineal diachronic scheme that privileges printed texts over oral tales, de Blécourt loses sight of the complex interaction of oral and literary tales, whereas the Grimms were profoundly interested in determining the margins and meanings of art and natural poetry. They were also deeply concerned with allowing all types of tales to breathe and *all voices* to be heard.

At one point in de Blécourt's book, he argues that peasant informants never exhibited the capacity to retain a large repertoire of fairy tales or other tales for that matter. Hence, he asks, how was it possible to speak of an oral tradition of storytelling? Yet once the Grimms opened the dikes that dammed the oral folk tales, hundreds of unusual collections of folk tales appeared in the nineteenth century. By the 1870s, the great Sicilian folklorist Pitrè, who stemmed from a poor fisherman's family, collected fairy tales in dialect from illiterate lower-class women and men, who displayed large repertoires of tales, as did many of the peasant storytellers in France and eastern Europe. Where did all these Sicilian, French, and eastern European tales come from? Certainly not from books, and yet books may have played some role in their development. There is still a great deal of work to do if we want to grasp why fairy tales came into being and why they have stuck with us. Only judicious researchers with modest goals will enable us to understand the irresistibility and inexplicability of tales—still in demand of a great deal of explanation and interpretation.

Notes

Preface

1. See Deirdre Barrett, *Supernormal Stimuli: How Primal Urges Overran Their Evolutionary Purpose* (New York: W. W. Norton, 2010). Barrett observes: "Animal biology developed a concept that is crucial to understanding the problems instincts create when disconnected from their natural environment—that of the *supernormal stimulus*. . . . The essence of the supernormal stimulus is that the exaggerated intention can exert a stronger pull than the real thing" (3).

Chapter 1. The Cultural Evolution of Storytelling and Fairy Tales

1. See Jean-Louis Dessalles, *Why We Talk: The Evolutionary Origins of Language*, trans. James Grieve (Oxford: Oxford University Press, 2007), 139–210.
2. See, for instance, Ruth Bottigheimer, *Fairy Tales: A New History* (Albany: State University of New York, 2009); Wilem de Blécourt, *Tales of Magic, Tales of Print* (Manchester: Manchester University Press, 2011). I deal with these books in more detail in the appendixes.
3. Arthur Frank, *Letting Stories Breathe: A Socio-Narratology* (Chicago: University of Chicago Press, 2010).
4. See, for instance, Michael Holquist, ed., *The Dialogic Imagination: Four Essays*, trans. Caryl Emerson (Austin: University of Texas Press, 1981); Caryl Emerson, ed. and trans., *Problems of Dostoyevsky's Poetics* (Minneapolis: University of Minnesota Press, 1984).
5. Frank, *Letting Stories Breathe*, 14.
6. Ibid., 16.
7. Ibid., 17.
8. Marshall Poe, *A History of Communications: Media and Society from the Evolution of Speech to the Internet* (Cambridge: Cambridge University Press, 2011), 35.
9. Ibid., 18, 32.
10. See also Dan Sperber and Deirdre Wilson, *Relevance: Communication and Cognition*, 2nd ed. (London: Blackwell, 1995). The coauthors state: "The central claim of relevance theory is that the expectations of relevance raised by an utterance are precise enough, and predictable enough, to guide the hearer towards the speaker's meaning. The aim is to explain in cognitively realistic terms what these expectations

of relevance amount to, and how they might contribute to an empirically plausible account of comprehension" (608).

11. Desalles, *Why We Talk*, 354–55.
12. Michael Tomasello, *The Cultural Origins of Human Cognition* (Cambridge, MA: Harvard University Press, 1999), 150–51.
13. Walter Burkert, *Structure and History in Greek Mythology and Ritual* (Berkeley: University of California Press, 1979), 2.
14. Vladimir Propp, *Morphology of the Folktale*, ed. Louis Wagner and Alan Dundes, trans. Laurence Scott, 2nd rev. ed. (Austin: University of Texas Press, 1968).
15. Burkert, *Structure and History*, 10.
16. Ibid., 23.
17. Ibid., 18.
18. Niklas Holzberg, *The Ancient Fable*, trans. Christine Jackson-Holzberg (Bloomington: Indiana University Press, 2002), 15.
19. Leslie Kurke, *Aesopic Conversations: Popular Tradition, Cultural Dialogue, and the Invention of Greek Prose* (Princeton, NJ: Princeton University Press, 2011), 11. The reference is to James Scott, *Domination and the Arts of Resistance* (New Haven, CT: Yale University Press, 1990).
20. Thomas Noel, *Theories of the Fable in the Eighteenth Century* (New York: Columbia University Press, 1975), 1.
21. Annabel Patterson, *Fables of Power: Aesopian Writing and Political History* (Durham, NC: Duke University Press, 1991), 15–16.
22. André Jolles, *Einfache Formen: Legende/Sage/Mythe/Rätsel/Spruch/Kasus/Memorabile/Märchen/Witz*, 2nd ed. (1930; repr., Darmstadt: Wissenschaftliche Buchgesellschaft, 1958), 241.
23. On the fox, see Graham Anderson, *Fairytale in the Ancient World* (London: Routledge, 2000), 173–76; Hans-Jörg Uther, "The Fox in World Literature: Reflections on a 'Fictional Animal,'" *Asian Folklore Studies* 65, no. 2 (2006): 133–60. On the different portrayals, see Ines Köhler-Zülch, "Kater: Der gestiefelte K. (AATH545B)," in *Enzyklopädie des Märchens*, ed. Rolf Wilhelm Brednich (Berlin: de Gruyter, 1993), 7:1070–83. For an important analysis of the origins of "Puss in Boots," see also Pierre Saintyves, "Le Chat Botté ou L'Instauration d'un Roi," in *Les contes de Perrault et les récits parallèlles: Leurs origines* (Paris: Emile Nourry, 1923), 467–98.
24. Uther, "The Fox in World Literature," 150.
25. Köhler-Zülch, "Kater," 1070–83.
26. Dan Ben-Amos, "Straparola: The Revolution That Was Not," *Journal of American Folklore* 123, no. 490 (2010): 434–35.
27. For a full discussion of Straparola's tales, see Jack Zipes, "The Origins of the Fairy Tale in Italy: Straparola and Basile," in *Fairy Tales and the Art of Subversion: The Classical Genre for Children and the Process of Civilization*, 2nd rev. ed. (New York: Routledge, 2006), 13–28.
28. Bartolomeo Rossetti, ed., introduction to *Le piacevoli notti*, by Giovanfrancesco Straparola (Rome: Avanzini e Torraca, 1966), 12.
29. Richard Dawkins, *The Selfish Gene* (Oxford: Oxford University Press, 1976), 192.
30. For an interesting historical analysis of the development of the term "meme," see Marion Blute, *Darwinian Sociocultural Evolution: Solutions to Dilemmas in Cultural and Social Theory* (Cambridge: Cambridge University Press, 2010), 113–26.

31. Melvin Konner, *The Evolution of Childhood: Relationships, Emotion, Mind* (Cambridge, MA: Harvard University Press, 2010), 689.

32. Ibid., 701.

33. Michael Drout, "A Meme-Based Approach to Oral Traditional Theory," *Oral Tradition* 21, no. 2 (2006): 271.

34. Ibid., 276.

Chapter 2. The Meaning of Fairy Tale within the Evolution of Culture

1. Donald Haase, ed., "Fairy Tale," in *The Greenwood Encyclopedia of Folktales and Fairy Tales* (Westport, CT: Greenwood Press, 2008), 1:322.

2. For a thorough discussion of this term, see Nadine Jasmin, *Naissance du Conte Féminin. Mots et Merveilles: Les Contes de fées de Madame d'Aulnoy (1690–1698)* (Paris: Champion, 2002), 447–51.

3. See Nancy Palmer and Melvin Palmer, "The French *conte de fées* in England," *Studies in Short Fiction* 11, no. 1 (Winter 1974): 35–44; Nancy Palmer and Melvin Paler, "English Editions of French contes de fées in England," *Studies in Bibliography* 27 (1974): 227–32.

4. There is a crucial difference in French between conte de fées (tale about fairies) and *conte féerique* (fairy tale). The conte de fées purports to tell about the actions and deeds of fairies, while the conte féerique, a term that was not used by French writers, describes the narrative form.

5. See Jack Zipes, ed. and trans., *Beauties, Beasts, and Enchantment: Classic French Fairy Tales* (New York: New American Library, 1989). See also the superb collection of stories in Lewis Seifert and Domna Stanton, eds., *Enchanted Eloquence: Fairy Tales by Seventeenth-Century Women Writers* (Toronto: Iter, 2010).

6. See Anne Defrance and Jean-François Perrin, eds., *Le conte en ses paroles: La figuration de l'oralité dans le conte merveilleux du Classicisme aux Lumières* (Paris: Éditions Desjonquères, 2007). In particular, see the essays by Lewis Seifert, Jean-Paul Sermain, Christine Noille-Clauzade, Sophie Raynard, Jean Mainil, Françoise Gevrey, Anne Defrance, Julie Bloch, Raymonde Robert, and Christelle Bahier-Porte.

7. See Thomas Frederick Crane, *Italian Social Customs of the Sixteenth Century and Their Influences on the Literatures of Europe* (New Haven, CT: Yale University Press, 1920): 263–322, 480–504; Seifert and Stanton, *Enchanted Eloquence*, 6–12.

8. See Constance Cagnat-Debœuf, preface to Madame Catherine Anne d'Aulnoy, *Contes de fées*, ed. Constance Cagnat-Debœuf (Paris: Gallimard, 2008), 7–44.

9. For a full discussion of the fairy tale's role within the civilizing process, see Jack Zipes, *Fairy Tales and the Art of Subversion: The Classical Genre for Children and the Process of Civilization*, 2nd rev. ed. (New York: Routledge, 2006).

10. Patricia Hannon, *Fabulous Identities: Women's Fairy Tales in Seventeenth-Century France* (Amsterdam: Rodopi, 1998), 171.

11. Anne Duggan, *Salonnières, Furies, and Fairies: The Politics of Gender and Cultural Change in Absolutist France* (Newark: University of Delaware Press, 2005); Holly Tucker, *Pregnant Fictions: Childbirth and the Fairy Tale in Early Modern France* (Detroit: Wayne State University Press, 2003). See also Catherine Marin, "Pouvoir et subversion féminine dans les contes de fées à l'époque classique en France" (PhD diss., University of Wisconsin at Madison, 1991); Lewis Seifert, "Création et réception des conteuses: du XVIIe au XVIIIe siècle," in *Tricentenaire Charles Perrault: Les grands contes du XVIIe siècle et leur fortune littéraire*, ed. Jean Perrot (Paris: In

Press Éditions, 1998), 191–202; Jack Zipes, "The Rise of the French Fairy Tale and the Decline of France," in *When Dreams Came True: Classical Fairy Tales and Their Tradition*, 2nd rev. ed. (New York: Routledge, 2007), 33–52.

12. Jacques Barchilon, introduction to Madame Catherine-Anne d'Aulnoy, *Contes*, ed. Philippe Hourcade (Paris: Société des Textes Français Modernes, 1997): 2:xxx.

13. Seifert and Stanton, *Enchanted Eloquence*, 9.

14. Duggan, *Salonnières, Furies, and Fairies*, 216.

15. Paul Ginsty, *La Féerie* (Paris: Louis-Michaud, 1910), 12.

16. See Michele Rak, *Da Cenerentola a Cappuccetto rosso: Breve storia illustrata della fiaba barocca* (Milan: Bruno Mondadori, 2007).

17. Duggan, *Salonnières, Furies, and Fairies*, 225. See Jean Mainil, *Madame d'Aulnoy et le Rire des Fées: Essai sur la Subversion Féerique et le Merveilleux Comique sous L'Ancien Régime* (Paris: Klimé, 2001).

18. Tucker, *Pregnant Fictions*, 56.

19. Zipes, *Beauties, Beasts, and Enchantment*, 477.

20. Nadine Jasmin, "Matière folklorique, matière médiévale," in *Naissance du Conte Féminin. Mots et Merveilles: Les Contes de fées de Madame d'Aulnoy (1690–1698)* (Paris: Champion, 2002), 194.

21. See Alfred Maury, *Les fées du Moyen Âge* (Paris: Ladrange, 1843), and *Croyances et Légendes du Moyen Âge* (Paris: Champion, 1896).

22. See Pierre Klossowski, *Diana at Her Bath: The Women of Rome*, trans. Sophie Hawkes and Stephen Sartarelli (New York: Marsilo, 1990), 107:

> Macrobius tells us that, according to Cornelius Labeo, *Bona Dea* is but another name for the goddess, *Maia*, mother of Mercury; that in the sacrifices (in the month of May) she is also called *Magna Mater*, and that she was seen ordering the construction of a temple under the name *Bona Dea*. The secret rites supposedly show that she represented the earth; while in the pontifical books she was referred to simultaneously as *Bona*, since she provides all nourishment; as *Ops* (another name for the Diana of Aricia) since she sustains life through her succor; as *Fauna* (*favet*), since she assists all living things in their needs; and as *Fauna* (*fando*: to speak), since newborns do not let their voices be heard until after having made contact with the earth.

23. See "The Obscure Goddess Online Directory," available at http://www.thaliatook .com/OGOD/fauna.html.

24. John Scheid, "The Religious Roles of Roman Women," in *A History of Women: From Ancient Goddesses to Christian Saints*, ed. Pauline Schmitt Pantel (Cambridge, MA: Harvard University Press, 1992), 392–93.

25. Leslie Ellen Jones, "Fairies," in *Medieval Folklore: A Guide to Myths, Legends, Tales, Beliefs, and Customs*, ed. Carl Lindahl, John McNamara, and John Lindow (Oxford: Oxford University Press, 2002), 128.

26. Laura Rangoni, *Le Fate* (Milan: Xenia Edizioni, 2004).

27. Laurence Harf-Lancner, *Les Fées au Moyen Âge: Morgane et Mélusine. La naissance des fées* (Paris: Honoré Champion, 1984), 42.

28. For two excellent studies of Mélusine, see Bea Lundt, *Mélusine und Merlin im Mittelalter: Entwürfe und Modelle weiblicher Existenz im Beziehungsdiskurs der Geschlechter* (Munich: Fink, 1991); Donald Maddox and Sara Sturm-Maddox, eds., *Mélusine of Lusignan: Founding Fiction in Late Medieval France* (Athens: University

of Georgia Press, 1996). There were numerous tales about Mélusine from the thirteenth through the nineteenth century. For a good summary of the most significant medieval version by Jean d'Arras, see Linda Foubister, "The Story of Melusine" (medieval France, 1394), in *Encyclopedia Mythica*, available at http://www.pantheon.org/areas/folklore/folktales/articles/melusine.html:

> The fairy, Melusine, was the daughter of the fairy *Pressyne* and King Elynas of Albany. She became the fairy Queen of the forest of Colombiers in the French region of Poitou. One day, she and two of her subjects were guarding their sacred fountain when a young man, Raymond of Poitiers, burst out of the forest. Melusine spent the night talking with Raymond, and by dawn, they were betrothed, but with one condition. Melusine requested that Raymond promise that he would never see her on a Saturday. He agreed, and they were married. Melusine brought her husband great wealth and prosperity. She built the fortress of Lusignan so quickly that it appeared to be made by magic. Over time, Melusine built many castles, fortresses, churches, towers and towns, each in a single night, throughout the region. She and Raymond had ten children, but each child was flawed. The eldest had one red eye and one blue eye, the next had an ear larger than the other, another had a lion's foot growing from his cheek, and another had but one eye. The sixth son was known as Geoffrey-with-the-great tooth, as he had a very large tooth. In spite of the deformities, the children were strong, talented and loved throughout the land.
>
> One day, Raymond's brother visited him and made Raymond very suspicious about the Saturday activities of his wife. So the next Saturday, Raymond sought his wife, finding her in her bath where he spied on her through a crack in the door. He was horrified to see that she had the body and tail of a serpent from her waist down. He said nothing until the day that their son, Geoffrey-with-the-great tooth, attacked a monastery and killed one hundred monks, including one of his brothers. Raymond accused Melusine of contaminating his line with her serpent nature, thus revealing that he had broken his promise to her. As a result, Melusine turned into a fifteen-foot serpent, circled the castle three times, wailing piteously, and then flew away. She would return at night to visit her children, then vanish. Raymond was never happy again. Melusine appeared at the castle, wailing, whenever a count of Lusignan was about to die or a new one to be born. It was said that the noble line which originated with Melusine will reign until the end of the world. Her children included the King of Cyprus, the King of Armenia, the King of Bohemia, the Duke of Luxembourg, and the Lord of Lusignan.

29. As was the case with Mélusine, there were many tales about the Fay Morgan in the Middle Ages. For a good summary of her significance, see Brian Edward Rise, "Morgan Le Fay," available at http://www.pantheon.org/articles/m/morgan_le_fay.html:

> Introduced in *Geoffrey of Monmouth*'s *Vita Merlini*, her name (there spelled "Morgen") implies ties to the realm of Fairy. She is also a magical figure as well as a priestess presiding over a sisterhood of nine inhabiting an enchanted isle. She receives the wounded king after the last battle and offers to cure him if he remains long enough.

There are many Celtic traditions evident here, not just of fairy queens ruling magic lands, but of actual sisterhoods of healers and miracle workers recorded in classical literature. Such a group might have been led by a priestess that served as the earthly manifestation of a goddess. Giraldus Cambrensis and other medieval authors were well aware of Morgan's divinity. Comparison of Welsh and non-Welsh Arthurian matter show her to be somewhat identified with Modron and ultimately with the river goddess Matrona, similar to and possibly derived from the Irish goddess Morrigan.

Christianity humanizes and eventually vilifies her. Early on she is a type of benevolent fairy that aids Arthur throughout his life, not just at the end. The Welsh claim her father to be the obscure Avallach, king of the magical island with its Welsh name, but he fades from legend. Morgan is essentially the sole personage of Avalon, the Isle of Apples. She is further humanized with the progress of Arthurian storytelling. The former goddess becomes a daughter of Ygerna and her first husband Gorlois, the Duke of Cornwall, making Morgan Arthur's half sister. Glastonbury's identification with Avalon leads to beliefs that she ruled in that area but romances place her in various locations. She becomes the owner of the Castle of Maidens, possibly near Edinburgh while a few continental romancers move her to the Mediterranean entirely. Sicily is one such place. She is named Fata Morgana by the Italians and that name is given to a mirage that appears in the Straits of Messina attributed to her magic in the past.

Medieval Christianity had a difficult time assimilating a benevolent enchantress, [thus] she becomes more and more sinister. She is now a witch taught the black arts by Merlin and is a bedevilment to Arthur and his knights with a special hatred towards Queen Guinevere. Oft times she is involved in a plan to ensnare a knight for her own pleasure by sending them into a "valley of no return," or against a mighty adversary. Other times she is married to Urien and bears a son, *Owain* or *Yvain*. Yet she never becomes purely evil. Many attractive qualities remain and Morgan is associated with art and culture. Despite the scheming and plotting at court, she is still the one who bears the wounded King to his place of healing on Avalon.

Part of Christianity's failure to understand the character of Morgan was their misapplied versions of morality. They imposed a Judeo-Christian ethical structure over a Celtic one and tried to eradicate the conflicts. The monks basically misunderstood the beliefs of Celtic rule. Women had equal if not greater power than men and were expected to take lovers. This is evident in the transcription of the Tain, the national epic of Ireland (except here scribal ignorance of Celtic ways actually preserved many of them). This is also the reason why Guinevere is seen as unfaithful rather than a free woman free to make her own choices in who she beds. Morgan necessarily becomes a witch to explain her sexuality.

30. For a thorough discussion of d'Aulnoy's knowledge and use of French folklore, see Raymonde Robert, "Madame d'Aulnoy et le Folklore: Le Puzzel des Motif Populaires," in *Le conte de fées littéraire en France de la fin du xvii à la fin xviii siècle* (Nancy: Presses Universitaires de Nancy, 1981), 108–21.

31. Seifert and Stanton, *Enchanted Eloquence*, 20.
32. Zipes, *Beauties, Beasts, and Enchantment*, 303.
33. Ibid., 307.
34. Ibid., 481.
35. Ibid., 399.
36. Ibid., 495.
37. Walter Burkert, *Creation of the Sacred: Tracks of Biology in Early Religions* (Cambridge, MA: Harvard University Press, 1996), 22.
38. Ibid., 56–79.
39. Ibid., 65.
40. Ibid., 70. See also P. G. Walsh's comments, cited in Lucius Apuleius, *The Golden Ass*, ed. and trans. P. G. Walsh (Oxford: Oxford University Press, 2008), xl–xli:

    > The basic themes of the beautiful girl with two jealous sisters, her courtship by an enchanted suitor reputed to be a monster, the enforced separation from him because of the breaking of a taboo, the oppression by a witch who imposes impossible trials upon her, and the ultimate reconciliation with her lover, can all be paralleled in widespread versions of folklore tales; the existence of a North African version is of particular interest. It was Apuleius' brilliant achievement to convert this *Märchen* into a *Kunstmärchen* for his special purpose of illuminating the career of Lucius.

41. Kate Distin, *Cultural Evolution* (Cambridge: Cambridge University Press, 1995), 209.
42. Ibid., 224.
43. Ibid., 224–25.
44. See the Wikepedia entry "Fairies," available at http://en.wikipedia.org/wiki/Disney_Fairies. The films, books, and games in this series are particularly insipid, depleting all meaning from the term "fairy." See Joanna Weiss, "Fear of Fairy Tales," *Boston Globe*, September 21, 2008, available at http://www.boston.com/boston globe/ideas/articles/2008/09/21/fear_of_fairy_tales/. She remarks: "Yet something important is lost when a child's introduction to fairy tales comes in such white-washed form. It's not just Rapunzel: In toys, movies, and books, the old fairy tales are being systematically stripped of their darker complexities. Rapunzel has become a lobotomized girl in a pleasant tower playroom; Cinderella is another pretty lady in a ball gown, like some model on 'Project Runway.' "

Chapter 3. Remaking "Bluebeard," or Good-bye to Perrault

1. Michael Drout, "A Meme-Based Approach to Oral Traditional Theory," *Oral Tradition* 21, no. 2 (2006): 269. For a comprehensive discussion of memes and fairy tales, see Jack Zipes, *Why Fairy Tales Stick: The Evolution and Relevance of a Genre* (New York: Routledge, 2006). For a comprehensive study of memes, see Kate Distin, *The Selfish Meme* (Cambridge: Cambridge University Press, 2005).
2. Drout, "A Meme-Based Approach," 271.
3. See Graham Anderson, "Butchering Girls," in *Fairytale in the Ancient World* (London: Routledge, 2000), 97–100.
4. Pierre Saintyves, "La Barbe-Bleue ou La Tentation Rituelle," in *Le contes de Perrault et les récits parallèles: Leur origines* (Paris: E. Nourry, 1923), 359–96.
5. Arthur Frank, *Letting Stories Breathe: A Socio-Narratology* (Chicago: University of Chicago Press, 2010), 53.

6. Constantine Verevis, *Film Remakes* (Edinburgh: University of Edinburgh Press, 2006), vii.

7. Ibid., 29.

8. Ute Heidmann and Jean-Michel Adam, *Textualité et Intertextualité des contes: Perrault, Apulée, La Fontaine, Lhéritier* (Paris: Garnier, 2010), 19.

9. See Saintyves, *Le contes de Perrault et les récits parallèles*. Saintyves provides ample evidence for the influence of oral tales, as does Raymonde Robert, *Le conte de fées littéraire en France de la fin du xvii à la fin xviii siècle* (Nancy: Presses Universitaires de Nancy, 1981).

10. Heidmann and Adam, *Textualité et Intertextualité des contes*, 34–35.

11. See the significant chapter "The Core of a Tale," in Walter Burkert, *Creation of the Sacred: Tracks of Biology in Early Religions* (Cambridge, MA: Harvard University Press, 1996), 56–79.

12. See Shuli Barzilai, "The Snake-Charmer's Wife in *Genesis Rabbah*," in *Tales of Bluebeard and His Wives from Late Antiquity to Postmodern Times* (London: Routledge, 2009), 1–21.

13. Verevis, *Film Remakes*, 29.

14. Douglas Keesey, *Catherine Breillat* (Manchester: Manchester University Press, 2001), 151.

15. See, for example, the interview with Nicolas Poinsot, "La scandaleuse, Catherine Breillat lance Barbe-Bleue au festival du film fantastique de Neuchâtel," available at http//www.lesquotidiennes.com/culture/la-scandeleuse-catherine-breillat-lance-barbe-bleue, in which Breillat states:

> Comme beaucoup de contes, celui-ci aborde un thème essentiel. Pour ma sœur et moi, il a toujours été notre préféré, depuis l'enfance. On le lisait à haute voix et on se mettait à pleurer ensemble avant d'arriver à la fin. D'une certaine façon, il s'adresse surtout aux petites filles. Il leur montre comment apprendre à aimer l'homme qui va les tuer. Leurs illusionsm elles les perdent très vite, parc qu'à quatorze ans, beaucoup se trouvent déjà vieilles. En fait ce film mûrissait dans ma tête depuis une dizaine d'années, mais il a véritablement commencé à prendre fore en 2005.

16. See Jack Zipes, "Bluebeard's Original Sin and the Rise of Serial Killing, Mass Murder, and Fascism," in *The Enchanted Screen: The Unknown History of the Fairy-Tale Film* (New York: Routledge, 2011), 158–71.

17. Anderson, *Fairytale in the Ancient World*, 102.

18. Frank, *Letting Stories Breathe*, 3.

19. Barzilai, "The Snake-Charmer's Wife," 5.

20. See Zipes, *Why Fairy Tales Stick*, 155–94. See also Philip Lewis, *Seeing through the Mother Goose Tales: Visual Turns in the Writings of Charles Perrault* (Stanford, CA: Stanford University Press, 1996).

21. Barzilai, "The Snake-Charmer's Wife," 8.

Chapter 4. Witch as Fairy/Fairy as Witch

1. See Giordano Berti, "La stregoneria nell'eta moderna," in *Storia della Stregoneria: Origini, Credenze, Persecuzioni e Rinascita nel Mondo Contemporaneo* (Milan: Arnoldo Mondadori, 2010), 193–222. See also James Lewis, ed., *Magical Religion and*

Modern Witchcraft (Albany: State University of New York, 1996); Ronald Hutton, *The Triumph of the Moon: A History of Modern Pagan Witchcraft* (Oxford: Oxford University Press, 1999).

2. Among the numerous books on this topic, see Anne Baring and Jules Cashford, *The Myth of the Goddess: Evolution of an Image* (London: Viking, 1991); Pauline Schmitt Pantel, ed., *A History of Women: From Ancient Goddesses to Christian Saints*, trans. Arthur Goldhammer (Cambridge, MA: Harvard University Press, 1992).

3. Laura Verdi, "Dalla Grande Madre alle fate delle fiabe," in *Le Grandi Madri*, ed. Tolda Giani Gallino (Milan: Feltrinelli, 1989), 171.

4. Leslie Ellen Jones, "Fairies," in *Medieval Folklore: A Guide to Myths, Legends, Tales, Beliefs, and Customs*, ed. Carl Lindahl, John McNamara, and John Lindow (Oxford: Oxford University Press, 2002.), 128.

5. Maren Clausen-Stolzenburg, *Märchen und mittelalterliche Literaturtradition* (Heidelberg: Universitätsverlag C. Winter, 1995), 308.

6. Monika Kropej, "Contemporary Legends from the Slovene Karst in Comparison with Fairylore and Belief Traditions," *Studia Mythologica Slavica* 8 (2005): 234.

7. It would be impossible to cite all the excellent studies that have been published. For good overviews, see Julio Caro Baroja, *The World of Witches*, trans. O.N.V. Glendinning (Chicago: University of Chicago Press, 1964); Ben Ankarloo and Gustav Henningsen, eds., *Early Modern European Witchcraft: Centres and Peripheries* (Oxford: Clarendon Press, 1990); Valerie Flint, *The Rise of Magic in Early Medieval Europe* (Princeton, NJ: Princeton University Press, 1991); P. G. Maxwell-Stuart, *Witchcraft in Europe and the New World, 1400–1800* (Houndmills, UK: Palgrave, 2001); Darren Oldridge, ed., *The Witchcraft Reader* (London: Routledge, 2002); Giordano Berti, *Storia della Stregoneria: Origini, Credenze, Persecuzioni e Rinascita nel Mondo Contemporaneo* (Milan: Arnoldo Mondatori, 2010).

8. See Jeffrey St. Clair, introduction to *Fear of the Animal Planet: The Hidden History of Resistance*, by Jason Hribal (Oakland, CA: AK Press, 2010), 1–19; Joyce Salisbury, *The Beast Within: Animals in the Middle Ages* (London: Routledge, 1994); W. W. Hyde, "The Prosecution and Punishment of Animals and Lifeless Things in the Middle Ages and Modern Times," *University of Pennsylvania Law Review* 64, no. 7 (1914): 690–730.

9. See Jean Seznec, *The Survival of the Pagan Gods: The Mythological Tradition and Its Place in Renaissance Humanism and Art*, trans. Barbara Sessions (New York: Harper and Row, 1953).

10. Diane Purkiss, *The Witch in History: Early Modern and Twentieth-Century Representations* (London: Routledge, 1996), 160.

11. For an excellent comprehensive study of Russian collectors and tales, see Yuruy Matveyevich Sokolov, *Russian Folklore*, trans. Catherine Ruth Smith (Hatboro, PA: Folklore Associates, 1966).

12. For much better and more complete translations of *The Historical Roots of the Wonder Tale* with excellent introductions, see Vladimir Propp, *Die historischen Wurzeln des Zaubermärchens*, trans. Martin Pfeiffer (Munich: Hanser, 1987); Vladimir Propp, *Les Racines Historiques du Conte Merveilleux*, trans. Lise Gruek-Apert, preface Daniel Fabre and Jean-Claude Schmitt (Paris: Gallimard, 1983).

13. Vladimir Propp, *The Russian Folktale*, trans. Sibelan Forrester (Detroit: Wayne State University Press, 2012). See also the Italian translation: Vladimir Propp, *La fiaba russa*, ed. and trans. Franca Crestani, intro. Kirill Chistov (Turin: Einaudi, 1990).

14. Kirill Chistov, "V. Ya. Propp—Legend and Fact," *International Folklore Review* 4 (1986): 17.

15. See Hans-Jörg Uther, *The Types of International Folktales: A Classification and Bibliography*, 3 vols., Ff Communications no. 284 (Helsinki: Suomalainen Tiedeakatemia, 2004). These volumes constitute a revision of Antti Aarne and Stith Thompson, *The Types of the Folktale: A Classification and a Bibliography*, 2nd rev. ed., Ff Communications no. 3 (Helsinki: Suomalainen Tiedeakatemia, 1961).

16. Vladimir Propp, *Theory and History of Folklore*, ed. Anatoly Liberman, trans. Adriadna Y. Martin and Richard P. Martin (Minneapolis: University of Minnesota Press, 1984), 117.

17. Michael Drout, *How Tradition Works: A Meme-Based Cultural Poetics of the Anglo-Saxon Tenth Century* (Tempe: Arizona Center for Medieval and Renaissance Studies, 2006), 16–17.

18. Vladimir Propp, *The Russian Folktale*, trans. Sibelan Forrester (Detroit: Wayne State University Press, forthcoming); Forrester's book is still in page proofs. For the Italian translation, see Vladimir Propp, *La fiaba russa*, ed. and trans. Franca Crestani, intro. Kirill Chistov (Turin: Einaudi, 1990), 202–3.

19. Joanna Hubbs, *Mother Russia: The Feminine Myth in Russian Culture* (Bloomington: Indiana University Press, 1988), 36.

20. Ibid., 37.

21. Andreas Johns, *Baba Yaga: The Ambiguous Mother and Witch of the Russian Folktale* (New York: Peter Lang, 2004), 258. See also the entire conclusion to Johns's book; ibid., 257–75.

22. For good accounts of his life and work, see Richard Dorson, *The British Folklorists: A History* (Chicago: University of Chicago Press, 1968), 387–91; Patrick Waddington, "Ralston, William Ralston Sheldon (1828–1889)," *Oxford Dictionary of National Biography* (Oxford: Oxford University Press, 2004); William Ryan, "William Ralston: Russian Magic and Folklore in England," in *Russian Magic at the British Library: Books, Manuscripts, Scholars, Travellers. The Panizzi Lectures 2005*, lecture 1 (London: British Library, 2005), 1–39.

23. W. R. S. Ralston, *Russian Folk Tales* (London: Smith, Elder, and Company, 1873), 163.

24. Gustav Henningsen, "'Ladies from the Outside': An Archaic Pattern of the Witches' Sabbath," in *Early Modern European Witchcraft: Centres and Peripheries*, ed. Ben Ankarloo and Gustav Henningsen (Oxford: Clarendon Press, 1990), 195.

25. Ibid., 198, 207.

26. For good discussions about shamanism and fairy tales, see Heino Gehrts and Gabriele Lademann-Priemer, eds., *Schamanentum und Zaubermärchen* (Kassel: Eric Röth Verlag, 1986); Carl A. P. Ruck, Blaise Daniel Staples, José Alfredo González Celdrán, and Mark Alwin Hoffman, *The Hidden World: Survival of Pagan Shamanic Themes in European Fairytales* (Durham, NC: Carolina Academic Press, 2007).

27. Carlo Ginzburg, "Deciphering the Witches' Sabbat," in *The Witchcraft Reader*, ed. Darren Oldrige (London: Routledge, 2002), 122.

28. Ibid., 126.

29. Éva Pócs, "The Alternative World of the Witches' Sabbat," in *The Witchcraft Reader*, ed. Darren Oldrige (London: Routledge, 2002), 133.

30. Ibid. See also Gábor Klaniczay, "Shamanistic Elements in Central Europe," in *The Uses of Supernatural Power: The Transformation of Popular Religion in Medieval*

and Early-Modern Europe, trans. Susan Singerman (Princeton, NJ: Princeton University Press, 1990), 129–50.

31. See Peter Dinzelbacher, *Heilige oder Hexen? Schicksale auffälliger Frauen in Mittelalter und Frühneuzeit* (Zurich: Artemis and Winkler, 1995); Richard Kieckhefer, "The Holy and the Unholy: Sainthood, Witchcraft, and Magic in Late Medieval Europe," in *Christendom and Its Discontents: Exclusion, Persecution, and Rebellion, 1000–1500*, ed. Scott Waugh and Peter Diehl (Cambridge: Cambridge University Press, 1996), 310–37.

32. Berti, *Storia della Stregoneria*, 219–20.

33. See Heidi Anne Heiner, ed., *Rapunzel and Other Maiden in the Tower Tales from around the World* (Charleston, SC: SurLaLunePress, 2010).

34. Linda Hults, *The Witch as Muse: Art, Gender, and Power in Early Modern Europe* (Philadelphia: University of Pennsylvania Press, 2005), 15–16. See Stuart Clark, *Thinking with Demons: The Idea of Witchcraft in Early Modern Europe* (Oxford: Oxford University Press, 1977).

Chapter 5. The Tales of Innocent Persecuted Heroines and Their Neglected Female Storytellers and Collectors

1. Antti Aarne and Stith Thompson, *The Types of the Folktale: A Classification and a Bibliography*, 2nd rev. ed., Ff Communications no. 3 (Helsinki: Suomalainen Tiedeakatemia, 1961). See also the revised version: Hans-Jörg Uther, *The Types of International Folktales: A Classification and Bibliography*, 3 vols., Ff Communications no. 284 (Helsinki: Suomalainen Tiedeakatemia, 2004). Uther no longer describes tale type 510 in the same way as Aarne and Thompson. Strangely, in the index, he notes about fifteen other tale types that can be categorized as tales about innocent persecuted women without listing "Cinderella" and "Peau d'Âne," and yet in his information for tale type 510, he indicates how "Cinderella" and "Peau d'Âne" are related to these tales by listing them under 510A and 510B.

2. Steven Swann Jones, "The Innocent Persecuted Heroine Genre: An Analysis of Its Structure and Themes," *Western Folklore* 52, no. 1 (January 1993): 39.

3. Laura Gonzenbach, *Beautiful Angiola: The Great Treasury of Sicilian Folk and Fairy Tales Collected by Laura Gonzenbach*, trans. and ed. Jack Zipes (New York: Routledge, 2004), 18–20.

4. Marie-Louise Tenèze and Georges Delarue, eds., *Nannette Lévesque, conteuse et chanteuse du pays des sources de la Loire. La collecte de Victor Smith 1871–1876* (Paris: Gallimard, 2000), 127–29.

5. Božena Němcová, "The Twelve Months," in *The Key of Gold: 23 Czech Folk Tales*, ed. and trans. Josef Baudis (London: George Allen and Unwin, 1917), 1–15.

6. Rachel Busk, *Roman Legends: A Collection of the Fables and Folk-Lore of Rome* (Boston: Estes and Lauriat, 1877), 84–90.

7. See, for instance, the following excellent collections: Angela Carter, ed., *The Virago Book of Fairy Tales* (London: Virago Press, 1990), and *Strange Things Sometimes Still Happen: Fairy Tales from around the World* (London: Faber and Faber, 1993); Kathleen Ragan, *Fearless Girls, Wise Women, and Beloved Sisters: Heroines in Folktales from around the World* (New York: W. W. Norton, 1998).

8. There is only scant biographical information about Busk. The two best sources at present are Richard Dorson, *The British Folklorists: A History* (Chicago: University of Chicago Press, 1968), 381–87; Venetia Newall, "Rachel Busk," in *Enzyklopädie des Märchens*, ed. Kurt Ranke (Berlin: de Gruyter, 1979), 2:1054–55.

9. Rachel Busk, *Roman Legends: A Collection of the Fables and Folk-Lore of Rome* (Boston: Estes and Lauriat, 1877), 71. This was the first US edition of *The Folk-Lore of Rome, Collected by Word of Mouth from the People.*

10. For more information about her life and works, see Milada Součková, *The Czech Romantics* (The Hague: Mouton, 1958); Jirí Morava, *Sehnsucht in meiner Seele: Božena Němcová, Dichterin: Ein Frauenschicksal in Alt-Österreich* (Innsbruck: Haymon, 1995).

11. Součková, *The Czech Romantics*, 135.

12. Ibid., 137.

13. The tales in this paperback volume were first published separately in two hardback editions: Gonzenbach, *Beautiful Angiola*, and *The Robber with a Witch's Head: More Stories from the Great Treasury of Sicilian Folk and Fairy Tales*, trans. and ed. Jack Zipes (New York: Routledge, 2004). The paperback edition contains two additional dialect tales.

14. See Jack Zipes, "Hansel and Gretel: On Translating Abandonment, Fear, and Hunger," in *Why Fairy Tales Stick: The Evolution and Relevance of a Genre* (New York: Routledge, 2006), 195–222.

15. See John Ellis, *One Fairy Story Too Many: The Brothers Grimm and Their Tales* (Chicago: University of Chicago Press, 1983).

16. Gonzenbach, *Beautiful Angiola*, 560.

17. Ibid., 106.

Chapter 6. Giuseppe Pitrè and the Great Collectors of Folk Tales in the Nineteenth Century

1. Simon Bronner, *American Folklore Studies: An Intellectual History* (Lawrence: University Press of Kansas, 1986), 2.

2. For a comprehensive study of the different publications, see Manfred Grätz, *Das Märchen in der deutschen Aufklärung: Vom Feenmärchen zum Volksmärchen* (Stuttgart: J. B. Metzler, 1988).

3. Jacob Grimm, *Circular wegen Aufsamlung der Volkspoesie*, ed. Ludwig Denecke, afterword Kurt Ranke (Kassel: Brother Grimm Museum, 1968), 3–4.

4. See the interesting essay with the correspondence between Taylor and the Brothers Grimm in Otto Hartwig, "Zur ersten englischen Übersetzung der Kinder- und Hausmärchen der Brüder Grimm," *Centralblatt für Bibliothekswesen* 15, nos. 1–2 (January–February 1898): 1–16.

5. David Blamires, "The Early Reception of the Grimms' *Kinder- und Hausmärchen* in England," *Bulletin of the John Rylands University Library of Manchester* 71, no. 3 (1989): 69.

6. Thomas Frederick Crane, "Giuseppe Pitrè and Sicilian Folk-Lore," *Nation* 103, no. 2671 (1916): 234.

7. Walter Keller, "Zum Andenken an Giuseppe Pitrè," *SAVk* 21 (1917): 94–96.

8. Alberto Mario Cirese, "Giuseppe Pitrè tra storia locale e antropologia," in *Pitrè e Salomone Marino* (Palermo: Flaccovio, 1968), 34. ("Atti del Convegno di studi per il 50 Anniversario della morte di Giuseppe Pitrè e Salvatore Salomone-Marino," Palermo, November 25–27, 1966.)

9. See Richard Dorson, *The British Folklorists: A History* (Chicago: University of Chicago Press, 1968); Giuseppe Cocchiara, *Storia del folklore in Europa* (Turin: Editore Borginghieri, 1952), translated by John McDaniel, as *The History of Folklore in Europe* (1952; repr., Philadelphia: Institute for the Study of Human Issues, 1981).

10. Giuseppe Pitrè, *La famiglia, la casa, la vita del popolo siciliano* (Palermo: Lauriel, 1913), 437–38.

11. Giuseppe Cocchiara, *Pitrè, la Sicilia e il folklore* (Messina: D'Alma, 1951), 142.

12. Giuseppe Pitrè, *La Demopsicologia e la sua storia*, ed. Loredana Bellantonio (Palermo: Documenta Edizioni, 2001), 34–35, 36.

13. Here the storyteller, Elisabetta (Sabedda) Sanfratello, interjects that she has given the mother in the story her own name, as a name "for example," and then feels compelled to add that, of course, she herself was not present for the story's actions.

14. Giuseppe Pitrè, *The Collected Sicilian Folk and Fairy Tales of Giuseppe Pitrè*, ed. and trans. Jack Zipes and Joseph Russo (New York: Routledge, 2008), 1:123–27.

Chapter 7. Fairy-Tale Collisions, or the Explosion of a Genre

1. See, for example, Jane Martineau, ed., *Victorian Fairy Painting* (London: Merrell Holberton, 1997); Christopher Wood, *Fairies in Victorian Art* (Woodbridge, UK: Antique Collectors' Club, 2000).

2. There have been several other important fairy-tale exhibits in the past ten years. See, for instance, Fairy Tales: From the Dark Wood to Happily Ever After, curated by Kris Waldherr at the Brooklyn Academy, 2009, available at http://www.kriswaldherr.com/press/ftpress.html. This chapter is a more extensive version of an essay that I wrote for the Frist Center's catalog of the exhibit. See Mark Scala, ed., *Fairy Tales, Monsters, and the Genetic Imagination* (Nashville, TN: Vanderbilt University Press, 2012).

3. John McEwen, *Paula Rego*, 3rd ed. (London: Phaidon, 2006), 289.

4. Cited in ibid., 138.

5. Marina Warner, introduction to *Nursery Rhymes*, by Paula Rego (London: Thames and Hudson, 1994), 8.

6. See Art 21, "Kiki Smith Biography," available at http//www.pbs.org.art 21/artists/smith/index.html.

7. Claire Prussian, "Artist's Statement," available at http://claireprussian.com/statement.html.

8. See Sarah Bonner, "Visualising Little Red Riding Hood," *Moveable Type*, available at http://www.ucl.ac.uk/english/graduate/issue/2/sarah.html.

9. See Navid Nuur and Lisa Alena Vieten, eds., *Aftérouge* (Rotterdam: Piet Zwart Institute, 2006), 5. The editors write:

> The book *Aftérouge* arose from a fascination with images and stories that are part of our collective memory. This led to an interest in association. . . . More than fifty visual contributions are included in this book, all based on personal associations with the memory of the same story, the familiar fairy tale Little Red Riding Hood. In assembling the visual contributions we expressly requested images that would not so much illustrate the story itself, but are based on the memory of the story. Images that in a certain sense are comparable with afterimages, or with echoes, distorted repetitions.

10. See http://www.deviantart.com/.

11. See http://www.6amhoover.com/index_flash.html.

12. See *PRISM international* 47, no. 2 (Winter 2009).

13. See http://mcraemorton.com/home.html.

14. For an excellent study of these photos, see Li Cornfeld, "Shooting Heroines: On Dina Goldstein's Fallen Princesses" (talk at the From Portraits to Pinups:

Representations of Women in Art and Popular Culture conference, Brooklyn Museum, May 13, 2011).

15. See Johanna Burton, ed., *Cindy Sherman* (Cambridge, MA: MIT Press, 2006); Julie Rouart, ed., *Cindy Sherman* (Paris: Flammarion, 2006).

16. See Miwa Yanagi, *Fairy Tale: Strange Stories of Women Young and Old* (Kyoto: Seigensha Art Publishing, 2007).

17. See "Polixeni Papapetrou," available at http://polixenipapetrou.net/text.php#Fairy_Tales2004-2006. This Web site includes short, interesting essays on Papapetrou's work by Adrian Martin, Béatrice Andrieux, and Vivienne Webb.

18. Rima Staines, "Drawing the Old Woman in the Woods," *Marvels and Tales* 24, no. 2 (2010): 336–37.

19. Meghan Body, "Artist Statements," available at http://www.lookingglasslabs.com/statementC.html.

20. Walter Martin and Paloma Muñoz, "Islands: The Art of Martin and and Muñoz—An Interview with the Artists," *Penleaf* (February–March 2008).

21. Joseph Wolin, "The Haunting: Marcel Dzama's Traumatic Fantasy Worlds," *Canadian Art* (Fall 2008): 95.

Appendix A. Sensationalist Scholarship

1. See Giovan Francesco Straparola, *Le piacevoli notti*, ed. Donato Pirovano (Rome: Salerno, 2000), xlvii.

2. Jack Zipes, *Fairy Tales and the Art of Subversion: The Classical Genre for Children and the Process of Civilization*, 2nd rev. ed. (New York: Routledge, 2006), 14.

3. Cited in Straparola, *Le piacevoli notti*, xlvii

4. See Jan Ziolkowski, "Straparola and the Fairy Tale: Between Literary and Oral Traditions," *Journal of American Folklore* 123, no. 490 (2010): 377–97; Francisco Vaz da Silva, "The Invention of Fairy Tales," *Journal of American Folklore* 123, no. 490 (2010): 398–425; Dan Ben-Amos, "Straparola: The Revolution That Was Not," *Journal of American Folklore* 123, no. 490 (2010): 426–46; Ruth Bottigheimer, "Fairy Godfather, Fairy-Tale History, and Fairy-Tale Scholarship: A Response to Dan Ben-Amos, Jan M. Ziolkowski, and Francisco Vaz da Silva," *Journal of American Folklore* 123, no. 490 (2010): 447–96.

5. Ziolkowski, "Straparola and the Fairy Tale," 377.

6. Ibid., 380.

7. Ibid., 385.

8. Ibid., 395.

9. Cited in Straparola, *Le piacevoli notti*, li.

10. Vaz da Silva, "The Invention of Fairy Tales," 404.

11. Ben-Amos, "Straparola," 430.

12. Ibid., 434.

13. Darren Oldridge, *Strange Histories: The Trial of the Pig, the Walking Dead, and Other Matters of Fact from the Medieval and Renaissance Worlds* (London: Routledge, 2005), 4.

14. Ben-Amos, "Straparola," 435.

15. Ruth Bottigheimer, *Fairy Tales: A New History* (Albany: State University of New York, 2009), 1.

16. Ibid., 4.

17. Ibid., 10, 11–12.
18. See Vladimir Propp, *Morphology of the Folktale*, ed. Louis Wagner and Alan Dundes, trans. Laurence Scott, 2nd rev. ed. (Austin: University of Texas Press, 1968); Claude Lévi-Strauss, *Structural Anthropology*, trans. Claire Jacobson and Brooke Grundfest Schoepf (New York: Doubleday, 1963); Claude Brémond, *L'Analyse structurale du récit* (Paris: Seuil, 1997); Louis Marin, *Food for Thought* (Baltimore: Johns Hopkins University Press, 1989); Steven Swann Jones, *The Fairy Tale: The Magic Mirror of Imagination* (New York: Twayne, 1995).
19. Bottigheimer, *Fairy Tales*, 16–17.
20. See Laurence Harf-Lancner, *Les Fées au Moyen Âge: Morgane et Mélusine. La naissance des fées* (Paris: Honoré Champion, 1984).
21. Bottigheimer, *Fairy Tales*, 45.
22. See Steffen Martus, *Die Brüder Grimm: Eine Biographie* (Berlin: Rowohlt, 2009).
23. See Raymonde Robert, *Le conte de fées littéraire en France de la fin du xvii à la fin xviii siècle. Supplément bibliographique 1980-2000 établi par Nadine Jasmin avec la collaboration de Claire Debru* (Paris: Champion, 2002); Anne Defrance and Jean-François Perrin, eds., *Le conte en ses paroles: La figuration de l'oralité dans le conte merveilleux du Classicisme aux Lumières* (Paris: Éditions Desjonquères, 2007).
24. Bottigheimer, *Fairy Tales*, 73.
25. For two important essays concerned with the oral components of Italian fairy tales, see Cristina Lavinio, "La fiaba tra oralità e scrittura: aspetti linguistici and stilistici," in *Oralità e Scrittura nel Sistema Letterario*, ed. Giovanna Cerina, Cristina Lavinio, and Luisa Mulas (Rome: Bulzoni, 1982), 91–114; Giovanna Cerina, "La fiaba tra oralità e scrittura: aspetti semiotici," in *Oralità e Scrittura nel Sistema Letterario*, ed. Giovanna Cerina, Cristina Lavinio, and Luisa Mulas (Rome: Bulzoni, 1982), 115–32. See also Luciano Morbiato, ed., *La Fiaba e altri Frammenti di Narrazione popolare* (Florence: Olschki, 2006).
26. Bottigheimer, *Fairy Tales*, 103.
27. Ibid., 107.
28. Cristina Bacchilega, "Authorizing Fairy-Tale History? Disciplinary Debates and the Politics of Inequality" (paper presented at the American Folklore Association meeting in Nashville, October 16, 2010). Haase, who responded to Bacchilega's paper, also made some perceptive remarks about Bottigheimer's rhetoric of assertion at this session. See also Cristina Bacchilega, review of *Fairy Tales: A New History*, by Ruth Bottigheimer, *Children's Literature Association Quarterly* 35, no. 4 (Winter 2010): 468–71.
29. Michael Tomasello, *The Origins of Communication* (Cambridge, MA: MIT Press, 2008), 9–10.
30. Ibid., 39.
31. Paul McMichael Nurse, *Eastern Dreams: How the Arabian Nights Came to the World* (Toronto: Viking Canada, 2010), 23.
32. Ibid., 46.
33. Brian Richardson, *Printing, Writers, and Readers in Renaissance Italy* (Cambridge: Cambridge University Press, 1999), 108.
34. R. A. Houston, *Literacy in Early Modern Europe: Culture and Education, 1500–1800*, 2nd ed. (London: Longman, 2002), 4.

Appendix B. Reductionist Scholarship

1. See Willem de Blécourt, *Tales of Magic, Tales in Print: On the Genealogy of Fairy Tales and the Brothers Grimm* (Manchester: Manchester University Press, 2012). Thanks to Matthew Frost, commissioning editor of the humanities at Manchester University Press, I received de Blécourt's manuscript before it went into production, but not in time to see the final page proofs. Therefore, I have cited (with Frost's permission) the manuscript chapter and page numbers, so readers should be aware that my references may not correspond with the same passages in the book. Frost has assured me that de Blécourt's general theses are the same.

2. de Blécourt, *Tales of Magic, Tales in Print*, chap. 1, 2, 7, 10.

3. Hans-Jörg Uther, *The Types of International Folktales: A Classification and Bibliography*, 3 vols., Ff Communications no. 284 (Helsinki: Suomalainen Tiedeakatemia, 2004). This is a revision of Antti Aarne and Stith Thompson, *The Types of the Folktale: A Classification and a Bibliography*, 2nd rev. ed., Ff Communications no. 3 (Helsinki: Suomalainen Tiedeakatemia, 1961). Aarne began this project in 1910 with his book *Verzeichnis der Märchentypen*.

4. See Rudolf Schenda, *Volk ohne Buch: Studien zur Sozialgeschichte der populären Lesestoffe 1770–1910* (Frankfurt am Main: Klostermann, 1970), and "Die Zivilizierung der Kommunikationswesen: Überlegungen anhand französischer Quellen des 18. und 19. Jahrhunderts," in *Volksdichtung zwischen Mündlichkeit und Schriftlichkeit*, ed. Lutz Röhrich and Erika Lindig (Tübingen: Gunter Narr Verlag, 1989), 17–34.

5. See Albert Wesselski, *Märchen des Mittelalters* (Berlin: Stubenrauch, 1925), and *Versuch einer Theorie des Märchens* (Reichenberg: Sudendt. Verlag, 1931).

6. See Jack Haney, *An Introduction to the Russian Folktale* (Armonk, NY: M. E. Sharpe, 1999); Vladimir Propp, *La fiaba russa*, ed, and trans. Franca Crestani, intro. Kirill Chistov (Turin: Einaudi, 1990), and the forthcoming English translation, *The Russian Fairy Tale*, trans. Sibelan Forrester (Detroit: Wayne State University Press); Andreas Johns, *Baba Yaga: The Ambiguous Mother and Witch of the Russian Folktale* (New York: Peter Lang, 2004). They all demonstrate the fallaciousness of de Blécourt's remarks.

7. de Blécourt, *Tales of Magic, Tales in Print*, chap. 3, 10, 15.

8. Ibid., chap. 6, 10.

9. Ibid., chap. 7, 1. See Warren Roberts, *The Tale of the Kind and the Unkind Girls: Aa-Th 480 and Related Tales*, ed. Alan Dundes (1958; repr., Detroit: Wayne State University Press, 1994).

10. See Johns, *Baba Yaga*; Joanna Hubbs, *Mother Russia: The Feminine Myth in Russian Culture* (Bloomington: Indiana University Press, 1988).

11. de Blécourt, *Tales of Magic, Tales in Print*, chap. 7, 25.

12. Ibid., epilogue, 1.

13. I am not certain that Schenda would have agreed with de Blécourt's theses, and he was skeptical about Grätz's book, *Das Märchen in der deutschen Aufklärung: Vom Feenmärchen zum Volksmärchen* (Stuttgart: J. B. Metzler, 1988).

14. de Blécourt, *Tales of Magic, Tales in Print*, chap. 1, 23–24.

15. See Giuseppe Cocchiara, *The History of Folklore in Europe*, trans. John McDaniel (1952; repr., Philadelphia: Institute for the Study of Human Issues, 1981). For more recent debates and discussions within Germany, see Lutz Röhrich and Erika Lindig, eds., *Volksdichtung zwischen Mündlichkeit und Schriftlichkeit* (Tübingen: Gunter Narr Verlag, 1989); Regina Bendix and Ulrich Marzolph, eds., *Hören, Lesen, Sehen,*

Spüren: Märchenrezeption im europäischen Vergleich (Baltmannsweiler: Schneider, 2008).

16. See Richard Reitzenstein, "Das Märchen von Armor und Psyche bei Apuleius (1912)," in *Amor und Psyche*, ed. Gerhard Binder and Reinhold Merkelbach (Darmstadt: Wissenschaftliche Buchgesellschaft, 1968), 87–158; P. G. Walsh, introduction to *The Golden Ass*, by Lucius Apuleius, ed. and trans. P. G. Walsh (Oxford: Oxford University Press, 1994), xi–lv; Joel C. Relihan, "To the Reader: A Brief History of *Cupid and Psyche*," in *The Tale of Cupid and Psyche*, by Lucius Apuleius, trans. Joel C. Relihan (Indianapolis: Hackett, 2009), xv–xxiii.

17. See Paul McMichael Nurse, *Eastern Dreams: How the Arabian Nights Came to the World* (Toronto: Viking Canada, 2010); Christa Tuczay, "Motifs in *The Arabian Nights* and in Ancient and Medieval European Literature: A Comparison," *Folklore* 116, no. 3 (December 2005): 272–91.

18. See Jean Seznec, *The Survival of the Pagan Gods: The Mythological Tradition and Its Place in Renaissance Humanism and Art*, trans. Barbara Sessions (New York: Harper and Row, 1953).

19. See Harvey Graff, ed., *Literacy and Social Development in the West* (Cambridge: Cambridge University Press, 1981); Alfred Messerli and Roger Chartier, eds., *Lesen und Schreiben in Europa 1500–1900: Vergleichende Perspektiven* (Basel: Schwabe, 2000); R. A Houston, *Literacy in Early Modern Europe: Culture and Education, 1500–1800*, 2nd ed. (London: Longman, 2002).

20. Françoise Waquet, *Parler comme un livre: L'oralité et le savoir (XVIe–XXe siècle)* (Paris: Albin Michel 2003), 9.

21. See Jerry Toner, *Popular Culture in Ancient Rome* (London: Polity, 2009); Peter Burke, *Popular Culture in Early Modern Europe*, 3rd rev. ed. (Farnham, UK: Ashgate, 2009); Danièle Alexandre-Bidon and Didier Lett, *Children in the Middle Ages: Fifth--Fifteenth Centuries*, trans. Jody Gladding (Notre Dame, IN: University of Notre Dame Press, 1999); Danièle Alexandre-Bidon and Marie-Thérèse Lorcin, *Le Quotidien aut temps des fabliaux* (Paris: Picard, 2003).

22. See Heinz Rölleke, *"Wo das Wünschen noch geholfen hat": Gesammelte Aufsätze zu den "Kinder- und Hausmärchen" der Brüder Grimm* (Bonn: Bouvier, 1985), "Neue Erkenntnisse zum Beiträgerkreis der Grimmschen Märchen," in *Volksdichtung zwischen Mündlichkeit und Schriftlichkeit*, ed. Lutz Röhrich and Erika Lindig (Tübingen: Gunter Narr Verlag, 1989), 49–66, and *Die Märchen der Brüder Grimm: Quellen und Studien* (Trier: Wissenschaftlicher Verlag Trier, 2000).

23. Rölleke, "Neue Erkenntnisse zum Beiträgerkreis der Grimmschen Märchen," 85.

24. Jürgen Beyer, "Are Folklorists Studying the Tales of the Folk?" *Folklore* 122, no. 1 (April 2011): 46.

25. Rölleke, *Die Märchen der Brüder Grimm*, 61.

26. Cited in Reinhold Steig, ed., *Achim von Arnim und die ihm nahe standen* (Stuttgart: J. G. Cotta'schen Buchhandlung, 1904), 271.

27. For a full account of the exchange with Arnim, see ibid., 115–44, 213–73.

28. Jens Sennewald, *Das Buch, das wird sind: Zur Poetik der "Kinder- und Hausmärchen," gesammelt durch die Brüder Grimm* (Würzburg: Könighausen and Neumann, 2004), 346.

29. Ibid., 28.

Bibliography

Literature

Afanasyev, Aleksandr Nikolaevich. *Narodnuiya Russkiya Skazki* [*Russian Popular Tales*]. Moscow, 1860–63.

Apuleius, Lucius. *The Golden Ass*. Translated and edited by Jack Lindsay. Bloomington: Indiana University Press, 1962.

———. *The Golden Ass*. Edited and translated by P. G. Walsh. Oxford: Oxford University Press, 1995.

———. *The Tale of Cupid and Psyche*. Translated by Joel C. Relihan. Indianapolis: Hackett, 2009.

Asbjørnsen, Peter Christen, and Jorgen Moe. *Norske folke-eventyr*. Christiania: J. Dahl, 1852.

Baring-Gould, Sabine, ed. *Notes on the Folklore of the Northern Countries of England and the Borders*, by W. Henderson, with an appendix on household stories by Sabine Baring-Gould. London, 1866.

Barrie, J. M. *Peter Pan, or the Boy Who Would Not Grow Up*. Introduction by Andrew Birkin. Illustrations by Paula Rego. London: Folio Society, 1992.

Basile, Giambattista. *Lo Cunto de li cunti overo Lo trattenemiento de peccerille*. 5 vols. Naples: Ottavio Beltrano, 1634–36.

———. *The Pentamerone of Giambattista Basile*. Translated and edited by N. M. Penzer. 2 vols. London: John Lane and the Bodley Head, 1932.

———. *The Tale of Tales, or Entertainment for Little Ones*. Translated by Nancy Canepa. Illustrated by Carmelo Lettere. Detroit: Wayne State University Press, 2007.

Bendix, Regina, and Ulrich Marzolph, eds. *Hören, Lesen, Sehen, Spüren: Märchenrezeption im europäischen Vergleich*. Baltmannsweiler: Schneider, 2008.

Benfey, Theodor. *Pantschatantra: fünf Bücher indischer Fabeln, Märchen, und Erzählungen*. Leipzig, Brockhaus, 1859.

Bladé, Jean-François. *Contes et Proverbes recueillis en Armagnac*. Paris: Franck, 1867.

Busk, Rachel, ed. *Roman Legends: A Collection of the Fables and Folk-Lore of Rome*. Boston: Estes and Lauriat, 1877.

Carter, Angela, ed. *The Virago Book of Fairy Tales*. London: Virago Press, 1990.

———. *Strange Things Sometimes Still Happen: Fairy Tales from around the World*. London: Faber and Faber, 1993.

Chudinsky, E. A. *Russkiya Narodnuiya Skazki* [*Russian Popular Tales*]. Moscow, 1864.

Comparetti, Domenico. *Novelline Popolari Italiane*. Bologna: Forni, 1875.

Coronedi-Berti, Carolina. *Novelle popolari bolognesi*. Bologna: Fava and Garagnai, 1874.

———. *Favole bolognesi*. Bologna: Forni, 1883.

Crane, Thomas Frederick, ed. *Italian Popular Tales*. Boston: Houghton Mifflin, 1889.

Curtin, Jeremiah. *Myths and Folklore of Ireland*. Boston: Little, Brown and Company, 1890.

d'Aulnoy, Madame Catherine-Anne. *Contes de fées*. Edited by Constance Cagnat-Debœuf. Paris: Gallimard, 2008.

De Gubernatis, Angelo. *Le Novelline di Santo Stefano*. Turin: Negro, 1869.

———. *Zoological Mythology, or the Legenda of Animals*. London: Trübner, 1872.

Deulin, Charles. *Les Contes de ma Mère l'Oye avant Perrault*. Paris: Dentu, 1878.

Dietrich, Anton. *Russische Volksmärchen*. Introduction by Jacob Grimm. Leipzig: Weidmanschnsche Buchhandlung, 1831.

———. *Russian Popular Tales*. Introduction by Jacob Grimm. London: Chaptman and Hall, 1857.

Fleutiaux, Pierrette. *Métamorphoses de la reine*. Paris: Gallimard, 1985.

Gonzenbach, Laura. *Sicilianische Märchen*. 2 vols. Leipzig: W. Engelmann, 1870.

———. *Beautiful Angiola: The Lost Sicilian Folk and Fairy Tales of Laura Gonzenbach*. Translated and edited by Jack Zipes. New York: Routledge, 2006.

Gottschalck, Kaspar Friedrich. *Deutsche Volksmärchen*. Leipzig, 1846.

Grimm, Albert Ludwig. *Kindermährchen*. Heidelberg: Morhr und Zimmer, 1809.

———. *Lina's Mährchenbuch*. Frankfurt am Main: Wilmans, 1816.

Grimm, Jacob, and Wilhelm Grimm. *Kinder- und Hausmärchen. Gesammelt durch die Brüder Grimm*. Berlin: Realschulbuchhandlung, 1812.

———. *Kinder- und Hausmärchen. Gesammelt durch die Brüder Grimm*. Vol. 2. Berlin: Realschulbuchhandlung, 1815.

———. *German Popular Stories, Translated from the Kinder- und Hausmärchen*. Translated by Edgar Taylor. London: C. Baldwin, 1823.

———. *Kinder- und Hausmärchen. Gesammelt durch die Brüder Grimm*. 7th rev. and exp. ed. 2 vols. Göttingen: Dieterich, 1857.

———. *The Complete Fairy Tales of the Brothers Grimm*. Edited and translated by Jack Zipes. 3rd rev. ed. New York: Bantam, 2003.

Grundtvig, Sven. *Gamle danske minder i folkemunde*. Copenhagen: Akademisk Forlag, 1854.

Haltrich, Josef, ed. *Deutsche Volksmärchen aus dem Sachsenlande in Siebenbürgen*. Hermannstadt: Krafft, 1885.

Haney, Jack, ed. and trans. *Russian Wondertales: Tales of Heroes and Villains*. Vol. 1. Armonk, NY: M. E. Sharpe, 2001.

———. *Russian Wondertales: Tales of Magic and the Supernatural*. Vol. 2. Armonk, NY: M. E. Sharpe, 2001.

———. *Russian Wondertales: Russian Tales of Love and Life*. Armonk, NY: M. E. Sharpe, 2006.

Heiner, Heidi Anne, ed. *Bluebeard Tales from around the World: Fairy Tales, Myths, Legends and Other Tales about Dangerous Suitors and Husbands*. Charleston, SC: SurLaLune Press, 2011.

———. *Rapunzel and Other Maiden in the Tower Tales from around the World*. Charleston, SC: SurLaLune Press, 2011.

Imbriani, Vittorio. *La novellaja fiorentina*. Livorno: F. Vigo, 1871.

——. *La novellaja milanese*. Bologna, 1871.

Jacobs, Joseph. *English Fairy Tales*. London: Nutt, 1890.

——. *Irish Fairy Tales*. London: Nutt, 1892.

Kennedy, Patrick. *Irish Fireside Folktales* [1870]. Edited by Karin von der Schulenburg. Cork, Ireland : Mercier Press, 1969.

Khudiakov, Ivan Aleksandrovich. *Velikorusskiya Skazki [Great Russian Tales]*. Moscow, 1860–62.

Knust, Hermann. *Italienische Märchen*. In *Jahrbuch für romanische und englische Literatur*, edited by Reinhold Köhler, 7:381–401. 1866.

Lover, Samuel. *Legends and Stories of Ireland*. London: Baldwin and Cradock, 1837.

Němcová, Božena. *The Key of Gold: 23 Czech Folk Tales*. Edited and translated by Josef Baudis. London: George Allen and Unwin, 1917.

——. *The Disobedient Kids and Other Czecho-Slovak Fairy Tales*. Edited and translated by William Tolman and V. Smetánka. Prague: Koĉi, 1921.

——. *Das goldene Spinnrad und andere tsechische und slowakische Märchen*. Edited and translated by Günther Janosch. Leipzig: Paul List, 1967.

Panzer, Friedrich. *Bayerische Sagen und Bräuche*. Munich: Kaiser, 1848.

Pedroso, Consiglieri. *Portuguese Folk-Tales*. 1882.

Perrault, Charles. *Griseldis, nouvelle. Avec le conte de Peau d'Ane, et celui des Souhaits ridicules*. Paris: Jean Baptiste Coignard, 1694.

——. *Histoires ou contes du temps passè*. Paris: Claude Barbin, 1697.

——. *Contes de Perrault*. Edited by Gilbert Rouger. Paris: Garnier, 1967.

——. *Contes*. Edited by Jean Pierre Collinet. 1281. Reprint, Paris: Gallimard, 1981.

——. *Contes*. Edited by Marc Soriano. Paris: Flammarion, 1989.

——. *Contes*. Edited by Catherine Magnien. Paris: Le Livre de Poche, 1990.

——. *Contes de ma Mère l'Oye*. Edited by Hélène Tronc. Paris: Gallimard, 2006.

Pitrè, Giuseppe. *Canti popolari siciliani*. Palermo: Giornale di Sicilia, 1868.

——. *Fiabe e Leggende Populari Siciliani*. Palermo: Lauriel, 1870.

——. *Canti popolari siciliani*. Palermo: Lauriel, 1871.

——. *Studi di poesia popolare*. Palermo: Lauriel, 1872.

——. *Fiabe, novelle e racconti populari siciliani*. 4 vols. Palermo: Lauriel, 1875.

——. *Il Vespro Siciliano nelle tradizioni popolari della Sicilia*. Palermo: Lauriel, 1882.

——. *Fiabe e Leggende popolari siciliane*. Palermo: Lauriel, 1888.

——. *Proverbi motti e scongiuri del popolo siciliano*. Palermo: 1910.

——. *The Collected Sicilian Folk and Fairy Tales of Giuseppe Pitrè*. Edited and translated by Jack Zipes and Joseph Russo. 2 vols. New York: Routledge, 2008.

Pröhle, Heinrich. *Kinder und Volksmärchen*. Leipzig: Avenarius and Mendelssohn, 1853.

Ragan, Kathleen. *Fearless Girls, Wise Women, and Beloved Sisters: Heroines in Folktales from around the World*. New York: W. W. Norton, 1998.

Ralston, W. R. S., ed. *Russian Folk Tales*. London: Smith, Elder, and Company, 1873.

Ranke, Kurt, ed. *Folktales of Germany*. Translated by Lotte Baumann. Chicago: University of Chicago Press, 1966.

Ritson, Joseph. *Fairy Tales*. London: Payne and Foss, Pall-Mall, and Pickering, 1831.

Röhrich, Lutz, ed. *Erzählungen des späten Mittelalters und ihr Weiterleben in Literatur und Volksdichtung bis zur Gegenwart: Sagen Märchen, Exempel und Schwänke mit einem Kommentar*. Bern: Francke Verlag, 1967.

Schambach, Georg, and Wilhelm Müller. *Niedersächsiche Sagen und Märchen*. Göttingen: Vandenhoeck and Ruprecht, 1855.

Schneller, Christian. *Märchen und Sagen aus Wälschtirol*. Innsbruck: Wagner, 1867.

Seifert, Lewis, and Domna Stanton, eds. *Enchanted Eloquence: Fairy Tales by Seventeenth-Century Women Writers*. Toronto: Iter, 2010.

Shirane, Haruo, ed. *The Demon at Agi Bridge and Other Japanese Tales*. Translated by Burton Watson. New York: Columbia University Press, 2010.

Simrock, Karl Joseph. *Deutsche Märchen*. Stuttgart, 1864.

Stahl, Karoline. *Fabeln, Mährchen und Erzählungen für Kinder*. Nuremberg, 1818.

Straparola, Giovan Francesco. *Le piacevoli notti*. 2 vols. Venice: Comin da Trino, 1550/1553.

———. *The Facetious Nights of Straparola*. Translated by William G. Waters. Illustrated by Jules Garnier and E. R. Hughes. 4 vols. London: Lawrence and Bullen, 1894.

———. *Le piacevoli notti*. Edited by Bartolomeo Rossetti. Rome: Avanzini e Torraca, 1966.

———. *Le piacevoli notti*. Edited by Pastore Stocchi. Rome-Bari: Laterza, 1979.

———. *Le piacevoli notti*. Edited by Donato Pirovano. 2 vols. Rome: Salerno, 2000.

Suttermeister, Otto. *Kinder- und Hausmärchen aus der Schweiz*. Aarau: Sauerländer, 1869.

Tenèze, Marie-Louise, and Georges Delarue, eds. *Nannette Lévesque, conteuse et chanteuse du pays des sources de la Loire. La collecte de Victor Smith 1871–1876*. Paris: Gallimard, 2000.

Vernaleken, Theodor. *Alpenmärchen*. Munich: Borowsky, 1863.

Vonbun, Franz Josef. *Volkssagen aus Vorarlberg*. Innsbruck: Witting, 1850.

Widter, Georg, and Adam Wolf. *Volksmärchen aus Venetien*. Vienna: K. K. Hof und Staatsdrückerei, 1864. Also in *Jahrbuch für romanische und englische Literatur*, edited by Reinhold Köhler, 7:1–36, 121–54, 249–90. 1866.

Wolf, Johann Wilhelm, ed. *Deutsche Märchen und Sagen*. Leipzig: F. A. Brockhaus, 1845.

Zingerle, Ignanz Vinzenz, and Joseph Zingerle. *Tirols Volksdichtungen und Volksbräuche*. Innsbruck: Wagner, 1852.

Zipes, Jack, ed. and trans. *Beauties, Beasts, and Enchantment: Classic French Fairy Tales*. New York: New American Library, 1989.

———, ed. *The Great Fairy Tale Tradition: From Straparola and Basile to the Brothers Grimm*. New York: Norton, 2001.

Criticism

Aarne, Antti, and Stith Thompson. *The Types of the Folktale: A Classification and a Bibliography*. 2nd rev. ed. Ff Communications no. 3. Helsinki: Suomalainen Tiedeakatemia, 1961.

Alexandre-Bidon, Danièle, and Didier Lett. *Children in the Middle Ages: Fifth–Fifteenth Centuries*. Translated by Jody Gladding. Notre Dame, IN: University of Notre Dame Press, 1999.

Alexandre-Bidon, Danièle, and Marie-Thérèse Lorcin. *Le Quotidien aut temps des fabliaux*. Paris: Picard, 2003.

Anderson, Graham. *Fairytale in the Ancient World*. London: Routledge, 2000.

———. *Greek and Roman Folklore: A Handbook*. Westport, CT: Greenwood Press, 2006.

———. *Folktale as a Source of Graeco-Roman Fiction*. Lewiston, NY: Edward Mellen Press, 2007.

Ankarloo, Ben, and Gustav Henningsen, eds. *Early Modern European Witchcraft: Centres and Peripheries*. Oxford: Clarendon Press, 1990.

Armstrong, Karen. *A Short History of Myth*. Edinburgh: Canongate: 2005.

Art 21. "Kiki Smith Biography." Available at http//www.pbs.org.art 21/artists/smith/index.html.

Bacchilega, Cristina. Review of *Fairy Tales: A New History*, by Ruth Bottigheimer. *Children's Literature Association Quarterly* 35, no. 4 (Winter 2010): 468–71.

Baker-Sperry, Lori, and Liz Grauenholz. "The Pervasiveness and Persistence of the Feminine Beauty Ideal in Children's Fairy Tales." *Gender and Society* 17 (2003): 711–26.

Baring, Anne, and Jules Cashford. *The Myth of the Goddess: Evolution of an Image*. London: Viking, 1991.

Baroja, Julio Caro. *The World of Witches*. Translated by O.N.V. Glendinning. Chicago: University of Chicago Press, 1964.

Barrett, Deirdre. *Supernormal Stimuli: How Primal Urges Overran Their Evolutionary Purpose*. New York: W. W. Norton, 2010.

Barzilai, Shuli. *Tales of Bluebeard and His Wives from Late Antiquity to Postmodern Times*. London: Routledge, 2009.

———. Review of *Fairy Tales: A New History*, by Ruth Bottigheimer. *Marvels and Tales* 25, no. 1 (2011): 171–74.

Bauman, Zygmunt. *Culture in a Liquid Modern World*. Translated by Lydia Bauman. Cambridge: Polity Press, 2011.

Becker, Ricarda. *Die weibliche Initiation im ostslawischen Zaubermärchen: Ein Beitrag zur Funktion und Symbolik des weiblichen Aspektes im Märchen unter besonderer Berücksichtigung der Figur der Baba-Jaga*. Wiesbaden: Harrassowitz, 1990.

Bédier, Joseph. *Les Fabliaux. Études de littérature populaire et d'histoire littéraire du moyen age*. Paris: Bouillon, 1893.

Ben-Amos, Dan. "Introduction: The European Fairy-Tale Tradition between Orality and Literacy." *Journal of American Folklore* 123, no. 490 (2010): 373–76.

———. "Straparola: The Revolution That Was Not." *Journal of American Folklore* 123, no. 490 (2010): 426–46.

Bennett, Gillian. *Traditions of Belief: Women, Folklore, and the Supernatural Today*. London: Penguin Books, 1987.

Benson, Stephen, *Cycles of Influence: Fiction, Folktale, Theory*. Detroit: Wayne State University Press, 2003.

Berger, Pamela. *The Goddess Obscured: Transformation of the Grain Protectress from Goddess to Saint*. Boston: Beacon, 1985.

Berti, Giordano. *Storia della Stregoneria: Origini, Credenze, Persecuzioni e Rinascita nel Mondo Contemporaneo*. Milan: Arnoldo Mondatori, 2010.

Bettini, Maurizio, and Luigi Spina. *Il mito delle Siren: Immagini e racconti dall Grecia a oggi*. Turin: Einaudi, 2007.

Beyer, Jürgen. "Are Folklorists Studying the Tales of the Folk?" *Folklore* 122, no. 1 (April 2011): 25–54.

Bickerton, Derek. "Language Evolution: A Brief Guide for Linguistics." *Lingua* 117, no. 3 (2007): 510–26.

Billington, Sandra, and Miranda Green, eds. *The Concept of the Goddess*. London: Routledge, 1996.

Binder, Gerhard, and Reinhold Merkelbach, eds. *Amor und Psyche*. Darmstadt: Wissen-schaftliche Buchgesellschaft, 1968.

Blackmore, Susan. *The Meme Machine*. Foreword by Richard Dawkins. Oxford: Oxford University Press, 2000.

Blamires, David. "The Early Reception of the Grimms' *Kinder- und Hausmärchen* in England." *Bulletin of the John Rylands University Library of Manchester* 71, no. 3 (1989): 63–77.

Blinderman, Barry, and Timothy Porges, eds. *Pixerina Witcherina*. Normal: University Galleries of Illinois State University, 2002.

Blute, Marion. *Darwinian Sociocultural Evolution: Solutions to Dilemmas in Cultural and Social Theory*. Cambridge: Cambridge University Press, 2010.

Bonner, Sarah. "Visualizing Little Red Riding Hood." *Moveable Type*. Available at http://www.ucl.ac.uk/english/graduate/issue/2/sarah.htm.

Boody, Meghan. "Artist Statements." Available at http://www.lookingglasslabs.com/statementC.html.

Bottigheimer, Ruth. *Fairy Godfather: Straparola, Venice, and the Fairy Tale*. Philadel-phia: University of Pennsylvania Press, 2002.

———. "Perrault aux travail." In *Le conte en ses paroles: La figuration de l'oralité dans le conte merveilleux du Classicisme aux Lumières*, edited by Anne Defrance and Jean-François Perrin, 21–33, 150–62. Paris: Éditions Desjonquères, 2007.

———. *Fairy Tales: A New History*. Albany: State University of New York, 2009.

———. "*Fairy Godfather*, Fairy-Tale History, and Fairy-Tale Scholarship: A Response to Dan Ben-Amos, Jan M. Ziolkowski, and Francisco Vaz da Silva." *Journal of American Folklore* 123, no. 490 (2010): 447–96.

Boyer, Pascal. *Religion Explained: The Evolutionary Origins of Religious Thought*. New York: Basic Books, 2001.

Boyer, Pascal, and James Wertsch. *Memory in Mind and Culture*. Cambridge: Cam-bridge University Press, 2009.

Brasey, Édpuar. *Fées et Elfes*. Paris: Pygmalion, 1999.

Brémond, Claude. *L'Analyse structurale du récit*. Paris: Seuil, 1997.

Bronner, Simon. *American Folklore Studies: An Intellectual History*. Lawrence: Univer-sity Press of Kansas, 1986.

Burke, Peter. *Popular Culture in Early Modern Europe*. 3rd rev. ed. Farnham, UK: Ash-gate, 2009.

Burkert, Walter. *Structure and History in Greek Mythology and Ritual*. Berkeley: Univer-sity of California Press, 1979.

———. *Creation of the Sacred: Tracks of Biology in Early Religions*. Cambridge, MA: Har-vard University Press, 1996.

Burton, Johanna, ed. *Cindy Sherman*. Cambridge, MA: MIT Press, 2006.

Buss, David M. "Sex Differences in Human Mate Preferences: Evolutionary Hypotheses Tested in 37 Cultures." *Behavioral and Brain Sciences* 12 (1989): 1–49.

———. *The Evolution of Desire*. New York: Basic Books, 2003.

Cagnat-Debœuf, Constance, ed. Preface to *Contes de fées*, by Madame d'Aulnoy, 7–44. Paris: Gallimard, 2008.

Carruthers, Peter. *Human Knowledge and Human Nature*. Oxford: Oxford University Press, 1992.

Carruthers, Peter, Stephen Laurence, and Stephen Stich, eds. *The Innate Mind: Culture and Cognition*. Vol. 2. Oxford: Oxford University Press, 2006.

———. *The Innate Mind: Structure and Contents.* Vol. 1. Oxford: Oxford University Press, 2006.

———. *The Innate Mind: Foundations and the Future.* Vol. 3. Oxford: Oxford University Press, 2007.

Carstairs-McCarthy, Andrew. "Language Evolution: What Linguists Can Contribute." *Lingua* 117, no. 3 (2007): 503–9.

Carver, Robert H. F. *The Protean Ass: The Metamorphoses of Apuleius from Antiquity to the Renaissance.* Oxford: Oxford University Press, 2007.

Chadwick, Whitney. *Women, Art, and Society.* Rev. ed. London: Thames and Hudson, 1997.

Cerina, Giovanna. "La fiaba tra oralità e scrittura: aspetti semiotici." In *Oralità e Scrittura nel Sistema Letterario*, edited by Giovanna Cerina, Cristina Lavinio, and Luisa Mulas, 115–32. Rome: Bulzoni, 1982.

Cerina, Giovanna, Cristina Lavinio, and Luisa Mulas, eds. *Oralità e Scrittura nel Sistema Letterario.* Rome: Bulzoni, 1982.

Chartier, Roger, ed. *Les usages de l'imprimé.* Paris: Fayard, 1987.

Chojnacki, Stanley. *Women and Men in Renaissance Venice: Twelve Essays on Patrician Society.* Baltimore: Johns Hopkins University Press, 2000.

Chistov, Kirill. "V. Ya. Propp—Legend and Fact." *International Folklore Review* 4 (1986): 17.

———. "V. Ja. Propp, studioso della fiaba." In *La fiaba russa*, edited and translated by Franca Crestani, vii–xxx. Turin: Einaudi, 1990.

Cirese, Alberto Mario. "Giuseppe Pitrè tra storia locale e antropologia." In *Pitrè e Salomone Marino*, 19–49. Palermo: Flaccovio, 1968. ("Atti del Convegno di studi per il 50 Anniversario della morte di Giuseppe Pitrè e Salvatore Salomone-Marino," Palermo, November 25–27, 1966.)

———. "Giuseppe Pitrè." In *Letteratura italiana. I critici. Per la storia della filogie e della critica moderna in Italia*, edited by Gianni Grana, 1:279–300. Milan: Marzorati, 1969.

Clark, Stuart. *Thinking with Demons: The Idea of Witchcraft in Early Modern Europe.* Oxford: Oxford University Press, 1997.

Clausen-Stolzenburg, Maren. *Märchen und mittelalterliche Literaturtradition.* Heidelberg: Universitätsverlag C. Winter, 1995.

Cocchiara, Giuseppe. *La Vita e l'arte del popolo siciliano nel Museo Pitrè.* Palermo: F. Ciuni, 1938.

———. *Pitrè, la Sicilia e il folklore.* Messina: D'Anna, 1951.

———. *Storia del folklore in Europa.* Turin: Editore Borginghieri, 1952.

———. *The History of Folklore in Europe.* Translated by John McDaniel. 1952; repr., Philadelphia: Institute for the Study of Human Issues, 1981.

Coldwell, Paul. *Paula Rego Printmaker.* London: Marlborough Graphics, 2005.

Cornfeld, Li. "Shooting Heroines: On Dina Goldstein's Fallen Princesses." Talk at the From Portraits to Pinups: Representations of Women in Art and Popular Culture conference, Brooklyn Museum, May 13, 2011.

Crane, Thomas Frederick. "Sicilian Folk-Lore." *Lippincott's Magazine* 18, no. 4 (October 1876): 433–43.

———. "Giuseppe Pitrè and Sicilian Folk-Lore." *Nation* 103, no. 2671 (1916): 234–36.

———. *Italian Social Customs of the Sixteen Century and Their Influence on the Literatures of Europe.* New Haven, CT: Yale University Press, 1920.

Daly, Martin, and Wilson, Margo. *The Truth about Cinderella: A Darwinian View of Parental Love*. London: Wiedenfeld and Nicolson, 1998.

Davies, Mererid Puew. *The Tale of Bluebeard in German Literature: From the Eighteenth Century to the Present*. New York: Oxford University Press, 2001.

Davies, Owen. *Cunning-Folk: Popular Magic in English History*. London: Hambledon and London, 2003.

de Blécourt, Willem. *Tales of Magic, Tales in Print: On the Genealogy of Fairy Tales and the Brothers Grimm*. Manchester: Manchester University Press, 2012.

Defrance, Anne, and Jean-François Perrin, eds. *Le conte en ses paroles: La figuration de l'oralité dans le conte merveilleux du Classicisme aux Lumières*. Paris: Éditions Desjonquères, 2007.

Denecke, Ludwig, ed. *Brüder Grimm Gedenken*. Vol. 2. Marburg: N. G. Elwert, 1975.

Deresiewicz, William. "Adaptation: On Literary Darwinism." *Nation*, June 8, 2009, 27.

Dessalles, Jean-Louis. *Why We Talk: The Evolutionary Origins of Language*. Translated by James Grieve. Oxford: Oxford University Press, 2007.

Deviant Art. Available at http://www.deviantart.com/.

Dinzelbacher, Peter. *Heilige oder Hexen? Schicksale auffälliger Frauen in Mittelalter und Frühneuzeit*. Zurich: Artemis and Winkler, 1995.

Dinzelbacher, Peter, and Hans-Dieter Mück, eds. *Volkskultur des europäischen Spätmittelalters*. Stuttgart: Alfred Kröner, 1987.

Distin, Kate. *The Selfish Meme*. Cambridge: Cambridge University Press, 2005.

———. *Cultural Evolution*. Cambridge: Cambridge University Press, 2011.

Dorson, Richard. *The British Folklorists: A History*. Chicago: University of Chicago Press, 1968.

Drout, Michael. "A Meme-Based Approach to Oral Traditional Theory." *Oral Tradition* 21, no. 2 (2006): 269–94.

———. *How Tradition Works: A Meme-Based Cultural Poetics of the Anglo-Saxon Tenth Century*. Tempe: Arizona Center for Medieval and Renaissance Studies, 2006.

Durham, William. *Coevolution: Genes, Culture, and Human Diversity*. Stanford, CA: Stanford University Press, 1991.

Easterlin, Nancy. "Hans Christian Andersen's Fish Out of Water." *Philosophy and Literature* 25 (2001): 251–77.

Ellis, John. *One Fairy Story Too Many: The Brothers Grimm and Their Tales*. Chicago: University of Chicago Press, 1983.

Engberg, Siri, ed. *Kiki Smith: A Gathering, 1980–2005*. Minneapolis: Walker Art Center, 2006.

Evans-Wentz, Walter Yeeling. *The Fairy-Faith in Celtic Countries*. Atlantic Highlands, NJ: Humanities Press, 1978.

Falassi, Alessandro. *Folklore by the Fireside: Text and Context of the Tuscan Veglia*. Austin: University of Texas Press, 1980.

Febvre, Lucien, and Henri-Jean Martin. *The Coming of the Book: The Impact of Printing 1450–1800*. Translated by David Gerard. London: New Left Books, 1976.

Feustel, Elke. *Rätselprinzessinnen und schlafende Schönheiten: Typologie und Funktionen der weiblichen Figuren in den Kinder- und Hausmärchen der Brüder Grimm*. Hildesheim: Olms-Weidmann, 2004.

Flint, Valerie. *The Rise of Magic in Early Medieval Europe*. Princeton, NJ: Princeton University Press, 1991.

Foley, John Miles. *The Theory of Oral Composition: History and Methodology.* Bloomington: Indiana University Press, 1988.

Franco, Hilário, Jr. *Nel Paese di Cuccagna: La societá medievale tra il sogno e la vita quo-
tidiana.* Rome: Città Nuova, 1998.

Frank, Arthur. *Letting Stories Breathe: A Socio-Narratology.* Chicago: University of Chicago Press, 2010.

Fitch, W. Tecumseh. *The Evolution of Language.* Cambridge: Cambridge University
Press, 2010.

Gaisser, Julia Haig. *The Fortunes of Apuleius and the Golden Ass: A Study in Transmission
and Reception.* Princeton, NJ: Princeton University Press, 2008.

Gallino, Tilde Giani, ed. *Le Grandi Madri.* Milan: Feltrinelli, 1989.

Gaskill, Malcolm. *Witchcraft: A Very Short Introduction.* Oxford: Oxford University
Press, 2010.

Gehrts, Heino, and Gabriele Lademann-Priemer, eds. *Schamanentum und Zaubermärchen.* Kassel: Eric Röth Verlag, 1986.

Gerlach, Hildegard. "Hexe." In *Enzyklopädie des Märchens,* edited by Rolf Wilhelm
Brednich, 6:959–91. Berlin: de Gruyter, 1990.

Gilchrist, Cherry. *Russian Magic: Living Folk Traditions of an Enchanted Landscape.*
Wheaton, IL: Theosophical Publishing House, 2009.

Ginzburg, Carlo. *Ecstasies: Deciphering the Witches' Sabbath.* Translated by Raymond
Rosenthal. New York: Penguin, 1991.

———. "Deciphering the Witches' Sabbath." In *The Witchcraft Reader,* edited by Darren
Oldridge, 120–28. London: Routledge, 2002.

Gittes, Katharine. *Framing the Canterbury Tales: Chaucer and the Medieval Frame Tradition.* Westport, CT: Greenwood Press, 1991.

Goody, Jack. *The Theft of History.* Cambridge: Cambridge University Press, 2006.

Gottschall, Jonathan. "Patterns of Characterization in Folk Tales across Geographic
Regions and Levels of Cultural Complexity: Literature as a Neglected Source of
Quantitative Data." *Human Nature* 14, no. 3 (2003): 365–82.

———. "The Heroine with a Thousand Faces: Universal Trends in the Characterization
of Female Folk Tale Protagonists." *Evolutionary Psychology* 3 (2005): 85–103.

———. "The 'Beauty Myth' Is No Myth: Emphasis on Male-Female Attractiveness in
World Folktales." *Human Nature* 19, no. 2 (2008): 174–88.

Gottschall, Jonathan, Johanna Martin, Hadley Quish, and Jon Rea. "Sex Differences in
Mate Choice Criteria Are Reflected in Folktales from around the World and in Historical European Literature." *Evolution and Human Behavior* 25, no. 2 (2004): 102–12.

Grätz, Manfred. *Das Märchen in der deutschen Aufklärung: Vom Feenmärchen zum
Volksmärchen.* Stuttgart: J. B. Metzler, 1988.

Graff, Harvey, ed. *Literacy and Social Development in the West.* Cambridge: Cambridge
University Press, 1981.

Graham, William. "Summation." *Oral Tradition* 25, no. 1 (2010): 1–8.

Gray, Jonathan. *Show Sold Separately: Promos, Spoilers, and Other Media Paratexts.* New
York: New York University Press, 2010.

Grenby, M. O. "Tame Fairies Make Good Teachers: The Popularity of Early British Fairy
Tales." *Lion and the Unicorn* 30 (2006): 1–24.

Grimassi, Raven. *Italian Witchcraft: The Old Religion of Southern Europe.* 2nd ed. Wood-
bury, MN: Llewellyn Publications, 2010.

Grimm, Jacob. *Circular wegen Aufsamlung der Volkspoesie*. Edited by Ludwig Denecke. Afterword by Kurt Ranke. Kassel: Brother Grimm Museum, 1968.

Haase, Donald. "Fairy Tale." In *The Greenwood Encyclopedia of Folktales and Fairy Tales*, edited by Donald Haase, 1:322. Westport, CT: Greenwood Press, 2008.

———. "Decolonizing Fairy-Tale Studies." *Marvels and Tales* 24, no. 1 (2010): 17–38.

Haase, Donald, ed. *The Greenwood Encyclopedia of Folktales and Fairy Tales*. 3 vols. Westport, CT: Greenwood Press, 2008.

Haenlein, Carl, ed. *Kiki Smith: All Creatures Great and Small*. Hannover: Kestner Gesellschaft, 1998.

Hall, Alaric. *Elves in Anglo-Saxon England: Matters of Belief, Health, Gender, and Identity*. Woodbridge, UK: Boydell Press, 2007.

Haney, Jack V. *An Introduction to the Russian Folktale*. Armonk, NY: M. E. Sharpe, 1999.

Hansen, William. *Ariadne's Thread: A Guide to International Tales Found in Classical Literature*. Ithaca, NY: Cornell University Press, 2002.

Harf-Lancner, Laurence. *Les Fées au Moyen Âge: Morgane et Mélusine. La naissance des fées*. Paris: Honoré Champion, 1984.

Harris, Ruth, and Lyndal Roper, eds. *The Art of Survival: Gender and History in Europe, 1450–2000*. Oxford: Oxford University Press, 2006.

Harris, Stephen, and Gloria Platzner. *Classical Mythology: Images and Insights*. 2nd ed. Mountain View, CA: Mayfield, 1998.

Hartwig, Otto. "Zur ersten englischen Übersetzung der Kinder- und Haumärchen der Brüder Grimm." *Centralblatt für Bibliothekswesen* 15, nos. 1–2 (January–February 1898): 1–16.

Heidmann, Ute, and Jean-Michel Adam. *Textualité et intertextualité des contes: Perrault, Apulée, La Fontaine, Lhéritier*. Paris: Garnier, 2010.

Henningsen, Gustav. *The Witches' Advocate: Basque Witchcraft and the Spanish Inquisition (1609–1614)*. Reno, NV: University of Nevada Press, 1980.

———. "'Ladies from the Outside': An Archaic Pattern of the Witches' Sabbath." In *Early Modern European Witchcraft: Centres and Peripheries*, edited by Ben Ankarloo and Gustav Henningsen, 191–215. Oxford: Clarendon Press, 1990.

Hermansson, Casie. *Bluebeard: A Reader's Guide to the English Tradition*. JacksonUniversity Press of Mississippi, 2009.

Hixon, Martha. "Rewriting History." *Children's Literature* 38 (2010): 231–36.

Houston, R. A. *Literacy in Early Modern Europe: Culture and Education, 1500–1800*. 2nd ed. London: Longman, 2002.

Howard, Jennifer. "From 'Once Upon a Time' to 'Happily Ever After.'" *Chronicle of Higher Education* 55, no. 37 (2009): B6–8.

Hribal, Jason. *Fear of the Animal Planet: The Hidden History of Animal Resistance*. Oakland, CA: AK Press, 2010.

Hubbs, Joanna. *Mother Russia: The Feminine Myth in Russian Culture*. Bloomington: Indiana University Press, 1988.

Hults, Linda. *The Witch as Muse: Art, Gender, and Power in Early Modern Europe*. Philadelphia: University of Pennsylvania Press, 2005.

Hutton, Ronald. *The Triumph of the Moon: A History of Modern Pagan Witchcraft*. Oxford: Oxford University Press, 1999.

D'Humières, Catherine, ed. *D'un conte à l'autre, d'une génération á l'autre*. Clermont-Ferrand: Presses Universitaires Blaise Pascal, 2008.

Hyde, W. W. "The Prosecution and Punishment of Animals and Lifeless Things in the Middle Ages and Modern Times." *University of Pennsylvania Law Review* 64, no. 7 (1914): 690–730.

Ivanits, Linda. *Russian Folk Belief*. Armonk, NY: M. E. Sharpe, 1989.

Jahn, Pamela Jahn. "Bluebeard: Interview with Catherine Breillat." *Electric Sheep*, July 16, 2010. Available at http://www.electricsheepmagazine.co.uk/features/2010/0716/bluebeard.

Jasmin, Nadine. *Naissance du Conte Féminin. Mots et Merveilles: Les Contes de fées de Madame d'Aulnoy (1690–1698)*. Paris: Champion, 2002.

Johns, Andrea. *Baba Yaga: The Ambiguous Mother and Witch of the Russian Folktale*. New York: Peter Lang, 2004.

Jolles, André. *Rätsel/Spruch/Kasus/Memorabile/Märchen/Witz*. 2nd ed. 1930. Reprint, Darmstadt: Wissenschaftliche Buchgesellschaft, 1958.

Jones, Leslie Ellen. "Fairies." In *Medieval Folklore: A Guide to Myths, Legends, Tales, Beliefs, and Customs*, edited by Carl Lindahl, John McNamara, and John Lindow, 128–30. Oxford: Oxford University Press, 2002.

Jones, Steven Swann. "The Innocent Persecuted Heroine Genre: An Analysis of Its Structure and Themes." *Western Folklore* 52, no. 1 (January 1993): 39.

———. *The Fairy Tale: The Magic Mirror of Imagination*. New York: Twayne, 1995.

Joosen, Vanessa. *Critical and Creative Perspectives on Fairy Tales: An Intertextual Dialogue between Fairy-Tale Scholarship and Postmodern Readings*. Detroit: Wayne State University Press, 2011.

Keesey, Douglas. *Catherine Breillat*. Manchester: Manchester University Press, 2009.

Keller, Walter. "Zum Andenken an Giuseppe Pitrè," *SAVk* 21 (1917): 94–96.

Kieckhefer, Richard. "The Holy and the Unholy: Sainthood, Witchcraft, and Magic in Medieval Europe." In *Christendom and Its Discontents: Exclusion, Persecution, and Rebellion, 1000–1500*, edited by Scott Waugh and Peter Diehl, 310–37. Cambridge: Cambridge University Press, 1996.

———. *Magic in the Middle Ages*. Cambridge: Cambridge University Press, 2000.

———. "Witchcraft." In *Medieval Folklore: A Guide to Myths, Legends, Tales, Beliefs, and Customs*, edited by Carl Lindahl, John McNamara, and John Lindow, 438–40. Oxford: Oxford University Press, 2002.

Kingston, Angela, ed. *Fairy Tale: Contemporary Art and Enchantment*. Walsall, UK: New Art Gallery Walsall, 2007.

Klaniczay, Gábor. *The Uses of Supernatural Power: The Transformation of Popular Religion in Medieval and Early Modern Europe*. Translated by Susan Singerman. Princeton, NJ: Princeton University Press, 1990.

———. "The Decline of Witches and the Rise of Vampires." In *The Witchcraft Reader*, edited by Darren Oldridge, 387–98. London: Routledge, 2002.

Köhler-Zülch, Ines. "Kater: Der gestiefelte K. (AaTh545B)." In *Enzyklopädie des Märchens*, edited by Rolf Wilhelm Brednich, 7:1070–83. Berlin: de Gruyter, 1993.

Klossowski, Pierre. *Diana at Her Bath: The Women of Rome*. Translated by Sophie Hawkes and Stephen Sartarelli. New York: Marsilio, 1998.

Konner, Melvin. *The Evolution of Childhood: Relationships, Emotion, Mind*. Cambridge, MA: Harvard University Press, 2010.

Kropej, Monika. "Contemporary Legends from the Slovene Karst in Comparison with Fairylore and Belief Traditions." *Studia Mythologica Slavica* 8 (2005): 227–50.

Kurke, Leslie. *Aesopic Conversations: Popular Tradition, Cultural Dialogue, and the Invention of Greek Prose.* Princeton, NJ: Princeton University Press, 2011.

Larson, Richard, Viviane Déprez, and Hiroko Yamakido, eds. *The Evolution of Language: Biolinguistic Perspectives.* Cambridge: Cambridge University Press, 2010.

Lathey, Gillian. *The Role of Translators in Children's Literature: Invisible Storytellers.* New York: Routledge, 2010.

Lavinio, Cristina. "La fiaba tra oralità e scrittura: aspetti linguistici and stilistici." In *Oralità e Scrittura nel Sistema Letterario,* edited by Giovanna Cerina, Cristina Lavinio, and Luisa Mulas, 91–114. Rome: Bulzoni, 1982.

Le Goff, Jacques. *Pour un autre Moyen Age.* Paris: Gallimard, 1977.

Le Goff, Jacques, and Emmanuel Le Roy Ladurie. "Mélusine maternelle et défricheuse." *Annales* 26, no. 3.4 (1971): 587–622.

Lecouteux, Claude. *Fées, Sorcières et Loups-Garous au Moyen Age.* Paris: Imago, 1992.

———. *Au-delà du Merveilleux: Des Croyances du Moyen Age.* Paris: Presses de l'Université Paris-Sorbonne, 1995.

———. *Chasses Fantastiques et Cohortes de la Nuit au Moyen Age.* Paris: Imago, 1999.

Leishman, Donna. Available at http://www.6amhoover.com/index_flash.html.

Leland, Charles. *Etruscan Roman Remains in Popular Tradition.* New York: Charles Scribner's Sons, 1892.

Lévi-Strauss, Claude. *Structural Anthropology.* Translated by Claire Jacobson and Brooke Grundfest Schoepf. New York: Doubleday, 1963.

Lewis, James, ed. *Magical Religion and Modern Witchcraft.* Albany: State University of New York Press, 1996.

Lewis, Philip. *Seeing through the Mother Goose Tales: Visual Turns in the Writings of Charles Perrault.* Stanford, CA: Stanford University Press, 1996.

Lindahl, Carl, John McNamara, and John Lindow, eds. *Medieval Folklore: A Guide to Myths, Legends, Tales, Beliefs, and Customs.* Oxford: Oxford University Press, 2002.

Lundt, Bea. *Melusine und Merlin im Mittelalter: Entwürfe und Modelle weiblicher Existenz im Beziehungsdiskurs der Geschlechter.* Munich: Fink, 1991.

———. "Undine geht—Melusine kommt. Feministische Märchen Rezeption am Beispiel der Erzähltradition von einer Meerjungfrau." In *Hören, Lesen, Sehen, Spüren: Märchenrezeption im europäischen Vergleich,* edited by Regina Bendix and Ulrich Marzolph, 20–46. Baltmannsweiler: Schneider, 2008.

Mace, Ruth, Clare Holden, and Stephen Shennan, eds. *The Evolution of Cultural Diversity: A Phylogenetic Approach.* London: UCL Press, 2005.

Maddox, Donald, and Sara Sturm-Maddox, eds. *Melusine of Lusignan: Founding Fiction in Late Medieval France.* Athens: University of Georgia Press, 1996.

Marin, Louis. *Food for Thought.* Baltimore: Johns Hopkins University Press, 1989.

Martin, Walter, and Paloma Muñoz. "Islands: The Art of Martin and Muñoz—An Interview with the Artists." *Penleaf* (February–March 2008).

Martineau, Jane, ed. *Victorian Fairy Painting.* London: Merrell Holberton, 1997.

Martus, Steffen. *Die Brüder Grimm: Eine Biographie.* Berlin: Rowohlt, 2009.

Marzolph, Ulrich, ed. *Strategien des populären Erzählens.* Berlin: LIT Verlag, 2010.

Max, D. T. "The Literary Darwinists." *New York Times Magazine,* November 6, 2005, 74–79.

Maxwell-Stuart, P. G. *Witchcraft in Europe and the New World, 1400–1800.* Houndmills, UK: Palgrave, 2001.

McClure, George. *The Culture of Profession in Late Renaissance Italy*. Toronto: University of Toronto Press, 2004.

McEwen, John. *Paula Rego*. 3rd ed. London: Phaidon, 2006.

———. *Paula Rego Behind the Scenes*. London: Phaidon, 2008.

Messerli, Alfred, and Roger Chartier, eds. *Lesen und Schreiben in Europea 1500–1900: Vergleichende Perspektiven*. Basel: Schwabe, 2000.

Mesoudi, Alex. *Cultural Evolution: How Darwinian Theory Can Explain Human Culture and Synthesize the Social Sciences*. Chicago: University of Chicago Press, 2011.

Michaelis-Jena, Ruth. "Edgar and John Edward Taylor, die ersten englischen Übersetzer der Kinder- und Hausmärchen." In *Brüder Grimm Gedenken*, edited by Ludwig Denecke, 183–202. Marburg: N. G. Elwert, 1975.

Morava, Jirí. *Sehnsucht in meiner Seele: Božena Němcová, Dichterin: Ein Frauenschicksal in Alt-Österreich*. Innsbruck: Haymon, 1995.

Morbiato, Luciano, ed. *La Fiaba e altri Frammenti di Narrazione popolare*. Florence: Olschki, 2006.

Morton, Sarah McRae. Available at http://mcraemorton.com/home.html.

Murray, Margaret. *The Witch-Cult in Western Europe*. Oxford: Oxford University Press, 1921.

Narváez, Peter, and Martin Laba, eds. *Media Sense: The Folklore-Popular Culture Continuum*. Bowling Green, OH: Bowling Green State University Popular Press, 1986.

Newall, Venetia, ed. *The Witch Figure*. London: Routledge and Kegan Paul, 1973.

———. "Rachel Busk." In *Enzyklopädie des Märchens*, edited by Kurt Ranke, 2:1054–55. Berlin: de Gruyter, 1979.

Nurse, Paul McMichael. *Eastern Dreams: How the Arabian Nights Came to the World*. Toronto: Viking Canada, 2010.

Nuur, Navid, and Lisa Alena Vieten, eds. *Aftérouge*. Rotterdam: Piet Zwart Institute, 2006.

O'Brien, Michael, and Stephen Shennan, eds. *Innovations in Cultural Systems: Contributions from Evolutionary Anthropology*. Cambridge, MA: MIT Press, 2010.

Oldridge, Darren, ed. *The Witchcraft Reader*. London: Routledge, 2002.

———. *Strange Histories: The Trial of the Pig, the Walking Dead, and Other Matters of Fact from the Medieval and Renaissance Worlds*. London: Routledge, 2005.

Packer, Alison, Stella Beddoe, and Lianne Jarrett, eds. *Fairies in Legend and the Arts*. London: Cameron and Tayleur, 1980.

Pantel, Pauline Schmitt, ed. *A History of Women: From Ancient Goddesses to Christian Saints*. Translated by Arthur Goldhammer. Cambridge, MA: Harvard University Press, 1992.

Paris, Gaston. *Les Contes Orientaux dans la Littérature Française*. Paris: Franck, 1875.

Pinker, Steven. *How the Mind Works*. New York: W. W. Norton, 1999.

Pitrè, Giuseppe. *Guglielmo I e Il Vespro siciliano nelle tradizioni popolari della Sicilia*. Palermo: Lauriel, 1873.

———. *Che cos'è il folklore*. Edited by Giuseppe Bonomo. Palermo,1965.

———. *La Demopsicologia e la sua storia*. Edited by Loredana Bellantonio. Palermo: Documenta Edizioni, 2001.

———. *Monarci, Monache e Preti nei "cunti" del popolo siciliano*. Preface and translated by Lucio Zinna. Palermo: Antares, 2005.

Pitrè, Maria D'Alia. "Vita e opera di Giuseppe Pitrè." *Etnostoria* 1, no. 2 (1995): 138–75.

Pócs, Éva. "The Alternative World of the Witches' Sabbat." In *The Witchcraft Reader*, edited by Darren Oldridge, 129–35. London: Routledge, 2002.

Poe, Marshall. *A History of Communications: Media and Society from the Evolution of Speech to the Internet*. Cambridge: Cambridge University Press, 2011.

Poinsot, Nicolas, "La scandaleuse, Catherine Breillat lance Barbe-Bleue au festival du film fantastique de Neuchâtel." Available at http//www.lesquotidiennes.com/culture/la-scandeleuse-catherine-breillat-lance-barbe-bleue.

Posner, Helaine, and Kiki Smith. *Kiki Smith: Telling Tales*. New York: International Center of Photography, 2001.

Propp, Vladimir. *Morphology of the Folktale*. Edited by Louis Wagner and Alan Dundes. Translated by Laurence Scott. 2nd rev. ed. Austin: University of Texas Press, 1968.

———. "Les Transformations des Contes Fantastiques." In *Théorie de la littérature*, edited by Tzvetan Todorov, 234–62. Paris: Seuil, 1965.

———. *Les Racines Historiques du Conte Merveilleux*. Translated by Lise Gruek-Apert. Preface by Daniel Fabre and Jean-Claude Schmitt. Paris: Gallimard, 1983.

———. *Theory and History of Folklore*. Edited by Anatoly Liberman. Translated by Adriadna Y. Martin and Richard P. Martin. Minneapolis: University of Minnesota Press, 1984.

———. *Die historischen Wurzeln des Zaubermärchens*. Translated by Martin Pfeiffer. Munich: Hanser, 1987.

———. *La fiaba russa*. Edited and translated by Franca Crestani. Introduction by Kirill Chistov. Turin: Einaudi, 1990.

———. *The Russian Fairy Tale*. Translated by Sibelan Forrester. Detroit: Wayne State University Press, forthcoming in 2012.

Prussian, Clair. "Artist's Statement." Available at http://claireprussian.com/statement.html.

Purkiss, Diane. *The Witch in History: Early Modern and Twentieth-Century Representations*. London: Routledge, 1996.

Ragan, Kathleen. "Reply." *Marvels and Tales* 23, no. 2 (2009): 445–50.

———. "What Happened to the Heroines in Folktales? An Analysis by Gender of a Multicultural Sample of Published Folktales Collected from Storytellers." *Marvels and Tales* 23, no. 2 (2009): 229–49.

Ralston, W. R. S. *The Songs of the Russian People: As Illustrative of Slavonic Mythology and Russian Social Life*. London: Ellis and Green, 1872.

Rangoni, Laura. *Le Fate*. Milan: Xenia, 2004.

Rego, Paula. *Nursery Rhymes*. Introduction by Marina Warner. London: Thames and Hudson, 1994.

Reitzenstein, Richard. "Das Märchen von Armor und Psyche bei Apuleius (1912)." In *Amor und Psyche*, edited by Gerhard Binder and Reinhold Merkelbach, 87–158. Darmstadt: Wissenschaftliche Buchgesellschaft, 1968.

Relihan, Joel C. "To the Reader: A Brief History of *Cupid and Psyche*." In *The Tale of Cupid and Psyche*, by Lucius Apuleius, xv–xxiii. Translated by Joel C. Relihan. Indianapolis: Hackett, 2009.

Richardson, Brian. *Printing, Writers, and Readers in Renaissance Italy*. Cambridge: Cambridge University Press, 1999.

Rigoli, Aurelio. *Il Concetto di sopravvenza nell'opera di Pitrè e altri studi di folklore*. Caltanissetta-Rome: Salvatore Sciascia, 1963.

———. "Pitrè e la bibliografia delle tradizioni popolari d'Italia." In *Pitrè e Palermo: La Dinamica del cambiamento*, edited by Anamaria Amitrano Bavarese, 17–37. Rome: Bulzoni, 1986.

Robert, Raymonde. *Le conte de fées littéraire en France de la fin du xvii à la fin xviii siècle*. Nancy: Presses Universitaires de Nancy, 1981.

———. *Le conte de fées littéraire en France de la fin du xvii à la fin xviii siècle: Supplément bibliographique 1980–2000 établi par Nadine Jasmin avec la collaboration de Claire Debru*. 2nd ed. Paris: Honoré Champion, 2002.

Roberts, Warren. *The Tale of the Kind and the Unkind Girls: Aa-Th 480 and Related Tales*, edited by Alan Dundes. 1958; repr., Detroit: Wayne State University Press, 1994.

Röhrich, Lutz. "Erzählungen des Spätmittelalters zwischen Schriftlichkeit und Mündlichkeit." In *Volkskultur des europäischen Spätmittelalters*, edited by Peter Dinzelbacher and Hans-Dieter Mück, 199–222. Stuttgart: Alfred Kröner, 1987.

———. "Erzählforschung." In *Grundriss der Volkskunde: Einführung in die Forschungs-felder der europäischen Ethnologie*, 353–79. 2nd ed. Berlin: Dietrich Reimer, 1994.

Röhrich, Lutz, and Erika Lindig, eds. *Volksdichtung zwischen Mündlichkeit und Schrift-lichkeit*. Tübingen: Gunter Narr Verlag, 1989.

Rölleke, Heinz. *"Wo das Wünschen noch geholfen hat": Gesammelte Aufsätze zu den "Kinder- und Hausmärchen" der Brüder Grimm*. Bonn: Bouvier, 1985.

———. "Neue Erkenntnisse zum Beiträgerkreis der Grimmschen Märchen." In *Volks-dichtung zwischen Mündlichkeit und Schriftlichkeit*, edited by Lutz Röhrich and Erika Lindig, 49–66. Tübingen: Gunter Narr Verlag, 1989.

———. *Die Märchen der Brüder Grimm: Quellen und Studien*. Trier: Wissenschaftlicher Verlag Trier, 2000.

———. *Die Märchen der Brüder Grimm: Eine Einführung*. Stuttgart: Philipp Reclam, 2004.

Rösener, Werner. *Peasants in the Middle Ages*. Translated by Alexander Stützer. Urbana: University of Illinois Press, 1992.

———. *The Peasantry of Europe*. Translated by Thomas Barker. Oxford: Blackwell, 1994.

Roper, Lyndal. *Oedipus and the Devil: Witchcraft, Sexuality, and Religion in Early Mod-ern Europe*. London: Routledge, 1994.

———. *Witch Craze: Terror and Fantasy in Baroque Germany*. New Haven, CT: Yale Uni-versity Press, 2004.

Rosenthal, T. G. *Paula Rego: The Complete Graphic Work*. London: Thames and Hudson, 2003.

Rouart, Julie, ed. *Cindy Sherman*. Paris: Flammarion, 2006.

Ruck, Carl A. P., Blaise Daniel Staples, José Alfredo González Celdrán, and Mark Alwin Hoffman. *The Hidden World: Survival of Pagan Shamanic Themes in European Fairytales*. Durham, NC: Carolina Academic Press, 2007.

Rubini, Luisa. *Fiabe e mercanti in Sicilia. La raccolta di Laura Gonzenbach e la comunità tedesca nell'Ottocento*. Florence: Olschki, 1998.

———. "Giuseppe Pitrè" In *Enzyklopädie des Märchens: Handwörterbuch zu historischen und vergleichenden Erzählforschung*, edited by Rolf Wilhelm Brednich, 10:1063–69. Berlin: Walter de Gruyter, 2002.

Ryan, William. "William Ralston: Russian Magic and Folklore in England." In *Russian Magic at the British Library: Books, Manuscripts, Scholars, Travellers. The Panizzi Lectures 2005*, lecture 1, 1–39. London: British Library, 2005.

———. "Games, Pastimes, and Magic in Russia." *Folklore* 119, no. 1 (April 2008): 1–13.

Sacks, Oliver. "A Man of Letters: Why Was the Morning Paper Suddenly in a Foreign Language?" *New Yorker*, June 28, 2010, 22–28.

Saintyves, Pierre. *Le contes de Perrault et les récits parallèles: Leur origines*. Paris: E. Nourry, 1923.

Salisbury, Joyce. *The Beast Within: Animals in the Middle Ages*. London: Routledge, 1994.

Savarese, Annamaria Amitrano, ed. *Pitrè e Palermo: La Dinamica del cambiamento*. Rome: Bulzoni, 1986.

———, ed. *Orizzonte Folklore: L'opera di Giuseppe Pitrè*. Palermo: Mazzone, 1989.

Scala, Mark, ed. *Fairy Tales, Monsters, and the Genetic Imagination*. Nashville, TN: Vanderbilt University Press, 2012.

Schenda, Rudolf. *Volk ohne Buch: Studien zur Sozialgeschichte der populären Lesestoffe 1770–1910*. Frankfurt am Main: Klostermann, 1970.

———. "Die Zivilizierung der Kommunikationswesen: Überlegungen anhand französischer Quellen des 18. und 19. Jahrhunderts." In *Volksdichtung zwischen Mündlichkeit und Schriftlichkeit*, edited by Lutz Röhrich and Erika Lindig, 17–34. Tübingen: Gunter Narr Verlag, 1989.

Seifert, Lewis. "Entre l'écrit et l'oral: la réception des contes de fées 'classiques.'" In *Le conte en ses paroles: La figuration de l'oralité dans le conte merveilleux du Classicisme aux Lumières*, edited by Anne Defrance and Jean-François Perrin, 21–33. Paris: Éditions Desjonquères, 2007.

Seifert, Lewis, Catherine Velay-Vallantin, and Ruth Bottigheimer. "Comments on Fairy Tales and Oral Tradition." *Marvels and Tales* 20, no. 2 (2006): 276–84.

Sennewald, Jens. *Das Buch, das wir sind: Zur Poetik der "Kinder- und Hausmärchen," gesammelt durch die Brüder Grimm*. Würzburg: Könighausen and Neumann, 2004.

Seznec, Jean. *The Survival of the Pagan Gods: The Mythological Tradition and Its Place in Renaissance Humanism and Art*. Translated by Barbara Sessions. New York: Harper and Row, 1953.

Shennan, Stephen. *Genes, Memes, and Human History: Darwinian Archaeology and Cultural Evolution*. London: Thames and Hudson, 2002.

———. *Pattern and Process in Cultural Evolution*. Berkeley: University of California Press, 2009.

Simpson, Jacqueline. "On the Ambiguity of Elves." *Folklore* 122, no. 1 (April 2011): 76–83.

Sokolov, Yuriy Matveyevich. *Russian Folklore*. Translated by Catherine Ruth Smith. Hatboro, PA: Folklore Associates, 1966.

Součkova, Milada. *The Czech Romantics*. The Hague: Mouton, 1958.

Spence, Lewis. *British Fairy Origins: The Genesis and Development of Fairy Legends in British Tradition*. London: Watts and Company, 1946.

Sperber, Dan, and Lawrence Hirschfeld. "Culture and Modularity." In *The Innate Mind: Structure and Contents*, edited by Peter Carruthers, Stephen Laurence, and Steven Stich, 149–64. Oxford: Oxford University Press, 2006.

Sperber, Dan, and Deirdre Wilson. *Relevance: Communication and Cognition*. 2nd ed. London: Blackwell, 1995.

Spierenburg, Pieter. *The Broken Spell: A Cultural and Anthropological History of Preindustrial Europe*. New Brunswick, NJ: Rutgers University Press, 1991.

St. Clair, Jeffrey. "Let Us Now Praise Infamous Animals." In *Fear of the Animal Planet: The Hidden History of Animal Resistance*, by Jason Hribal, 1–20. Oakland, CA: AK Press, 2010.

Staines, Rima. "Drawing the Old Woman in the Woods." *Marvels and Tales* 24, no. 2 (2010): 336–40.

Stanonik, Marija. *Le Folklore littéraire: Approche pluridisciplinaire d'un phénomène syncrétique*. Translated by Florence Gacoin-Marks. Paris: L'Harmattan, 2009.

Steig, Reinhold, ed. *Achim von Arnim und die ihm nahe standen*. Vol. 3. Stuttgart: J. G. Cotta'schen Buchhandlung, 1904.

Sumpter, Caroline. "Fairy Tale and Folklore in the Nineteenth Century." *Literature Compass* 6, no. 3 (2009): 785–98.

Tatar, Maria. *Secrets beyond the Door: The Story of Bluebeard and His Wives*. Princeton, NJ: Princeton University Press, 2004.

Tomasello, Michael. *The Cultural Origins of Human Cognition*. Cambridge, MA: Harvard University Press, 1999.

———. *The Origins of Communication*. Cambridge, MA: MIT Press, 2008.

Toner, Jerry. *Popular Culture in Ancient Rome*. London: Polity, 2009.

Tooby, John, and Cosmides, Leda. "Does Beauty Build Adapted Minds? Toward an Evolutionary Theory of Aesthetics, Fiction, and the Arts." *SubStance* 94, no. 95 (2001): 6–27.

Trevor-Roper, H. R. *The European Witch-Craze of the of the Sixteenth and Seventeenth Centuries and Other Essays*. New York: Harper and Row, 1969.

Tuczay, Christa. *Magie und Magier im Mittelalter*. Munich: Eugen Diederichs Verlag, 1992.

———. "Motifs in *The Arabian Nights* and in Ancient and Medieval European Literature: A Comparison." *Folklore* 116, no. 3 (December 2005): 272–91.

Tylor, Edward B. *Researches into the Early History of Mankind*. London, Murray, 1865.

———. *Primitive Culture: Researches into the Development of Mythology, Philosophy, Religion, Language, Art, and Custom*. London: Murray, 1871.

Uther, Hans-Jörg. *The Types of International Folktales: A Classification and Bibliography*. 3 vols. Ff Communications no. 284. Helsinki: Suomalainen Tiedeakatemia, 2004.

———. "The Fox in World Literature: Reflections on a 'Fictional Animal.'" *Asian Folklore Studies* 65, no. 2 (2006): 133–60.

———. *Handbuch zu den "Kinder- und Hausmärchen" der Brüder Grimm: Entstehung—Wirkung—Interpretation*. Berlin: Walter de Gruyter, 2008.

———. "Tale Type." In *The Greenwood Encyclopedia of Folktales and Fairy Tales*, edited by Donald, Haase, 3:937–42. Westport, CT: Greenwood Press, 2008.

Van Gennep, Arnold. *Coutumes et croyances populaires en France*. Paris: le Chemin vert, 1980.

Vaz da Silva, Francisco. "The Invention of Fairy Tales." *Journal of American Folklore* 123, no. 490 (2010): 398–425.

Verdi, Laura. *Il regno incantato: il contesto sociale e culturale della fiaba in Europa*. Padova: Centro Studi Sociologica Religiosa di Padova, 1980.

———. "Dalla Grande Madre alle fate delle fiabe." In *Le Grandi Madri*, edited by Tilda Giani Gallino, 171–77. Milan: Feltrinelli, 1989.

Verevis, Constantine. *Film Remakes*. Edinburgh: Edinburgh University Press, 2006.

Walsh, P. G. Introduction to *The Golden Ass*, by Lucius Apuleius, xi–lv. Edited and translated by P. G. Walsh. Oxford: Oxford University Press, 1994.

Waquet, Françoise. *Parler comme un livre: L'oralité et le savoir (XVIe—XXe siècle)*. Paris: Albin Michel, 2003.

Warner, Marina. Introduction to *Nursery Rhymes*, by Paula Rego, 7–10. London: Thames and Hudson, 1994.

Waugh, Scott, and Peter Diehl, eds. *Christendom and Its Discontents: Exclusion, Persecution, and Rebellion, 1000–1500*. Cambridge: Cambridge University Press, 1996.

Weitman, Wendy. *Kiki Smith: Prints, Books, and Things*. New York: Museum of Modern Art, 2003.

Wesselski, Albert. *Märchen des Mittelalters*. Berlin: Stubenrauch, 1925.

———. *Versuch einer Theorie des Märchens*. Reichenberg: Sudendt. Verlag, 1931.

Wheeler, Michael, John Ziman, and Margaret Boden, eds. *The Evolution of Cultural Entities*. Oxford: Oxford University Press, 2002.

Wolf, Eric. *Europe and the People without History*. Berkeley: University of California Press, 1997.

Wolin, Joseph. "The Haunting: Marcel Dzama's Traumatic Fantasy Works." *Canadian Art* (Fall 2008): 94–100.

Wood, Christopher. *Fairies in Victorian Art*. Woodbridge, UK: Antique Collectors' Club, 2000.

Yanagi, Miwa. *Fairy Tale: Strange Stories of Women Young and Old*. Kyoto: Seigensha Art Publishing, 2007.

Ziman, John, ed. *Technological Innovation as an Evolutionary Process*. Cambridge: Cambridge University Press, 2000.

Ziolkowski, Jan. "Straparola and the Fairy Tale: Between Literary and Oral Traditions." *Journal of American Folklore* 123, no. 490 (2010): 377–97.

Zipes, Jack. *Why Fairy Tales Stick: The Evolution and Relevance of a Genre*. New York: Routledge, 2006.

———. *Fairy Tales and the Art of Subversion: The Classical Genre for Children and the Process of Civilization*. 2nd rev. ed. New York: Routledge, 2006.

———. "What Makes a Repulsive Frog So Appealing: Memetics and Fairy Tales." *Journal of Folklore Research* 45, no. 2 (2008): 109–43.

———. *The Enchanted Screen: The Unknown History of the Fairy-Tale Film*. New York: Routledge, 2011.

Zirnbauer, Heinz. "Grimms Märchen mit englischen Augen. Eine Studie zur Entwicklung der Illustration von Grimms Märchen in englischer Übersetzung von 1823 bis 1970." In *Brüder Grimm Gedenken*, edited by Ludwig Denecke, 203–41. Marburg: N. G. Elwert, 1975.

Zunshine, Lisa. *Why We Read Fiction: Theory of Mind and the Novel (Theory and Interpretation of Narrative)*. Columbus: Ohio State University Press, 2006.

———, ed. *Introduction to Cognitive Cultural Studies*. Baltimore: Johns Hopkins University Press, 2010.

Index

Printed in the USA
CPSIA information can be obtained
at www.ICGtesting.com
JSHW081450010823
45760JS00002B/62